# CODE KORAL

# CODE KORAL

Cara Saylor Polk

**ARPress**
ILLUMINATING IDEAS.
EMPOWERING VOICES

**ARPress**
45 Dan Road Suite 5
Canton MA 02021

Hotline:  1(888) 8210229
Fax:       1(508) 545-7580

Ordering Information:
Quantity sales. Special discounts are available on quantity purchases by corporations, associations, and others. For details, contact the publisher at the address above.

Printed in the United States of America.

ISBN-13:      Softcover      979-8-89356-299-6
              eBook          979-8-89356-298-9

Library of Congress Control Number: 2024903341

# BLURBS

"Code Koral" is a fast-paced Cold War thriller that grabs you by the throat and doesn't let go. A deep-cover American spy, a defecting Soviet hockey team, and a duplicitous Secretary of State tangle in a rich mix of intrigue and betrayal Jason Bourne move over. Peter Porter has come to town." Bob Drogin, national correspondent, Los Angeles Times, author of "Curveball: Spies, Lies and the con man who caused a war." (Bob has 2 Pulitzer prizes and 2 Robert F. Kennedy awards)

"A gripping suspense that makes you miss the good old days of the Cold War when we had more serious dangers to worry about than suicidal fanatics with bombs." Doug Pardue, award-winning investigative reporter and editor, Post Courier, Charleston, SC.

On unfolding villainy: "Trollop couldn't have done it better and he was very good at that kind of thing." John Bross, General Counsel, CIA (dec'd)

"I loved this book. In "Code Koral," Cara Saylor Polk has written a page-turner that sizzles with intrigue. Set in the period of Cold War Soviet- American distrust, the book captures the intrigue, emotions and political hubris that shaped events in the 1970's. But the story also ties in events from WWII and even the White Revolution to shape the characters and enrich the plot. "Code Koral" is a book that will keep readers mesmerized until the satisfying end." Ric Tulsky, Pulitzer-Prize winning investigative reporter, The Philadelphia Inquirer (Director, Medill School of Journalism, Northwestern University).

"Politics, passion and pursuit. Reading is believing. The parallels with the hidden history of Don Draper in TV's "Mad Men" are also intriguing." Joan Mower, Director of Development and International Media Training, USIA (Voice of America) Washington, DC.

"I was about to be furious over the double-crosses and I didn't know how she would turn those around in the last few pages. But all was well." Barbara Krimgold, National Director, Kellogg's Health Scholars Program.

This book is wonderful! Absolutely fantastic! I am now halfway through and don't want to stop.

I have to tell you I keep saying to myself . . . "This is wonderful writing and I actually know that author." That makes it so much fun. I read over paragraphs and say to myself . . . "How does Cara know all about this?" I am SO impressed—so impressed. Then, of course, I want to know if any of this has any semblance of truth. Did some of these people really live? I hope so.

I like this book so much because your spies really use their wits—and you let us use ours to get there too. I love how you take me down the road and have me thinking I get it and then you surprise me . . . again and again. Move over Agatha Christie . . . here comes Cara Saylor Polk. It's a spy novel, it is a great mystery, it is a history lesson and so much more. This book has intrigue, great characters who actually love their country and make great sacrifices and still have a heart, but more, it relies on good old-fashioned spooks who use their wits instead of all the hi-tech toys to get the job done. I can't put it down, but I will be sad when it ends because there won't be anymore. I hate that about good books— you love them and then they are gone. I will be waiting—none too patiently—for the sequel! Lea Thompson, emmy-award winning Investigative Reporter, formerly of NBC, now with her own production company.

# Author's Note

This is a book of faction, a term I use for fiction based on fact. There was a WWII and a General Eisenhower. There was a switch and a hidden file that no longer exists. There were Wings of the Soviet Hockey team who defected, perhaps not in this exact way. There was a Secretary of State whose name sounded a lot like Bollinger. Perhaps the character is patterned on him. There was, and perhaps still is, a safe house very much as described.

I wrote this book 35 years ago on the edge of perestroika. It was sold to a small publishing house which melted away suddenly. Perhaps it was too soon for the tale to be told. Perhaps too many characters would have been placed at risk unless I waited until they were no more.

There were more discussions with insiders than archival research. Talesare meant to be intriguing. I hope this one is for you, the reader.

Cara Saylor Polk,
March 2010

# Dedications

To the old guard who recognized ideals as well as operations andBrian Eagle, perhaps not his real name, a man who could fall asleep while smoking his pipe without dropping an ash, and to my dearest friend, John Bross, who weighed well the value of all living things.

To my beloved late father, born 1917, whose last note to me on the publication of my first novel read: "May this be the start of a long line of books that you will write for the enlightenment of all and the enjoyment of many." I'm working on it.

John "Johnny" Bross 1921–1990

Harold Murray Saylor 1917–2001

"I would rather excel in knowledge and virtue
than in power and glory."

– Alexander the Great in a letter to his old teacher, Aristotle.

To begin at the end . . .

Rubin took a quick step backward as the small flame blazed, threatening his favorite Liberty tie. He had bought the tie-on sale at Harrods for two pounds in the late sixties. He liked to think of the tie as one of a kind by now. Rubin was also a prudent man.

His movements were as autonomous as his pulse. This departure had been programmed years before.

The vault's door hung open. Rubin's attention was focused on the burning file and microfilm, now raging hot in the microcosmic world of the metal tray he had unhinged from the old paper shredder in the back storage room, tagged for Friday's trash removal.

The tab on the old manila file folder swelled with the heat. "KORAL— CkO—" briefly appeared embossed before the words turned to slate-colored ash.

There were no copies. Rubin Silverstein's incendiary farewell as director of Soviet Counterintelligence for the National Security Council would never reach the agency's logs. Code Koral had, and would, remain outside official status, unmentioned in reports, only brief summaries added to the one-copy- only file. All top-level and presidential reports had been oral, including the covert summary of April 18, 1945. On orders from Colonel Waterbury, Rubin, as one of the ten-day-wonder captains of WW II, has privately reported to General Eisenhower on the significance of Code Koral.

The scene had stayed with Rubin like a private psychic film, always ready to be replayed. The general had expressed concern. "Is it too much to ask of one man, however bright and dedicated?"

Thick silence had followed the general's question, which still had no good answer.

Halfway between the present and his first big war, Rubin unlocked his window and shook the ashes into the night wind, ignoring an incongruous flash of guilt for littering. Code Koral had must die with his departure.

Methodically, he carried the tray into his private bathroom, flushing away the last gray particles before replacing the tray in position on the obsolete shredder. Content, he slipped on his overcoat, adjusted his glasses, and neatly pulled his tie back into place. His farewell fire would make an amusing anecdote during dinner with his old friend. Perhaps they could play chess over brandy. A game that was a game. Nice thought.

# ANDOVER, MASSACHUSETTS
## February 12, 1976
## 5:30 p.m.

A mist was rising, obscuring the stream and woods behind their century- old house, adding to the "neither-nor" mysteries of dusk. Dusk, like dawn, is the in-between time of ancient mythologies, neither night nor day, neither land nor water. She could picture an Irish warrior-king riding forth into the haunts of the New England woods, crossing the mystical razor edge between being and nonbeing, the place where the impossible becomes possible. Mattie shivered, her mind slipping back to cold Milwaukee winters and her mother's bedtime legends from the old country.

She sensed Brian approach and reach for his favorite spot where her cheek met her upper thigh. "Ouch!"

"How about a drink?" Brian, comfortable and down-to-earth, all six foot two inches of him, kissed the top of her curly red-gold hair. Mysticism vanished. She was again the lady of her very solid hearth, congratulating herself on adding a shampoo to her last-minute shower.

"Diet Pepsi?"

He nodded as he wrapped his strong arms around her from behind, following her gaze, but seeing only a dark backyard with tips of crab grass poking through the snow.

"Kids in?"

"Upstairs thawing out. They're really hyper over Yori's coming to dinner."

She turned back toward the kitchen. "Menu: Chopped egg and beluga caviar. Beef Stroganoff. Spicy white fish, veggies, and vodka-kirsch strawberry tart. Topped off with cinnamon coffee."

"Yuck!" Ten-year-old Brian, Jr., "B", bounded into the kitchen. "If you want to make him feel at home, why don't you cook something we eat around this home?"

Brian laughed as Mattie assured B the menu included hamburgers and french fries for him and Cloie.

B exited, pretzel in hand, to find his arrowhead collection to show Yori. Brian perched on the deep windowsill, his back to the evening mists as he watched Mattie prepare her final garnishes.

"I think it shows the Russians are coming around, don't you?" Brian asked without waiting for a reply. "To let the team members come to our homes shows a fairly liberal attitude. I'm surprised. I thought the KGB kept them locked up except when they played."

"Mmmm," Mattie concentrated on keeping the white fish shaped like a fish as she moved it to the serving dish.

"Yori's a pretty fantastic goalie," Brian continued. "We were fairly well matched. We played an even game."

Mattie glanced up from the fish, a twinkle in her green eyes. "Such modesty! Is that why they won 5-4?"

"Yori and I each allowed four goals scored against us. The fifth Wings's goal was scored against my relief man," Brian protested.

Deserting the hollandaise sauce and broccoli for a moment, she rewarded Brian with a quick hug. "You're the best," she stated.

"You're prejudiced," he objected without much conviction.

"Me and Sports Illustrated." She smiled as she returned to her mound of chopped eggs and caviar. The doorbell rang. "Right on time!" she panicked. "Stall him, Brian, while I finish the caviar."

"It's Yori!" Cloie's high-pitched eight-year-old voice echoed into the kitchen.

Dinner was a moderate success, the food outscoring the conversation. Unlike Mattie's image of the aggressive Wings's team, Yori was shy. Pulling him out and into the conversation took concerted family teamwork. Mattie allowed

Cloie to ramble on about Abraham Lincoln freeing the slaves; that had been part of her Lincoln's birthday school lessons. When Cloie asked him if there were ever slaves in Russia, Yori told her about the serfs in the days of the czars. Yori's English was stilted, but comprehensible. He spoke carefully in a studied manner Mattie found charming. Brian thought he seemed nervous, almost wary. Brian kept plugging, asking Yori questions about Russian training methods. Mattie began to sense the tension and broke family dinner table rules and allowed B to bring his arrowhead collection to the table. She wondered if a babushka and folk dance would ease the strain. Finally, she sent the children downstairs to the family room to play and left Yori to Brian's devices as she cleared the remnants of dessert and headed for the kitchen.

In the living room where Brian and Yori had taken their coffee, the conversation had hit an uncomfortable silence.

Brian looked around. The room was the same. The polished bar had lost none of its antique luster. The shag carpet, Mattie's favorite shade of green, still stretched thirty-two feet, six inches across the floor. He thought of Mattie's initial reaction to the room: "At last! A chance for our own bowling alley." But Brian loved the spaciousness, and Mattie, with the help of a biweekly cleaning woman, learned to love it too.

Yori was frozen in his chair, leaning forward, taut, as though waiting for an official to drop the puck. Brian cleared his throat, hesitated, tugged his earlobe, and finally spoke, "Has every member of your team thought this through?"

Yori smiled tightly and nodded. He and team captain, Ivan Malitinsky, had spent many tense hours confirming the commitments of their teammates. Although Yori and Ivan had discussed making the move two years before during the previous Wings's tour in the United States, they'd hesitated too long to make contact. This time they'd moved with certainty, carefully testing the feelings of their fellow players. Yori had "tested the waters," then Ivan plunged in with the initial suggestion. A few were lukewarm at first, but Ivan's dynamic personality and his accustomed position as team leader was keeping the would-be defectors in line. Vladimir Vladistock had been the last to agree and the first to insist on personal conditions.

Brian remembered how difficult it had been for the Bruins to keep the coach's surprise party under wraps for less than two weeks. The coach had become suspicious before the first week's planning had been completed.

"Yori, how are you keeping it quiet? And how did you ever get eighteen men to agree?"

"Nothing was said, and we contacted nobody among ourselves until we were here, away from our families and friends. Most of us are not married because the team travels, and we practice all the time in our homeland. It is difficult to have a wife. Many of the players are young. But we all know also that if we are to succeed, we must stay quiet. If the KGB becomes suspicious at all, our actions would be limited. I would not be here for dinner. If they had certain information that we wished to defect, we would pay heavily. It would not be nice for us." Yori took a deep breath and leaned forward intently. "We do not have many days. We are to fly back to Moscow in a week on February 19. It must all be done quickly—if it is to happen."

"That's not much time." Brian spoke slowly, weighing his words carefully. "I don't think there is any doubt or question that we would want you, but there must be problems we don't know about—legalities. Your guards. Have you worked out the details?"

Yori shook his head. "No, we must have help from your country's officials. Vladistock and Malitinsky won't leave without their families. They must be brought from Russia. We don't know how to get them out."

"Why hasn't your coach made contact? He meets with the NHL officials. Why me?"

"I am not so closely watched as our coach. At home his wife is suspected. Only because he is good as a coach does he come here."

"But in Russia you have incredible prestige, better homes, even more freedom than others from what I've heard. You have family, friends— your life."

"And here you get hundreds of thousands of dollars to play. And," his hand waved at the room, "look how you live. Plus, TV shows and girls." His grin was slow and wide. "Our players would like that."

A branch snapped outside the window. Yori moved to the window, pushed aside the woven Indian drapes, and peered for a moment at the car waiting outside. He didn't have much time.

Brian gnawed on his lower lip. "But Yori, here we are owned body and soul by the team owners. If they want, they can trade or sell us to another team. Once we sign contracts, we're all theirs."

"Unless you quit." Yori gripped his glass. "I want to quit. On the Wings, I am in the army, and I do what they say, or I am court-martialed. To quit would dishonor the team, myself, my friends."

Brian's thoughts raced. "How would it work for the others? Would you split up among our teams?"

Yori turned impatiently from the window. "This we do not know. How can we know before we talk with your hockey league? How do we know what your Mr. McDougal will say? If our conditions can be met, we shall defect."

"Defect."

The word echoed in the room.

The stereo was silent, the record finished. Right here, outside Boston, the topic for the night was defection to the free world. Brian's thoughts skated into confusion. Life was good. Mattie had stopped complaining about road trips. "One if by land and two if by sea, and I on the opposite shore will be, ready to ride and spread the alarm through every Middlesex village and farm for the country folk to be up and to arm." That's ridiculous, thought Brian. I haven't thought of that in twenty years. He broke training without hesitation, reached across the bar for a bottle of Cutty, and poured an inch plus on the melting ice remaining from his diet soda. "I don't know if I can handle this. What do you want me to do?"

Yori leaned closer, lowering his voice. "I want you to find out what they'll pay us to play on American teams. And if they can get Vladistock's wife and child and Malitinsky's mother out first. And I would like to be a coach for young people in a school. And there must be protection from . . ." Yori paused, uncertain. Their KGB escorts? Newsmen? There was no precedent for such a group defection. He remembered a Hungarian circus troupe making a dash across the border years before. But they were the famous Wings of the Soviets. Yori shivered and waited for Brian to respond.

"I don't know who is best to approach with this."

The Russian studied Brian's face. Brian studied his melting ice with equal concentration. Yori relaxed and waited. Brian was taking him seriously.

"We need somebody to trust, somebody you trust. Someone who knows the right people, even a government official."

Brian thought of Rob Carson, attorney for the New York Rangers who had been an interim NHL commissioner. Brian had been ten years behind Rob at Cornell, but they were friends. When it came to team mergers, sales, franchises, or even special drafts and contracts, Rob would know what to do. Clandestine deals were the very successful sports lawyer's specialist.

"OK," said Brian. "I have a man in mind, but since we're playing this close to the chest, I won't give you his name until it's necessary."

Yori grinned as though he had just saved a shout-out. "You'll help us!"

"I'll try." Brian swallowed the last of his illicit scotch. "How do I get in touch with you next . . . on this matter?"

"You don't. It would be too suspect. They frown if we become too friendly with an American player. It is on the schedule for you to have Ivan Malitinsky, our captain, at your home for lunch. All of us are brothers in this. To talk to Ivan is to talk to me. Only one is not with us and he was hurt on the boards in Montreal. But he has been left at the hospital there and we believe will be sent home." Yori paused. "It was Ivan's stick that broke his ankle."

Mattie came to a running halt inside the arch to the living room, holding a large bag of potato chips.

"Hi. Don't mean to interrupt, but I wondered if Yori has tasted American potato chips."

Yori rose from the couch and bowed. "Madame." "Mattie," corrected Brian.

"Mattie," echoed Yori awkwardly. "I must go. We talk too long already."

"Please try one," she urged. "From the way you played, we should keep you here and turn you into a Bruin." She laughed.

Yori glanced at Brian for reassurance. He was unaccustomed to jesting Americans. Brian shrugged his shoulders and smiled. "It's OK, Yori. Indulge her. Try a chip."

Yori politely munched a chip. It lay salty and tasteless in his dry mouth. He turned to Mattie. "Thank you. I shall look forward to another time to enjoy your American chips." He methodically looked around the room, memorizing it for his teammates. He stood rigidly, looking younger than his thirty-three years.

Impulsively, Mattie leaned forward and kissed him on the cheek. "I hope the rest of your tour is sensational."

He swallowed hard to avoid choking on the chip and tried to smile. "Thank you." He looked at Brian and added, "For everything, 'til tomorrow."

Then he was gone into the waiting car.

Mattie dropped the bag of chips on the hall table and hugged Brian. "What's tomorrow?"

"You know, we're having Ivan Malitinsky over for lunch." Brian wanted to share Yori's conversation with Mattie, but he knew her cheerful midwestern optimism well. "Of course, they want to defect," she'd say. "Who wouldn't?" Then she'd push to help. Her "help" would be calling the Associated Press. He sighed, loving her, and hugged her again before heading for the study to call Rob Carson.

Rob wasn't in, Ellen told him. "It's important, Ellen, I must talk to him tonight."

"You sound uptight. Are the kids OK, Mattie?"

"We're all fine. It's nothing to do with us." I hope, he thought. "Just have him call the second he gets in." Brian had the feeling he'd said too much already. Anyone tuning in on the call would know Yori had just left.

An hour passed. No call. "Maybe I should fly to New York," he mused over a bowl of Jell-O.

"To New York? When?" Mattie smiled automatically.

There were no more flights that night. He'd never be able to get there, see Rob, and be back in time for lunch with Malitinsky. Where was Carson?

The phone jarred his thoughts.

Mattie answered it. Her mother. They chatted. Finally, Brian protested. "Mattie, I'm expecting a call. Talk to her tomorrow." Quickly saying good- bye, she turned to him. "Who?"

"Rob. Just a team matter." Mattie pulled her hair back and piled it on top of her head. "Could we go this weekend?"

"Rob might even be here tomorrow." "Oh? With Ellen?"

"League business. No Ellen."

"But he doesn't represent the league anymore, just the Rangers—not even the Bruins."

"Mattie, I don't know what it's about. I can't tell you what I don't know!" The phone jangled, matching his rising irritation. "I'll get it," he snapped. It was Rob. Mattie beat a retreat into the kitchen with the Jell-O dishes.

Rob calmed Brian's paranoia that the phones might be bugged as he made notes on the conditions and key points. He trusted Brian's judgment. If Brian said they were serious, they were.

Rob signed off, promising to keep Brian posted, and called Charles Mattimore, a friend from Princeton days, now an undersecretary with the State Department. Within the hour Mattimore, as specialist in Soviet affairs, was driving toward the White House to rendezvous with secretary of state Karl Bollinger and President Dodge. The Wings's cry for freedom was being heard.

NSA Director Rubin Silverstein was packing his briefcase to head home as an aide walked in holding the latest report from Israeli intelligence inside the USSR. In the spring of 1975, an electronic breakthrough enabled them to tune in on special Israeli transmissions. Combined with the code key purchased at great cost through an Israeli source, the reports from the efficient, highly organized Israeli operations were proving invaluable for corroboration as well as new information. Rubin was particularly interested in the recent mention of a KGB search for the leak regarding the Russian plan to infiltrate British MI Headquarters again. Two Russian plants had been ferreted out and arrested. The KGB was certain information was somehow leaked from a Russian source.

Rubin knew all too well that their suspicions were warranted. He skimmed the report. The Israelis wanted the facts and figures on the Russian arms shipments to Arafat as well as geological reports on the oil fields. The report recounted rumors that the Russians were getting nervous about dwindling well production without significant new fields being discovered. The extent of the potential energy crisis within the USSR would determine the strength of their push for influence in the Middle East. Genuine figures, not the politically inspired numbers reported in Pravda, were vital.

The Israelis were asking the right questions, and Rubin realized "Koral," their high-placed Russian mole, could deliver the critical information. Unless the heat was on, and he'd come under suspicion after decades of brilliant covert activities. Koral's January report gave no indication of difficulty regarding the "discovery" of the British operation, but Israeli intelligence was generally current and accurate. The KGB alarm must be very recent. He tucked the information in the back of his mind. He'd have to carefully consider the alternatives before asking Koral to take action if his position were in jeopardy.

Yawning, Rubin glanced at the security report sent over from the White House by Major J. L. Rhodes. Rubin thought of J. L. as his in-house mole. Currently number 2 man of WHCA, the White House Communications Agency, J. L. first came to Rubin's attention during a fact-finding mission in Vietnam. Then First Lieutenant Rhodes was assigned to him as guide and translator. Rubin soon realized that beneath the good-humored, seemingly casual facade, J. L. was tough, straight, and dedicated in the post-Vietnam months, Rubin made a special request for J. L.'s temporary assignment to NSA as a military consultant. During the confused clean-up intelligence operations, Rubin and J. L. developed a warm, mutual respect. J. L.'s beer-drinking and poker style life was an alien world to Rubin, and Rubin's occasional offerings to J. L. of opera or concert tickets fell on deaf ears. But they could count on each other as bosom buddies in affairs of state.

In 1964, J. L. transferred into WHCA with Rubin's blessings. He retained his function for Rubin as an NSA "consultant," but went undercover; payments were made in cash and recorded in the coded, classified source account. J. L.'s presence and activities helped Rubin stay on top of the political maneuverings, allowing him and the agency to sail through Watergate and other crises while others floundered. It was a relationship of mutual advantage, the only kind Rubin trusted.

Rubin picked up the security packet and dropped it in his briefcase. He'd lull himself to sleep with the Oval Office conversations of the day; J. L. would have noted in the tape log which ones were important to review. Sometimes, it was more entertaining than the Tonight Show. Rubin gave President Dodge better ratings as talk show host than he gave Carson. Dodge was at his best with two or three guests and a friendly audience. As Rubin signed out for the night, the president was entertaining two State Department guests, with only an inconspicuous wire recorder for an audience.

# THE OVAL OFFICE
## February 13
## 12:37 p.m.

"Are they serious?" President Dodge kicked at a paper clip on the floor that had escaped the attention of Housekeeping. "The whole hockey team wants to defect?"

"It appears so, sir," Undersecretary of State Charles Mattimore attested. "Carson's word is golden, and from all reports Brian Earle is no prankster. The very fact that there are no other intelligence reports or rumors indicates that the Soviet team is playing it very carefully and seriously." Mattimore appreciated and understood a dedicated, serious approach to life.

"What's this Earle like?" demanded Secretary of State Karl Bollinger. Charles flipped open his file on Earle and scanned it. "Brian Earle, twenty-nine, resides in Andover, Mass., and is co-captain of the Boston Bruins. The younger players call him "Poppa." Happily married, rare for an athlete, works with teenagers in Boston's drug rehabilitation program, more than the usual lip service of promotional appearances. A straight shooter. Second generation Serbian and Scotch-Irish, he's been born and bred a Western Pennsylvanian f Democrat—in both senses of the word."

"We can forgive him his party affiliation if he's a good solid American." Smiled Dodge.

Bollinger glared for a split second. The party politics of government were a constant irritant. "We're avoiding the real issue. If they're serious, and we'll find that out soon enough, we're put in the position of meeting their conditions and granting the asylum or rejecting it. Evidently, they want to be certain we'll accept them and

they'll be offered positions on American teams before they'll move." Bollinger, a self-appointed master of détente, closed his eyes. "I'm certain the Soviets would be furious. They might be able to keep it out of their state-controlled newspapers, but it wouldn't help. It would become known internally almost as soon as internationally. Bad for the Bear's image."

His stomach growled as he paused dramatically. After-theatre dinner had not yet been served as the call came from the White House. His reward for his empty stomach was ample blood to stir the sanguine corners of his brain and none of the logy apathy that beset him on schedule, an hour after dinner. He let his lids drop while he thought for a long moment before speaking.

"There must be a way, gentlemen, to turn this opportunity into something more than a plethora of athletes competing with American hockey players. Remember, we still don't know what NHL Commissioner McDougal's reaction will be. That's a contingent condition that we can't guarantee; and we certainly can't make dollar offers." He opened his eyes, slightly wrinkling his heavy brows, and stared at Mattimore. "Now, can we?"

Mattimore sighed. "The NHL hasn't been approached yet as far as I know. I told Whitehall to have everyone sit tight until we get back to them. As far as the money goes, we do have provisional funds for defectors—discretionary— until other arrangements are made."

"If they can be made," amended Bollinger. He looked more like an overgrown mouse than a cat, but his mental maneuverings were distinctively feline. Habitually, he sat quietly, eyes closed. Then with claws sheathed in velvet rhetoric, he sprang into discussions, hooking into the issues with the guttural remnants of German ghettos in the Bronx of the thirties.

"How quickly and quietly can we accomplish this defection? When do they have a few days between games?" Bollinger turned to the president. "Perhaps it could be arranged for the end of the tour."

Dodge met Bollinger's narrowed gaze. "What are you getting at, Karl? What difference does it make?"

"Perhaps worlds. We still have three crewmen from the surveillance plane we disowned in Siberian labor camps. It would make good press to have them 'home for Christmas.'" Bollinger lifted the right corner of his mouth. It might have passed for a smile.

Mattimore winced. "What good would it do to have them back? They've been drained dry as old women and they've hardly gained any new information in prison."

"I'm sure America would rejoice in print. There must be a deal to be made. The Soviets wouldn't like it voiced at home or abroad that their superstars wish to defect."

Mattimore reached behind his neck for his fifth vertebrae, the one that always bothered him when he dealt with Bollinger. It paralleled Bollinger's personality. The man inevitably reached weak spots. He also delighted in complicating operations. A team defection with worldwide impact and sophisticated conditions wasn't enough for him. He had to add his own brand of power politics. "Karl, are you saying we should accept the defection with the intention of trading them back? A double cross?"

"Watch your language. I'm only pointing out that we have a tough election coming up this year. We must make optimum use of every situation. But before we can play, we must hold the cards. The Soviets have no suspicion the team wants to defect?"

"None has been reported," affirmed Mattimore.

"I'll double-check all departments to be certain." Bollinger paused, sliding his tongue across his plump lower lip.

"Suppose we meet the conditions and get them out and the Soviets won't deal?" asked Mattimore.

"Then we have ourselves a star hockey team." Bollinger looked smug. "Any way you look at it, we win."

Mattimore fingered his tortoise frames. "Karl, that means proceeding as though we're going to grant asylum. Without the team, there's nothing to bargain with. We'll have to pull a network of agents off other assignments to meet their conditions and accept the defection covertly. By the time we've done that, there'll be a hundred places for a leak."

Bollinger bared his teeth in a semblance of a smile as he rose, pointing his left forefinger at Charles. "Of course, if there is a leak that blows this operation, it will be your responsibility. I'm making you security liaison for this operation." He revolved to face Dodge. "Do you agree, Mr. President?"

Dodge's mind had wandered for a moment. The antipathy between Bollinger and Mattimore disturbed him. "Had he been paying attention? he might have bristled at Bollinger's imperious directive to Mattimore. He'd been gathering mental wool as he reminisced on the Wings-Bruins game he'd watched on TV."

"The Wings have drive and spirit. They play an intelligent game, very calculated. If they want to become Americans," he paused, looking at Bollinger for confirmation. Bollinger nodded. "See if it's possible to meet their conditions, Karl."

Mattimore took a step forward. "Do you agree with Karl's thinking on this, Mr. President?"

Dodge didn't want to admit he'd only heard part of the conversation. "Give every assistance possible from your State Department resources, Charles."

"We're going to need the cooperation of NSA and the CIA and perhaps military intelligence."

"You'll have it. Karl, make a note right now to get Rubin and Bob Shields here by seven thirty tomorrow morning. I want you and Charles here too."

Bollinger's eyes gleamed. It would be his show. "Right away, Mr. President. In the meantime, we'll get the wheels in motion."

Dodge pushed his intercom. "Marcy, ring Mrs. Dodge and tell her I'm on my way. And have the kitchen send up hot milk, cheese, and Nabiscos." He rose, signaling the end of the session. "All clear, gentlemen?"

"All clear," echoed Bollinger.

Mattimore snapped shut his briefcase. "Good night, sir."

"Sleep well, Mr. President," added Bollinger as they followed Dodge from the office.

# MOSCOW KGB HEADQUARTERS
## February 13
## 7:00 a.m.

Colonel Sergei Padov drank the tea in front of him, wishing for some good strong coffee. He glanced up from his notes and addressed General Taikov, "Sir, I still believe the leaks are coming from the field. I'd like to scout around a bit."

The slight, birdlike general leaned forward intently. "Colonel Padov," he stated, "I'd like you to go further than that. I want you to take charge of this operation. We all agree there is a mole somewhere, a mole privy to the most classified documents. It does no good to mount diversionary misinformation if the Allies are getting the straight facts from an unquestionable source."

Padov's lean, high-cheeked face showed no emotion. "And when I find him, do I take him out or save him for bigger bait?"

"First, find him. He has to be under control before our Prague meetings. All the heads of security from all the member countries will be represented—some are deep cover. We can't talk policy, revamp codes, or touch anything sensitive if we suspect a plant. It's maddening. I'm beginning to suspect I talk at night and my wife is taking notes!"

Padov didn't smile at the general's attempt at humor. It was not in the character of Sergei Padov, director of KGB International Operations. "I'll clean up a few minor operations, sir, and delegate everything current. I'll ferret him out if I have to go back in the field myself."

"I suspect you'd like that," commented the general. "You'd rather be in the field playing nasty games yourself than planning strategies behind your desk, wouldn't you?" The general didn't wait for a response. "We all grow old, Colonel, and must move up or move out. But you're fit enough." He chuckled with double meaning. "My reports indicate that you still have the prowess of the young. Do what you must do. You will report only to me."

"I understand, sir. Until we know our target, any discussion could send him into deep cover."

"I have plans to use this mole to our advantage." Taikov's old claw like hands gripped the pencil. "But if there must be a sanction, Colonel, it will be yours. A present from an old man who still remembers the glories of the field." His face creased into a hundred small wrinkles. "That is all, Colonel. Use the korallion code, plus one. But stay in touch.

Padov rose to leave. The general stared up at the tall, lean officer. "Colonel, I shouldn't tell you this," he began, "but it might inspire you to greater heights of your most brutal efficiency. You're under strong consideration for a promotion to general. And I am carefully considering my own retirement, following our successes in Prague."

Padov tried to ignore the thrill of pride he felt, without success. He'd been born an achiever and he would die one. He hadn't given the prospect of reaching general much thought in his years with the KGB. He'd accepted each promotion and its accompanying advantages routinely. General Sergei Padov, he relished the concept. "I'll do my best to deserve your confidence, sir."

"Good hunting, Colonel." "Thank you, sir."

J. L. Rhodes enjoyed both his duties and his prestige as number 2 man of WHCA, the White House Communications Agency. He could have retired two years previously at forty-three with his twenty-year pension and gone to work for the State Department Security like some fellow WHCA members had, but he liked the White House association. The money wasn't great. It was military pay and majors didn't get rich. Without his "moonlight money" from his covert NSA double duties, he'd have a hard time fighting inflation. His men considered him straight and tough and a throwback to FDR days. Political differences aside, he liked the current president, Harry Dodge. Unlike the past two presidents, the man never requested the impossible. LBJ had been the worst, switching schedules at the last minute and driving WHCA and the Secret Service scrambling up walls and around cities without adequate time for security setups.

He reflected on last month's trip to Moscow, the first such trip since the Nixon days. It was the only time he'd ever seen Dodge uptight.

"He wasn't comfortable with the Soviets," J. L. had commented to his longtime mistress Linda during his monthly sojourn to Denver. "He's not xenophobic, generally, but he's got a lot of midwestern suspicion in his soul despite his words of détente. Sometimes I think he only echoes Bollinger. I guess it's understandable. During his years in the Senate, he spent his time with the agriculture and interstate trade subcommittees. Closest he got to Russia was approving the sale of wheat, but he only did that for a trade-off to help his land bank proposal."

"I didn't know you were a political philosopher," commented Linda while she mixed him another martini.

"I observe. I'm more than an Oval Office robot. I can't pinpoint it, Linda. He's never done anything wrong, but he's never taken strong stands on much either. His record in the Senate should read: Clean nose. Stayed out of trouble. Voted party line. Moderate conservative. Moderate liberal. Moderate intellect. Right now, he has moderate control of the government and maybe minimal control of Bollinger. What am I trying to say?" He answered his own question as Linda handed him his full glass, leaned over, and rubbed the top of his shiny head.

He brushed her hand away. "Stop it. You might cause hair to grow, and I'd ruin my reputation. Bald men are more virile, you know." He took a sip as he chuckled. "Dodge is a great guy to watch a football game with, but until someone lays out the international balance of power like a Super Bowl game, I don't think he'll get it."

J. L.'s WHCA responsibilities included assuring a semblance of technical order for media equipment and secured communications during presidential trips. He personally checked out all priority communication devices, including the infamous "red phone." The job was demanding, but it had its quotable moments for war stories. "At a spur-of-the moment press conference, LBJ decided to hold at the Houston airport," he'd recount for his friends' amusement, "the wind was destroying the mikes. This guy we'd dredged up as an assistant engineer from a local station kept trying to improvise wind shields from everything from cornflake boxes to rubber ducks. In desperation, the guy pulls a Trojan from his pocket and puts it over the mike. Good-bye wind distortion! We've called them those fuckin' emergency wind screens ever since!"

J. L. was in a serious mood this morning as he passed through White House corridors. His two-year extension was up in ninety days, and he had to make a decision to retire or stay. There were rumors floating that Congress was going to change some of the double-dipping rules, precluding retiring with full pension and getting another federal job. Aides' voices brought him back to the present.

"The president was up late last night with Mattimore and Bollinger. I wonder what's up."

"Something with the Soviets, I'd guess. It's Mattimore's area. They were back this morning with Shields and Silverstein. Must be heavy."

J. L. noted than any news reporter being escorted through the West Wing would have been privy to that piece of highly classified information. He made a mental note to get them properly chewed out.

He continued on to the Oval Office, nodded to the guard outside the door, and walked in. Chore time. He checked out the red phone, pulled out his sweeper and checked for any unwanted electronic ears, ending his sweep by one of several innocent-looking white phones. Since J. L. was responsible for all presidential phones lines, no one would have noticed anything out of the ordinary if they'd have walked in. He quickly unscrewed the mouthpiece, traded miniature discs, replaced it, and dialed a number.

"Umber-nay ive-fay?" answered Dougherty at NSA Headquarters. "Uck-fay ou'yay," replied J. L., his good humor returning. He'd laughed when Dougherty instigated pig Latin, but the man swore the inverted words, combined with sophisticated scramblers and basic codes made outside surveillance impossible.

"Atch-way auto-ays e-ray onse-pay o-tay raut-kay and-a Owl-ay. Eck-chay in-ay if-ay et-tay a-ay et-ay."

"A-OK," replied J. L.

Dougherty ended the connection and J. L. replaced the receiver while pocketing the disc. So, he was to keep an eye out for the Kraut and the Owl, Bollinger and Mattimore. Something was afoot. J. L. didn't waste time conjecturing. He'd know soon enough when he checked the recordings and encoded the log for Silverstein. Even though he was privy to all Oval Office conversations, J. L. still felt he never got the full picture on operations. So much was turned over to the president as summaries; other information was obviously read by the president and commented upon, but J. L. couldn't always determine the substance from the references. He'd had his suspicions during the Watergate days about Silverstein's use of the recordings, but he'd never asked about it. If Rubin had urged on the press with judiciously revealed information, J. L. could only applaud. "The man" as J.L. had always called Nixon, had become psychotic toward the end.

He'd chuckled to himself when General Bonekemper, WHCA commander, indignantly told him CIA director Bob Shields had requested assistance to put a CIA tap on the office.

"Bob told me," Bonekemper related to J. L., "after Watergate someone should keep an ear on the president and it's WHCA's duty to help. Imagine! Butterfield got into enough trouble when it was Nixon's own tape system!" J. L. was glad Bonekemper had stonewalled Shields since he trusted neither

Shields nor the CIA. Rubin Silverstein inspired confidence, and he seemed the least corruptible. Philosophically in accord with Shields, Rubin convinced

J. L. there had to be a monitor over the powermongers and the NSA and himself were the best bet. A presidential aide entered as J. L. put away the sweeper.

"All clean and quiet?" he asked J. L. "Heard from Lightbulb yet?"

When Dodge wasn't around, his aides delighted in referring to him by his Secret Service and WHCA code name. The first lady traditionally was given the privilege of selecting code names for the first family. J. L. had conferred with her as she struggled to find objects with the same first initial. "Give me a bright idea," she'd begged.

"How about a lightbulb?" he quipped. Amused, she decided that Lightbulb was an appropriate code name for her husband with his receding hairline. She called herself Lamp and their sixteen-year-old son Lantern. J. L. gladly allowed the first lady to take full credit for the nomenclatures.

"Not yet," J. L. replied to the aide.

"He's upstairs finishing breakfast. You should get a beep soon. They're heading for church en famille. Getting close to election," he added with chuckle.

Within five minutes, J. L. had double-checked all the lines opened in the church offices, ready for instant communications. He thought about requesting the Secret Service to handle the offering. What a moment in the annals of martyrdom if the president were gunned down by a terrorist "usher" while contributing to the ecumenical bureaucracy. But all that would be thoroughly checked. No usher would approach the president. In Washington,

D.C. this morning, church and state would remain separate. If the church weren't taxed by the state, neither would the president be publicly taxed by the church.

J. L. checked the updated itinerary. Everything looked in order.

# STATE DEPARTMENT WASHINGTON, D.C.

## February 13

## 8:30 a.m.

In his cream-colored State Department office, Mattimore put through Classified File Requests on all concerned parties. He signed the requisition slip and stared sightlessly at the impersonal form. Every time Bollinger gets involved, he thought, it's all ends against the middle, with no clear vision of the middle. One thing seemed certain. More than a dozen men, plus two women and a child, were asking for freedom against heavy odds. It would take the concerted efforts of the State Department, NSA, and the CIA to pull this one off, whatever was ultimately determined.

They were pulling out all stops. Charles wondered if it were worth it in light of Bollinger's gamesmanship. He had set up his board so that everyone from Mattimore to the president to the prospective defectors was pawns.

He buzzed for his aide Bob Moore to take the requisition over to NSA and return with the files.

Within minutes, the computer searched through its miniature memory cells. Computer operator Bruce Martin watched the printout.

VLADIR VLADISTOCK. AGE 24 LEFT WING, WINGS OF THE SOVIETS, NATIONAL HOCKEY TEAM. MARRIED 9/15/70, NADIA MAIKOP. SON, VLADIMIR, JR. BORN 5/7/73. ENROLLED STATE NURSERY SCHOOL #732. NADIA EMPLOYED AS NURSE, CENTRAL HOSPITAL 415, MOSCOW. RESIDENCE, NORTHWEST SECTOR 733029.1. UPPER MIDDLE CLASS. (489732-V)

BERTHE (RUKOWSKY) MALITINSKY. MOTHER OF WINGS OF THE SOVIET NATIONAL HOCKEY TEAM, CAPTAIN AND CENTER, IVAN MALITINSKY. AGE 54. INVOLVED WITH HUNGARIAN-BORN HUSBAND IN COUNTER-REVOLUTIONARY ACTIVITIES IN 1958. IVAN MALITINSKY, SR. INTERRED IN SIBERIA, CONFESSED, TRIED, AND SHOT 8/7/59.

IVAN, JR. PLACED IN SOVIET MILITARY ACADEMY 9/2/59. BERTHE CURRENTLY EMPLOYED, FABRIKA RUSSKI. WORKER. RESIDENCE, SOUTHEAST SECTOR 27947.6. /SEE ALSO IVAN MALI-TINSKY, SR; IVAN MALITINSKY, JR./ (326938-M)

Bruce sometimes wondered if the NSA computer had direct input from official Soviet files. He was continually amazed at the details spewed forth from the machine on American citizens, ranging from fourth-grade report cards to minor traffic violations. But he was even more intrigued by the rundowns on seemingly obscure foreigners. Why the interest in a nurse and old woman connected with the Soviet hockey team? The question would go no further than his mind. He'd learned years before to think loudly, talk quietly, and assume nothing.

# BOSTON
## February 13
## 9:00 a.m.

In the guest locker room of the Boston Bruins, Yori paced like a caged animal as he waited for Ivan, fear and worry glinting in his dark eyes. Ivan entered casually. Yori was on him in a moment, grasping his muscular arm. "Vasili's coming back," he hissed.

Ivan let the thought sink into his head. "I thought they were sending him directly home from the hospital in Montreal. Did you hear what changed the plan?"

Yori shrugged his shoulders. "Vasili himself, I guess. The coach told me it wasn't as bad a fracture as they thought at first. And Vasili wants to be part of the team for the final game, even if it means sitting it out on the bench."

Ivan's lips tightened for a second. "Bad break."
"Not bad enough," grumbled Yori.

"It's hard to judge those things," muttered Ivan. Then he raised his voice for the benefit of the trainer who entered. "I feel better knowing it's not too bad. It was my mistake that injured him, after all." He paused, taking in Yori's nervousness. "What you need," Ivan continued with hearty affirmation, "is a good workout to loosen you up! Am I ever going to drill that puck at you during practice!" He grinned at Yori. "I have to work up a good appetite for lunch with the American!"

# WASHINGTON D.C. NSA HEADQUARTERS
## February 13
## 9:07 a.m.

Rubin Silverstein read the files and memo sent over from Mattimore. He smiled as he realized Charles had sent him copies of NSA computer printouts pulled the day before. He skimmed the memo. Mattimore was in charge, but he'd concentrate on the U.S. operation while Rubin would handle the Russian. It confirmed the decisions made in the meeting. Charles was rarely inspired, Rubin realized, but he was reliable.

During the meeting, Shields had acknowledged that Rubin's elite intelligence forces had fewer security risks connected with them. They were the cream of the agent pools. Shields had lost a couple of ace agents to the NSA cadre. They agreed that the CIA would be on call for whatever backup Rubin or Charles might require. Mattimore had expressed his opinion that the

U.S. operation could be adequately handled with the State Department, WHCA, and the Secret Service working together, but promised to call on the CIA for problem-solving or reinforcements. All in all, it was a cooperative session.

The interagency meeting with the State Department, the Secret Service, NSA, and CIA heads was the most open meeting any of them had attended, with all concurring in their mistrust of the FBI. "Too many Hoover hangovers," Shields had phrased it.

Rubin tilted back in his swivel chair and stared at the diplomas his aide had insisted upon hanging—the PhD from Stanford, LLD from Georgetown, BA from Harvard. As his glance reached his Harvard document, his thoughts touched on Peter Porter, code "Koral." Rubin wished he had a better handle on the current KGB situation regarding their "leak." This morning's Israeli report reiterated the information that the search was on within the KGB ranks.

Rubin knew his man wouldn't cry "Uncle Sam" unless the situation was critical, but it might be too late by then. Peter was in the best position for quickly arranging the exodus of the hockey team's families. The information on the oil fields and arms shipments could be sent out through the underground routes, but each request, if the KGB were dragging the nets, could endanger Peter's position. If it weren't already shaky.

Rubin weighed the situation as he headed for his vault. He hadn't mentioned Peter or his possible role in this operation at the interagency meeting when he accepted leadership of the Russian operations. If he involved Peter, they could know after the fact. As far as they knew, there was no Peter.

Inside the vault, Rubin pulled aside a steel panel to uncover a special combination lock. He twirled the lock in sequence then used his private key to open it and extract a file marked in red with the single word Koral. No numbers. Koral would never become one of a number. The file had no duplicates or microfilm copies. It was unique, as unique as the subject, Peter Alexis Porter, born Peter Alexis Rimnok off- Protokov, Harvard, Class of '41, the same as Rubin.

Rubin returned to his desk with the file, letting his thoughts drift back decades. The Peter of their Harvard days had been part of the international set, sailing off to London for a summer of English debuts and steeplechases with his British relatives, chartering yachts for weekends on the Charles, booking the Stork Club for Friday night dinner parties in New York. Peter's world was a light-year away from the lifestyle of the brilliant young Jew on a scholarship who worked weekends in the library while his father presided over the Brighton Beach Synagogue and ran the best-stocked hardware store in Brooklyn.

Rubin met Peter their sophomore year on the debating team. Peter had an incisive mind combined with a flashing sense of humor. They'd debated each other during a practice session for the Cornell debates. It was the toughest debate either young man had ever experienced. The judges called it a draw, congratulating them and expressing gratitude that they would both be exercising their polemics for the same team. Rubin and Peter emerged with mutual respect, and Harvard came out ahead with an unbeatable team for the next three years. Rubin studied the black-and-white photos, trying to compare them with his mental images of the tall, handsome and brilliant young classmate of thirty-odd years before. Rubin's most vivid recollection was of Peter's eyes, an unusual shade of deep blue, almost black in the shadow of lashes that would have looked feminine in a weaker face. His eyes would darken in anger and lighten in the sun. He would still know him.

It gave Rubin a secret pleasure, as though he'd won a point in a debate after all these years, to know Peter had no inkling that his information was transmitted to Rubin.

Rubin pulled himself back into present time, skimming the files. G-2 U.S. military. Distinguished Service Medal. Purple Heart. Missing in action, September 6, 1945, Berlin. Presumed dead.

Rubin glanced back at the files. That must have destroyed his father. If I remember correctly, his old man was in munitions. Yes, there it is. Peter was destined to come home and take over the machines of war. He never made it, Rubin thought to himself, noting the old man had died in 1968. He remembered Peter's father as an elegant man with a wry sense of humor.

When Peter had taken Rubin along to the Porter offices in the Chrysler Building to pick up some "drinking money," Rubin had expected a richer version of a Russian butcher he'd known in Brooklyn, a solid bear of a man. Pierre Porter, as Peter's father had translated the Russian Protokov for himself, was a tall, slender man with sandy graying hair and hazel eyes. His humor was quick and wry. Rubin recalled the phrase he'd used as he handed Peter money: "Anything for my progeny directed toward the reigns of economic and political power. Now be discreet, my young gentlemen."

Rubin buzzed for Harelson, chief of international communications. Within minutes, courtesy of a wireless communications relayed to Moscow by a Rumanian trawler, OPERATION CONTACT was set in motion. Rubin would pull Peter out of the sea of Red suspicion before the net closed in and let him bring along a few smaller fish for Bollinger's publicity coup.

Colonel Sergei Padov studied the list he'd received moments before. General Taikov had a fixation on the 1953 fire in the KGB records room. There was no doubt it had been arson.

Taikov had ordered him to check all personnel in a position to leak classified information against the records of those whose files were destroyed. "Then triple-check the correlations," Taikov directed. "We might find our mole lurking there."

Padov pushed the theory that it was a leak rather than a long-term plant, but he conceded Taikov could be right and went ahead and ran a computer check. He studied the list, two hundred and eighty-seven names of current KGB employees whose records were immolated in the flames of treason over twenty years ago. Many of them had risen in the ranks. Padov smiled as he noticed both his and Taikov's names were on the list. It was a place to begin. He'd run the next check for correlation of critical categories to narrow it down. In the past ten years, there'd been major leaks on Cuban missiles, skirmishes with the Chinese, secret tests, various attempts to infiltrate Western intelligence agencies, and more. Padov was well aware of them. Some of them had placed his own operations on the carpet.

Padov did not believe the computer could hand them the source on a nice, neat printout. It could only point to the general possibilities. Then it would be time for careful analysis and review of the in-depth files. Computers couldn't put together subtleties where the subconscious would focus on a name or place and awaken devastating associations; it couldn't recall gut reactions. He smiled ruefully to himself. This wouldn't get him back in the field for a while.

Personally, he had an edge. Cryptology was his passion, and his mind was an encyclopedia of codes—Russian, American, English, Chinese, French, Cambodian, and others—balanced by his working knowledge of ten languages. Whether or not there was a plant, to assure his generalship and keep Taikov happy, he'd find one.

Relaxing a moment, his hand reached instinctively for the scar disfiguring the left side of his neck as he stretched for a moment, glancing at the medals carefully framed on his wall, medals awarded to Lieutenant Sergei Padov for valor in World War II. It had been a long thirty years. He rang for Konstantine.

Konstantine briskly entered the office, saluting precisely. "Sir?" In their eleven months of association, Sergei had never seen a single wrinkle in his aide's uniform. The man would fall apart in a world without starch. Once, Sergei thought he saw a stray dog hair on his shoulder, but as the aide moved closer, Sergei realized it was a trick of light streaming through the mesh wire of the subterranean headquarters. Sergei was privately amused that the KGB top offices were at basement level, a result of their underground inception, he conjectured. Konstantine, as well as being his aide, was covertly his KGB Control Operative, responsible to "control" for Sergei's activities. Had Konstantine known Sergei chaired the Control Committee, he wouldn't have been surprised. All of the KGB expected the checks and counterchecks. Sergei had suggested the procedure himself as another check for the system.

"Anything of interest in the morning report?" Sergei asked.

"Mostly routine, sir. Some crazy report of submarine sightings in the Black Sea that turned out to be a false alarm. The raid in Leningrad produced a library of illegal Jewish material and books. We've arrested twenty-three so far."

Sergei reached out his hand. "Let me read it myself."

The aide handed Sergei the computerized report, verbatim from Odessa. Sergei spoke as he studied the report, "Konstantine, call my driver and tell him to meet me at my apartment at one. Tell him his leave is postponed, Condition W priority."

Konstantine's eyes gleamed; Condition W was emergency procedures.

Sergei watched the avaricious interest in Konstantine's rounded young face with amusement. Then he dropped his bomb. "You are being transferred to Kiev to oversee the containment of the Jewish dissidents. You are to report to Colonel Malikov directly by 0900, February 15."

The young aide seemed to lose some starch as his jaw dropped an inch, slack with surprise. "But, sir, what will you do . . ." He paused, wondering if Control knew of his reassignment.

"I managed to survive somehow before you were assigned to me. I shall attempt to struggle through without you." A slight smile lifted the right corner of his mouth, causing a long dimple to crease his lean cheek. "You'll find it's been approved through Control if you check."

Konstantine nodded wordlessly, his hands crumpling the edges of the paper in his hands. Sergei asked, "Is that something you wished to show me?"

"Yes, sir," croaked the aide, finding his voice. He handed the memo to Sergei. "This memo's nearly a month old, sir. It must have gotten lost in a bureaucratic shuffle. I wondered if we should take any action on it."

Sergei dropped it on his desk with a cursory glance. A Red Army hockey team security matter. He'd deal with it later. He had work to do before he met his driver at one. "That will be all, Konstantine. I'll give you a good report for the work you have done."

"Thank you, sir." The aide turned to leave.

"And Konstantine, for your records, I plan to walk to the apartment at noon. I need the exercise and my mother is not well."

"Very good, sir." He hadn't known the colonel's mother was ill, but he knew she was in her eighties. It was as likely that the colonel had planned an assignation with his mistress Natasha, the thirty-year-old translator for the Kremlin. Konstantine relished the knowledge of his superior's secret life. His greatest asset was attention to details. His reports included everything from precise descriptions of Tasha's clothes to the decor of restaurants. He was enough of a red-blooded twenty-eight-year-old Moscovite to appreciate Tasha's beauty, but hypercritical enough to wish she'd comb her dark curls more often.

"Prepare a report on anything you are currently handling that will require follow-up. We'll review it this afternoon." Sergei was itching to get moving. "You are excused until then."

Konstantine saluted and hurried out to call Control and confirm his reassignment. He wondered who would be assigned the watch on Colonel Padov. It wouldn't matter to him in Kiev.

Sergei dialed a number, let it ring once, hung up, then dialed again. "Hello," a female voice answered.

"Mr. Vasolovich."

"I'm calling Moscow exchange 5112. This is the second wrong number!"
"Sorry, sir, you should check your directory."

"Thank you." He smiled as he hung up. Andrejeski would be there at
ten. By that time, he'd know the American request and have laid his plan. OP-
ERATION CONTACT. The one code which meant "out." He and Waterbury
had chuckled at the Black Sea meeting when he devised the submarine scare
code. "For time to surface," he'd quipped. Sergei found his thoughts slipping
into English as he thought about his parents and sister. Not Sergei's, he chided
himself, Peter's. The Baron and Baroness Pierre Rimnikoff-Protokov, Americanized into Porter. Were they still alive? Were his father's vast financial holdings
intact? What would I be like if I had followed the path my father had cleared
for me, a destiny of wealth and power? It was a futile question about a destiny
that Peter Sergei Alexis Porter denied on November 11, 1945, in the cold rains
outside St. Petersburg.

# NORTHERN RUSSIA
## October 28, 1945
## 4:00 p.m.

The autumn was mild for Northern Russia. Although the harvest was over, shocks of corn remained in the fields, reminding Peter of Halloween visits to German cousins in Upstate New York. In the long, tedious weeks since leaving Berlin, he'd developed a great fondness for the fourth-hand fifth-rate plow horse he'd bought for an exorbitant price from a greedy farmer on the outskirts of Berlin.

"If you pay dearly for something, you should treat it dearly," rationalized Peter as he awarded the geriatric creature his best woolen blanket and the name "General Patton." He soon hit upon the diminutive "GP," which he shortened to "Jeep," hoping the old horse would combine the heart of Patton with the reliability of a jeep. Jeep had come a long way with him.

Peter had always thought of himself as a loner. He had been cautioned as a child not to talk about his family or himself. Most of the time his thoughts were his own. The better part of valor.

Even so, compared with the close companionship of his military colleagues thrown together through war and a common enemy, the past forty-odd days had seemed bleak and interminable. Although many of his G-2 assignments in the previous three years had been lone wolf assignments, he had at least dealt with other human beings, even though that was only a minor part of his job. Members of the French underground, temporary landladies in crowded apartment buildings filled with transient refugees and black- m a r k e t opportunists—although the encounters lacked intimacy, they had their own brief reality of exchange. Not so for this journey. The unofficial trek into northern

Russia precluded all extraneous contacts.

His cover was that of a Soviet lieutenant, shell-shocked, fatigued, returning home. His name was Peter Padov. Padov had been the name of the gatekeeper at the Rimnikoff Estate outside St. Petersburg. "Peter Padov" was heading "home," without papers, confused. Bradley Waterbury, Peter's G-2 commander, agreed that "no papers" would stand scrutiny better than forgeries. "If you must do this thing," he'd added. They'd been through that "if" a dozen times before Waterbury conceded it had merit.

"Sir, it has a double purpose. First off, we've about won the war and I deserve a leave. I promised my mother I'd make every effort to find her sister and family, reach them, and see if there's any way to help them get out. Or"—here he'd paused for a moment, narrowing his eyes as he studied the reactions of his commander—"you've often said now is the time to infiltrate the Soviets before they seal off their borders. I must still have cousins and relatives who may not be sold on the new Soviet way, without the estates they remember. They might be ripe for enlisting as . . . communicators." Peter chose his words with precision.

Waterbury capitulated. There would be no surface recognition of Peter's journey. Only in the most highly classified files. The expedition would be, according to Peter, "a White Russian mole, burrowing his way home." The St. Petersburg contacts and codes were set.

In 1945, many military experts agreed that although the maturing Red Bear might be a recognized ally against Hitler, it was in no way to be considered a trusted friend. The seeds of Democratic-Communistic confrontations were being sown in ground already frozen and the fields were surrounded by hardening curtains of polemic. The United States was fighting World War II for ideals and freedom; the USSR, for land. The invasion of minds is less of a threat to a controlled society than is the disregard of territory.

"The French, on the other hand," mused Peter, "feel invasion of territory the lesser of the evils. And where, Monsieur Vichy-sois, will that place you in the postwar power plays? In the soup?"

Little did Peter know that mild and weary afternoon that this trick of mentally considering issues for his own amusement would be instrumental in preserving his sanity for the next three decades.

He stopped around four o'clock and extracted the pieces of his map from his pocket. He carefully fitted three sections together to form the outskirts of Leningrad, St. Petersburg. He wanted to confirm the lines and names already engraved in his mind. Fifteen miles to go. That would bring him to the estate around seven thirty in the evening. Perfect. Would they still be around? Would anyone remember them? Padov could be the key.

The image of his mother, soft and golden, confronted him. "That Hapsburg cousin," his grandmother would laugh, "pops up on the strangest faces." Sophie was as blond as her younger sister, Katya, was dark. If Katya were still alive, she'd be fifty-two. He remembered all the stories of the gay and beautiful Tanya who refused to leave with her unborn son.

When other children in the spacious Park Avenue apartments were lulled to sleep with Uncle Remus tales, Peter and his sister Nathalie were privy to tales of czars and noble uncles, brave officers in the czar's army like Colonel Rudolph Radovich, Katya's husband, shot down in the final minutes of the great White Russian stand in 1918.

Sophie had begged Katya to come to England and America with them. "Think of the child. Rudi would want you to be safe!"

Katya remained adamant. "For the sake of the child, our Russian son, I remain." Nothing moved her. "Go with God," she counseled Sophie, "for I fear God will have a difficult time in our new Russia." These were the last words she spoke to Sophie. As the car drove away, winding along the long road from the Rimnikoff estate, Sophie turned back, watching Katya solemnly watching them, unmoving. Sophie began to pray and continued to pray each day for the next half a century, for Katya's safety.

"Go and find her if you get an opportunity, Peter," Sophie pleaded as she sent her son to war. "If she wants to join us at last . . . I know it may be impossible . . ." She paused and looked down at the Oriental patterns of the carpet as a shadow seemed to pass over her. Peter sensed her deep sadness. Then she'd leaned toward him, looking intently into his eye, trying to pass him her own determination. "You must try, as though I were the one you had to find. She is our blood, and blood, pray God, must in the end be stronger than politics." Peter nodded and bit his tongue to stop himself from adding "Hapsburg cousin and all."

As he urged Jeep ahead to a faster walk, his thoughts raced ahead to the estate. The photographs of his mother and father with Katya and Rudi picnicking on the manicured lawns. His grandmother posing beside sterling samovars. Katya and his mother as children in the elegant playhouse. Katya and his mother in gowns, dressed for balls. His mother remembered their special playhouse fondly. "It was so elegant." She'd laugh. "And almost as large as this apartment."

# THE ESTATE
## October 28, 1945
## 7:32 p.m.

Katya knocked on the service entrance of the main house. For the thousandth time? three thousandth? It didn't matter. It had been safe all these years for Sergei, herself, and Uncle Alexis, God rest his soul, she added.

After Sophie and her parents had gone, she and Uncle Alexis were the only ones remaining besides the servants. As the Bolsheviks steadily completed the takeover, no aristocrat was safe. Reports reached them from district after district of the "sovietization," which featured harsh examples being made of former owners for the glory of the state. It became evident that they could not remain in the open.

In the early days of 1919, Uncle Alexis and Katya carefully made their plans. As the scholar in the family, Uncle Alexis had never taken time from his worldwide research excursions to marry and have a family. This gave him two advantages. Aside from his niece, he had no immediate family to worry about. Also, he'd spent most of his time abroad, so few people in the area recognized him.

"We must merge into the proletariat for our safety," he insisted to Katya. "As the mole on their cheeks and under their noses. Only there shall they never find us."

They made their sad farewells to the Chippendale and crystal and quietly moved into the gatekeeper's cottage by the entrance to the estate. They had dismissed their servants the week before, giving them handsome bonuses along with the explanation they were going to join the rest of their family outside

Russia.

Alexis seemed content to settle into the role of the retired gatekeeper. "I have done my traveling, Katya, and as a historian, I would hate to miss this new era in Russia. Love it or hate it, it is a historic first in the struggle to structured society. Can Communism work? Given the nature of man, I have my doubts. But it should be interesting."

It couldn't get worse, Katya decided as she ate another potato. Alexis had convinced her that her only safe disguise, to pass as the daughter of the gate-keeper Padov, was in fat.

"I know your vanity will suffer, child, but rather that than your life and the life of your child."

Being pregnant, it was easier to keep on eating. The starchy food helped fill the hollow that had lodged in her stomach as she watched Sophie and her parents drive away. As usual, Uncle Alexis proved to be correct. The extra pounds gave her a round, peasant quality she maintained even after Sergei was born. She privately considered it one of her greatest sacrifices, disguising the high cheekbones and lithe aristocratic figure.

"And you must roughen your hands!"

That too! Although she was doing all the cleaning and cooking, tending the vegetable gardens and the one remaining horse, she was careful to wear gloves and to take care of her nails. "That too, Uncle Alexis," she murmured as still another nail broke and the harsh soap they now used burned red spots on her sensitive skin. She was glad her mother had gone.

The simple ruse worked. When the Soviets took over the Rimnikov estate and converted it into a state school, they allowed Alexis and Katya to move into the playhouse in the gardens. Alexis, who was well qualified to be headmas-ter-plus, was appointed chief groundkeeper and Tanya was conscripted to do the school's mending. The administrators were delighted with her fine work on their shirts, but she didn't allow herself a single stitch of embroidery or patterns lest they become suspicious.

To Katya, it seemed little Sergei grew too quickly. She dreaded the day he would be sent off to a state school far away. Their luck held and he was assigned to the estate school, learning his lessons in the gracious rooms where, unknown to him, his mother and her family had lived, loved, and left.

Many years before, Katya stopped recounting stories of the Rimnikov family and the prerevolutionary days. Sergei had reacted defensively. "You speak like a decadent aristocrat," accused her twelve-year-old son of a White Russian war hero. "Our first loyalty must be to the state. If you keep talking subversively, I shall report you to my cell leader."

Katya shuddered into silence. The week before in the village, the Vladikoffs had been dragged from their cottage, branded as traitors by their eleven-year-old twins who received citations for their loyalty to the Soviet state. That would not happen to her!

Despite his Communist conditioning, Sergei continued to give her pleasure. He would steal carrots and turnips from the school gardens to give his mother extra rations. Food was scarce, and by 1935, she had completely regained the slender figure she had eaten away. By then she'd been accepted as the daughter of Alexis Padov, chief gardener. No one questioned her and she stayed away from the main buildings when strangers were there. No men were important to her except Alexis and Sergei. Once, a teacher at the estate school had tried to approach her, but she quickly rebuffed him. Romance had died for her on a bloody field. Occasionally she would dream of gayer times, of dances, and stolen kisses by her then-suitor Rudi. She would awaken and choke back tears as she realized it was only a distant dream.

"You are so much like your father." She would smile at Sergei. "Your brave father who died fighting for our Russia."

"I don't want to hear about my father," Sergei insisted. Katya had told him his father died fighting side by side with Prince Rudolph Paderovsky.

"Rudolph Paderovsky was a traitor to the State," Sergei announced one evening. Alexis and Katya exchanged worried glances. "If that is so, my father was also a traitor. From this moment, I have no father but the State."

Katya tried to explain, but Sergei only grew hostile. Gently, Alexis changed the subject, knowing no good could come from the discussion.

Traitor! thought Katya indignantly, picturing the proud intelligence of Rudi before he lost his life courageously in the last major frenzied attempt to prevent this new Russia from emerging with children's minds suckled by the State.

On Sergei's twenty-first birthday, Katya went to the secret cache she and Sophie had begged the carpenter to design decades before. They never dreamed their childhood whim would play a vital part in the drama of Katya's life. Although the paper notes of the czar were worthless than kindling, the gold, silver, and jewels were easily bartered in the alleys of St. Petersburg for medicine and warm clothing. She traded the silver and gold. She didn't touch the jewels. She didn't know what disaster could be great enough to force her to sell the jewels she considered Sergei's secret birthright. The jewels stood between her and insanity as she hoed her cabbages and mended poorly styled clothes. They represented her inner strength, glittering facets of the life she'd buried.

As she touched the corner closet's three releases in sequence and opened the voluminous drawer, which had been designed for large dolls and trains, she reached in and retrieved a small box bearing the hallmark Fabergé.

Between the soup and potatoes that evening, she handed the box to Sergei. Uncle Alexis held his peace. His council was "wait," but Katya insisted. "I must give him something of value!"

"This was your grandfather's watch." She smiled. "It is all gold and represents loyalty and purity of spirit."

Sergei leaped to his feet. "You had it hidden all these years!" He frowned in exasperation as she silently nodded. "You put us all in danger. It is illegal to hide valuables from the State. And if you turn it in now, they will ask why you have held it and wonder what else you have hidden."

Katya's reply was calm. "It is yours now, Sergei. It was so from the day you were born. What is done with it now is up to you."

"It is lucky we go to war tomorrow. Otherwise, I might have to deal with this. I don't like mysteries, but I cannot bring myself to question you further, right now."

He kept the watch and studied the Rimnikov crest and Fabergé hallmark. His mother had handed him a puzzle upon his majority. He couldn't picture her as the bastard daughter of a Rimnikov. Perhaps the old estate owner had given it to Alexis for a service. But Alexis had remained silent, unusual for the verbose old man. The party line voice in his head put a curtain upon his thoughts as he turned his attention to the battlefields of World War II Russia. He had enough to contend with from the Germans without worrying about his mother's family intrigues.

When in the spring of 1943 his commanding colonel noticed the watch, Sergei laughed and explained he'd plundered it from an old man one night. Sergei felt a flash of shame as the colonel laughed.

A few months later, Alexis suffered a severe stroke. Home on leave for several weeks, Sergei showed great gentleness toward the old man he believed to be his grandfather. While Katya went to collect her work from the school, he read to him and made tea. He felt a great loss when the old man died on the eleventh day of his leave. He never mentioned the watch.

# NORTHERN RUSSIA
## October 28, 1945
## 8:00 p.m.

As Peter turned Jeep into the road leading to the Rimnikov estate, he noticed a sign on the gatehouse, "State School 515." Of course. The State would have conscripted the property.

He tied Jeep to a tree and headed under cover of the surrounding woods for the west lawns and the playhouse. "If they are not there," Sophie had counseled him, "look in the secret drawer of the corner cupboard. It's impossible to open by accident. If Katya left a message, it would be there."

Surrounded by boxwood, the playhouse looked like the old photographs in Sophie's albums. The apple tree in the back was larger. As he cautiously crept closer, he noted that the paint was peeling, and the right front window had been filled in with waxed brown paper. It was dark, but evidently someone was using it. Stealthily, Peter approached the door. No sound came from inside. Breath held, he tried the knob. Open. Hand on his Soviet revolver, he stepped inside. Moonlight filtered in the side windows, mellowing the old room. Photographs flashed in his mind in luxurious comparison. No longer the lovely carved cherry furniture, dolls' houses, mechanical bears, and music boxes. Only one settee looked vaguely familiar, disguised by its frayed cover and worn polish. But the corner cupboard, minus glass panes and tin soldiers, was there! In his excitement, he knocked into a rickety chair crossing the room. "Damn!" he hissed and froze as the noise echoed in the silent room.

"Who's there?" a faint male voice called from the back room. The playhouse library, Peter quickly judged, wondering who the occupant could be. He heard bedsprings creak, followed by a sigh, as though someone were repositioning in an old bed.

It's too early for sleep, thought Peter. Perhaps someone is ill. He caught his breath. If someone were sick, then someone else must be around to tend to him.

His mind raced as his body remained motionless. He debated slipping back outside and returning later, taking the time to see who lived there and come back in when they left again—if the man in bed ever did.

If he's very sick or an invalid, he might not leave for weeks, he mused, and I don't have weeks.

The shadowy cupboard continued to flaunt its mystery. He wavered another moment then moved toward the cupboard. As his mother had carefully instructed him, he touched the releases in sequence. The dusty insides of the large drawer looked like a farmer's storage bin, filled with cardboard boxes printed with seed companies' names and lumpy brown paper bags.

Peter reached for the nearest bag. The paper crackled; his mouth went dry as adrenaline shot through him. He waited. Nothing stirred. Slowly, he inched his hand into the bag and pulled out a necklace. Aunt Katya's emeralds. Rudi's wedding present. He recognized them from her wedding portrait. Was she dead then? Did she have to leave so quickly she could take nothing and leave no note? Perhaps there was a note after all.

Suddenly the door opened, and Peter saw a woman framed for a moment in the moonlit rectangle.

"Sergei?" the woman gently called. "Are you asleep?" A weary sigh escaped from her lips as she moved into the room, setting her heavy basket on the table, facing away from Peter. He studied her from the shadowed corner by the cupboard.

Although dressed in bulky coarse clothing, she was slender, and in the night, her hair was dark and wavy. There was not a shade of doubt in Peter's mind, although he'd seen her face a brief moment, the woman was his "beautiful Aunt Katya," to quote his mother.

The Katya who smiled out from his mother's albums had been no more than twenty-two. Softened in the moonlight, she looked much the same. Peter's mind turned a corner. Who was in the study? Uncle Alexis? A new husband? A Soviet? His muscles tightened, preparing.

As she lighted the oil lamp on the table, she continued to face away from him. Soon she would see him. Three quick steps and he closed his hand over her mouth.

"Forgive me, Aunt Katya," he whispered in her ear, "but you must not shout." He gently pushed her away from him and turned her toward him, hand still on her mouth. In fear touched with curiosity, she viewed him silently, without resistance.

Peter smiled with a touch of mischief in spite of, or perhaps because of, the bizarre encounter. "I am your sister Sophie's son, your nephew Peter," he whispered.

He took a recent miniature of his mother from his breast pocket. Unusual for a Soviet soldier to carry, perhaps, but it was not as dangerous as a letter from an Americanized sister. She looked at the small painting carefully and slowly nodded as the implications of Peter's appearance began to touch her. He dropped his hand and stood quietly, his heart pounding as he tightened his grip on his gun.

"This way," she mouthed, silently heading toward the outside. "Mother!" The voice from the library halted them.

"Yes, Sergei!" she called back. "I just got back with more sewing." "It seemed so long," came the truculent response.

Katya motioned Peter to wait as she hurried past him into the back study. "You just came in? I thought I heard you before."

"Just this minute." She touched his feverish forehead. "How do you feel?"

"The pain does not change, and I've slept too much today to sleep more." He looked at her with a vulnerability she hadn't seen since he was in school. "Perhaps you would read to me?"

"First, tell me, are you as hungry as a bear in the night?" She'd asked this question every night for the first five years of his life. He weakly shook his head. "You must eat, Sergei. Dr. Zharkov will be here in the morning, and I want a good report from him! You must build up your strength."

"I wonder why they didn't send him off with the army." Sergei avoided the food issue. "They desperately need doctors."

She straightened the heavy old quilt. "He was the only doctor remaining in the district. The younger men were all called." She paused. "He's past eighty, my son. He wouldn't last long in the stress of battles. I am glad he is here. He delivered you, and me before that. He will not give your life away easily when he worked so hard to bring you here. We had a difficult day when you were born." She smiled, remembering the trauma without remembering the pain.

"He is not in the party, Mother, but he is a good man."

"It makes me happy to have you feel that way. Old loyalties are import-ant . . ." She paused, silently thanking her god that Dr. Zharkov had been near when the army hospital in Leningrad had no more room. Sergei, the wounded hero, had volunteered to go home to recuperate. She leaned down to kiss his forehead, then handed him a glass of water.

"Take off your coat, Mother. It's warm in here."

"I must go outside and get wood for the fire to make sure it stays that way.

And cold soup is not appetizing!"

"Please hurry. I'm tired of being alone." "Not long," she soothed.

In the main room, Peter waited, frozen like an Apache, praying his in-stinctive trust was wise. He did not move until Katya returned and motioned him to follow her outside.

Inside the small woodshed, she held the oil lantern with one hand and reached out to touch his cheek with the other. "Your eyes are so like your moth-er's, it's uncanny. They are dark blue, like Sergei's, not sky blue like hers, but the shape and expression are hers." Her eyes dimmed with nearly thirty years of unshed tears. "She and Stanislaus are well?"

Peter assured her they and Grandmamma Rimnikov were well; Grand-pappa Rimnikov had died ten years before.

"He never was strong. I often thought it would kill him to leave. He didn't want to. He did it for her, you know."

Peter hadn't known. He quickly explained his mission as it regarded her. Would she come back with him? His mother had never stopped praying and worrying. Life was good for them in America. He knew they could make it back. Would she come?

She did not address the question. She searched his dark eyes and asked, "And you, Peter, how did you get here? I cannot believe you are here. It is so difficult to get in or out of our country now. I wanted to write so many times, but I was afraid they would find us."

They covered dozens of years in a few minutes. She explained his cousin

Sergei was wounded and lying inside.

"Would Sergei turn me over to the military?"

"Perhaps," she paused. "You would find it hard to understand how your cousin has been trained from such a young boy. He thinks I am the daughter of the gardener Padov. Even when I gave him your grandfather's gold watch with the Rimnikov crest, he asked no questions. Perhaps he is afraid to know. I don't know. He has been nurtured by this new Soviet state and is as much a son of the party as of me. If this were not so, who knows what would have become of us."

"Come back with me. Let the party take care of Sergei."

"No, Peter. I have lived through this, and I shall continue to hold my peace each day. I pray that things will ease up soon so I can give Sergei what is his. No longer the land, but the gold and jewels. There are still bank accounts in Switzerland of mine and Rudi's that Sergei may have someday."

"May I stay for a while?"

Fear softened her voice. "No one must see you. You cannot stay in the upstairs. Sergei might hear you, but there is a basement room. It is very dark, a storage room. Once it held sleds and skates and carts . . . and had electricity. Now they don't repair the lines from the estate generator so we must use oil lamps." Peter gently probed to see if she knew anyone who might be sympathetic to the free world.

"Uncle Alexis would have been, but he is dead. Perhaps Dr. Zharkov. Although he is nearly eighty, he is alert, and in his heart, he is of the old school. He delivered both your mother and me." She smiled in the lamplight.

"Can I speak to him?"

"He'll be here tomorrow to attend to Sergei. I'll arrange it then. Now I must get back inside before Sergei gets nervous."

Peter spent the next ten days "underground, like a mole," he joked to Katya. Despite the frequent attention of Dr. Zharkov, Sergei's condition deteriorated. The fever rose as the infection spread. Zharkov and Peter met and discussed the current state of Russia, following the medical visits. Zharkov detested the Sovietization and the regulated opinions.

When Sergei died early in the morning, November eleventh, Zharkov challenged Peter. "Your country wishes to have agents among our people. I agree this would benefit the free world. And I will not be of use long. Who knows how soon I shall follow your cousin Sergei to the other side? Now consider this, my young friend. If your mother had been the one who stayed rather than Katya, it might be you lying there dead today. As the fates have decreed, you are alive . . . looking much like our Sergei. Your hair is half a shade lighter, but you basically have the same coloring, height, and build. If one considers that war and illness can change people, you could easily be taken for him."

Peter caught the drift of Zharkov's conversation. "You're suggesting I replace Sergei, use his identity as a cover?"

Thoughts flashed through Peter's mind from a dozen directions—images of his mother, father, and Nathalie crowded together with school memories, war memories, New York apartments, girlfriends, dances, USO bashes in Paris. Actively enter the military establishment of Russia? Never return to the United States? If he believed in the goals of the free world and Waterbury's dour predictions of the cold war, it was an incredible opportunity. He could become a vital source of information if he did at all well in the Russian system. But if he slipped once . . .

"We would coach you carefully," continued Zharkov. "Katya would take you through Sergei's life moment by moment. I would do my best on the system and the military."

If he chose to accept this role, he couldn't inform his family. They would be told he was missing. But wouldn't they want him to do everything possible to help Katya and the democratic system? His mother would understand, but his father, as a pragmatist, would argue against it. Peter would be turning away from an international business, from the power structure his father was building for him. What would his new life be like? No worse, he thought wryly, than being holed up in a basement for the past week and a half.

That night, in a cold drizzle, Katya, Zharkov, and Peter buried the shell of Sergei under an old, gnarled apple tree beside the playhouse. The tune "Don't sit under the apple tree with anyone else but me, 'til I come marching home" drifted through Peter's mind as his shovel bit into the cold earth. "No, no, no, don't go walking down lover's lane . . ." He remembered his last night in New York with his sister's friend, Sheila. She'd kissed him hard as they said goodnight, adding, "Come see me when you've won the war." He hadn't thought about her since and probably wouldn't again.

When the last piece of sod had been carefully replaced beside the trunk of the tree, which had been the happy site of a hundred picnics, Dr. Zharkov stepped a few feet back from the burial grounds and prayed for the immortal soul of "our brother Sergei." Then he turned to Peter. "You have decided?"

"We have buried Sergei. Now we must account for him." Dr. Zharkov nodded. "Long live Sergei Padov."

A sob caught in Katya's throat. She quickly stifled it with her hand, biting her lower lip, gazing from Dr. Zharkov to Peter.

"There is one more thing that must be done, Peter-Sergei," Zharkov continued, "if you have the stomach for it. It will prevent questions."

"You're the doctor. What is it?"

"Sergei was badly burned on his neck. The trauma from the burn weakened his resistance, added to his pain, and contributed to his death."

Peter nodded. Trained by expert American and British operatives, he had noticed every detail on the body, including the angry, inflamed tissue covering the left side of the neck. He took a deep breath, calming his racing heart and mind. "How will you do it?"

"With candle wax and brandy. I am permitted no anesthetics except in the hospital."

"Perhaps I could get some on the black market in St. Petersburg?" Katya suggested. "I mean Leningrad."

"If we had time. The invalid cannot be found missing. Sergei's superiors have a habit of checking in at odd times. It must be done tonight. Then Peter-Sergei shall become gravely ill, the infection spreading to his face, requiring bandages. Then a slow steady recovery."

"Shall we go inside?" asked Katya.

"At once," replied Zharkov. "And get me candles and brandy. You have both?"

Katya nodded as she led the way inside the playhouse.

Zharkov explained to Peter. "Candle wax will burn the skin steadily and deeply. Perhaps nine or ten applications will be needed. The brandy will help your pain.

The brandy helped only a little.

# MOSCOW
## February 14, 1976
## 11:00 a.m.

It didn't seem over thirty years ago to Peter. So much had happened in between. A marriage. Nina, his wife, dead from an explosion in a chemical warfare lab. Cold warfare. Guerilla warfare. Aunt Katya had been a pillar, filling in as surrogate mother for all of them. She stayed in the background, barely speaking at official receptions lest she seem too elegant for the simple peasant mother of a good Soviet officer throughout his long, steady rise to power in the KGB. Zharkov, finding a sympathetic Soviet dentist to de- Americanize his teeth. Setting fire to the KGB record room. Ordering the sanction of Western agents. "My friends" he would think as he signed their death orders. To have done less would have made him suspect. Walking the razor edge between a humanist and a tough KGB officer. He'd tried to play his role as Sergei Padov, ambitious, hard young KGB officer, as a character in a play, but it was an all-consuming role. It had become too easy; he was too hardened to the cruel methodology. Colonel Sergei Padov was closer than second nature.

He thought of his Soviet family. Aunt Katya was eighty-three and spritely. She would understand, whatever the repercussions. He closed his eyes, shutting out the images of his children Peter and Sophie. He rarely saw them except for special functions and ceremonies at their schools. There could be no farewells.

Peter tried to steel himself to remain patient, but he was chaffing to know what cataclysmic situation could call for surfacing. By eleven forty-five, he was climbing the stairs to their third-floor flat two at a time. Not quite as fast as fifteen years ago, he thought. Although he was in excellent condition, he perceived small slowdowns. "The midfifties aren't the midthirties," he'd reminded his mistress Tasha. Still, his taut stomach and firm muscles pleased him. He wasn't far removed from his field condition of a decade before.

In the kitchen, his aunt hummed an old Russian ballad as she mixed batter for Peter's favorite walnut cake. He followed the sound into the kitchen.

"Hello, Mother!" he announced himself. "Is that a surprise for me? You must be feeling better."

"Sergei! What are you doing home at this hour?"

Peter dipped his right forefinger into the batter for a taste.

"Keep your fingers out of there," chided Katya. "You'll never grow up."

Looking directly at her, Peter dropped his left eyelid slowly over his eye, a trick he'd practiced since childhood. "You didn't look well this morning, so I thought I'd stop by and see how you were."

Quickly, she picked up her cue. "How good of you to notice. I felt a little weak this morning, but now that I'm moving around, I feel better. At eighty-three, old bones move more slowly than young ones, especially in our Moscow winters."

It had been nearly a year since they'd rehearsed. Peter held his breath, waiting. Would she remember her lines?

"Oh, I almost forgot to tell you." Katya continued mixing the batter, adding more walnuts. "I called the electrician on the way to the market. He should be here soon."

Peter relaxed. They'd rehearsed this simple conversation a dozen times in as many years, but never here for the benefit of the KGB special wiring. The simple explanation would cover the lack of a phone call from Peter's office or the flat. The electrician had been cued by the powers behind Operation Contact.

The buzzer sounded. Peter pushed the archaic button and listened to the electrician announce himself. Peter instructed him to come to the third floor and buzzed him in. He then quickly headed for the parlor where he pulled the wires from a metal lamp resting on the sideboard.

In the kitchen, Katya's tired heart fluttered as she poured the batter into the baking pan while continuing to hum her old ballad. She could hear the footsteps climbing to the third floor. She heard Peter walk to the front door and open it, waiting.

"In here," Peter called as the man approached the third-floor landing.

"It's the living room lamp. There were sparks last night. I'm afraid of starting an electrical fire."

"Sparks are dangerous, very dangerous," acknowledged the man, "especially with wooden buildings."

Code completed, noted Peter to himself. Sparks, dangerous twice, and the mention of wood. Peter's apartment building was brick. The code was another check.

Peter felt adrenalin surge through him. This was the first friendly direct contact he'd had with a Western agent since 1962 during a Black Sea vacation when he'd worked out codes and procedures with Waterbury. He'd been grateful many times for that precautionary summit. It would have been extremely difficult to arrange after he'd been promoted up out of the field.

The electrician quickened his step as he followed Peter into the living room, stumbling on the edge of a small Persian rug. Peter reached out a hand to steady him. The electrician grabbed his hand as he steadied himself. Not a word was spoken as Peter felt him slip a small square of paper into his hand. Peter nodded slightly as he gestured toward the lamp. "The sparks came from this light."

The man examined the lamp for a moment. "The wire is damaged," he said. "It has blown out the socket. I have the proper wire with me now, but I'll have to come back tomorrow to replace the socket and check the main wiring. That could have been damaged also."

"As you will," Peter said. "My mother will let you out when you've finished. I must return to my office." Peter was eager to digest the details for the operation. He hurried into the kitchen to give Katya a quick kiss on the cheek and tell her what the repairman was doing. "See you at dinner, Mother. I can't wait for the cake!"

He restrained his impatience to read the message until he was safely inside Natasha's small rooms three blocks away. There he eagerly spread the tightly folded onionskin paper on the table and decoded the message.

The assignment had three parts. Information on arms shipments to the Middle East in detail. Accurate figures and prospects on the oil fields. And arranging the escape of one middle-aged mother and a wife and child of members of the Wings hockey team. The whole team planned to defect!

He smiled to himself. The premier and General Taikov would be furious. He'd enjoy watching their expressions. There was a fifth part. They wanted him to come out. It was an order. He knew it would be difficult to arrange everything to meet the schedule—barely five days—but it could be done. He already had the information on the arms and an update from the oil fields. He knew his figures were accurate, perhaps the only accurate figures in the country. Using Andrejeski and his personal elite network, he could arrange the exodus. He'd need fancy footwork, but it needn't blow his own cover. What possessed Headquarters to panic? Perhaps they'd gotten wind of the all- out hunt for a high-placed leak. And who were "they?"

After Waterbury's heart attack in 1968, he had no concept of who was running Headquarters. For all Peter knew, it could be someone who didn't have the same confidence in him. He couldn't leave now on the verge of taking over as head of the KGB. Taikov had as much as promised it to him. Although the information they needed was vital to get out, it wasn't. It couldn't be as import- ant as his current position. And he had the search for the mole under his own control. They would get their information and Wings relatives, but he would not blow his cover. What could they do? Court- martial him?

He chuckled at the thought as he he walked toward the bathroom, re- viewing possible plans for the operation mentally. He dropped the treated paper in the toilet and watched it rapidly dissolve before he flushed. At that moment, Peter heard the key turning in the lock. He deliberately let his muscles relax as he casually turned on the faucet, washed his hands, and dried them carefully, checking his thick, lightly silvered hair in the mirror with satisfaction. He rec- ognized Tasha's footsteps.

"Sergei!" Tasha's breath caught in her slender throat. "I didn't expect you . . ."

His effect on her was always the same. The physical attraction was so strong it interfered with her ability to speak whenever she first saw him, wheth- er they'd been apart for an hour or a week. All she wanted to do was move closer and melt into a hug.

He moved toward her as she leaned against the wall. She reached out her arms as he folded her against him, leaning into the wall. She felt the energy flow between them flood her body; his passion hardened against her. As the blood surged, his mind raced. What repercussions would Operation Contact have for her? If he had to blow his cover, would she be interned? If he needed her help, would she give it without question? Born in 1945, his year of decision, she'd grown up Sovietized, a party member in good standing. Her mind had been parented by the State, but her heart he knew was his. Despite the differences in their ages, he knew she loved him.

Between their breathless mergers, they stole minutes, hours, and occasional days sharing their thoughts. She was bright, courageous, and loyal. He could not marry her or bring her openly into his family. She was technically married to an army officer who ran a Siberian detention camp, in perfect irony, Peter thought. An ambitious young man, he had put his career first and Tasha a poor second. She rarely spoke of him, except to say he would fight a divorce. Peter hadn't pushed. As he approached his mid-fifties, his sense of fairness to her in relation to both his age and unique situation convinced him it was best to remain in the status quo. He had learned patience long before.

His mind darted even as his tongue searched sensuously across hers. In the crunch, he might have to take the group over the border himself. If possible, he should do it with minimum outside help. Only give them a time and place for contact. Most free world operatives were known and watched by the KGB. He couldn't risk contact with the knowns, and he didn't want to risk contacting the wrong people. If he had to take them out himself, it was unlikely he could return. He would have to return home. Home. For years, he'd blocked out thoughts of his American family. Were they alive? His mother would be eighty-six. Nathalie, his sister, middle-aged. It was difficult to imagine his pixie sister as a matron. An excited shiver ran down his spine. He blocked out the memories as he lost himself in the soft lips and tongue of Tasha's response.

"Whew," she murmured, breaking for breath. "What new drug are you experimenting with?"

He felt her taut nipples through her soft white blouse. She slid her hand from around his back and unfastened her buttons to give him easier access. "Mmmmmm."

"Mmmmmm?" He continued his rubbing explorations lower.

"Too many clothes," she muttered, tossing off her blouse, slipping off her shoes, and dropping her skirt. An eager minute later, she stood naked before him. Breathing heavily, he caressed her with his eyes, starting at the slender ankles, moving slowly up the smooth line of her body. "You are a whippet," he breathed, picturing the trim racing form of the finest of greyhounds.

She moved closer, reaching down to check the success of his erection. "Does that mean"—she chuckled deep in her throat—"that I am a bitch?"

He laughed in reply, picked her up, and carried her across the room to the bed. He gently dropped her and kneeled beside the bed, resting his head on her firm breasts, his tongue seeking the taste of her.

"Take off your clothes," she pleaded, fumbling with the buttons of his shirt.

"Not yet," he whispered hoarsely as he continued his sensual journey across her skin, "not until I have you over the wall with pleasure."

As head of the KGB, he could force the divorce and marry her with impunity. He could serve the best of both worlds. Then he turned his thoughts over to his nerve endings and responded instinctively.

Outside the flat, Konstantine made notations in his Control log. "SP stopped at his flat 11:45. 12:00 noon walked three blks to T's flat. T. arrived12:25." As he suspected. A quick session at lunch, he thought smugly. I should award the colonel a medal for virility. According to the files, Sergei was fifty-four with the appearance of a man in his midforties. Men who kept their shape and hair had a decided edge, Konstantine observed, and the colonel faithfully worked out in the KGB training room at least three times a week.

Konstantine had a lot to take care of in his few remaining hours. He decided he'd better dig up information on the Wings's hockey team relatives before the colonel returned. The colonel hadn't noticed the date on the memo Konstantine had given him earlier; it was over three weeks old. The inefficiency of the routing system infuriated the colonel. Depending on Padov's mood, heads would roll, and Konstantine's well-groomed head wasn't eager to be one of them.

By the time he finished all the routine work, it would be time to leave for the day. He was determined to run some additional computer checks on the potential moles. He called the officer of the day and requested permission to work late, explaining that it was his last day in Moscow and he wanted to leave everything in perfect order for the colonel. Permission was granted. Konstantine was calculating that if he came up with additional solid leads in the search for the mole, the colonel might revoke the unwanted assignment. He sensed he wasn't a favorite of the colonel, but the man was fair. If he came up with valuable information, there was a chance he'd be kept on. It made spending his last night poring through numbers and codes worth the tedium. Konstantine enjoyed detail work others found enervating under normal conditions. This time he had a concrete goal.

At ten minutes before two, Sergei slowed his pace as he entered Headquarters. Konstantine was sitting erect in his straight-backed chair, leafing through file folders. "Everything under control? No problems?"

"Yes, sir. No, sir," he answered in sequence.

As Sergei moved on into his office, his mind considered, rejected, and reconsidered possible plans. Nomadic disguises? The Black Sea yachts? Through Poland's old route? First, he had to track down the critical three: a middle-aged mother, a young wife, and a child.

He focused on the papers piled on his desk. Better attend to business as usual. There must be no change in pattern until time to move. Of course, he could pass back word that the assignment was impossible in the stipulated time. The thought hovered above his conscious mind like a thundercloud. It rumbled for a moment and was gone.

He glanced at the date on the memo on top of the pile, the one Konstantine handed him before lunch. "Konstantine!"

His aide appeared at attention in the doorway.

"This memo is three weeks old! When did we receive it?"

"I made a notation on the bottom, received it this morning. I've already assembled the pertinent information on the relatives involved. It is fortunate the hockey team is performing brilliantly, under total control from our security reports."

"The hockey team!" It flashed like lightning as Sergei scanned the memo. "Bring me the information you have collected immediately!" he barked.

Konstantine stiffly exited and returned carrying a neat list. "It's all there, sir."

"Very good."

Sergei studied the list. Konstantine was on the nose. It was all there. Names, residences, habits, work, everything. His guardian angel was working overtime this Monday morning. He looked back up at his aide. "The laxity of surveillance of the teams' relatives is criminal. I want them all interned immediately." He checked off several names. "Have these brought here and divide the others among the other Moscow facilities."

Konstantine nodded sharply. As if he hadn't anything else to do, he thought as he hurried from Padov's office.

Knowing Konstantine would be occupied with arrangements for picking up the Wings's relatives, Sergei used the time to substitute dummy files for the classified files on the oil fields and arms shipments. The files summarized both past and projected numbers. If he had to blow his cover, his loss would be felt. If he made it back to Moscow, mission accomplished, he could cover. The files were never removed. He only gave Taikov and the premier summary reports based on the originals.

# NEW YORK
## February 14
## 11:30 a.m.

NHL Commissioner Adam "Mac" McDougal carefully replaced the receiver in its cradle. Rob Carson. Hadn't seen him in years—three to be precise. At the farewell reception for Rob's interim term as NHL Commissioner, the changing of the guard. Rob had returned to private practice. Rob certainly was mysterious on the phone. Maybe he was negotiating a sale. Mac wondered who wanted in or out. At the worst, he'd get a good lunch out of it. Maybe he'd even wangle a weekend invitation for him and Nancy on the marvelous old Carson yacht on Martha's Vineyard. He'd heard a lot about it. Polished teak and mahogany. Build around 1927. Few around like that anymore.

He checked his Accutron. Twenty minutes before lunch. If he walked over, he'd arrive right on schedule. The exercise wouldn't hurt his growing executive paunch either.

Rob sat at a corner table, ordering a martini up as McDougal approached.

Rob smiled. "Timing. An interesting thing. For some things, critical. I'm glad you could make it."

"That's pretty heavy for a Monday lunch opening statement!" "True. We'll keep it light until we go upstairs to eat."

Over spinach salad and a fine herb omelet for both, McDougal secretly wished for a double thick prime rib, but echoed the diet fare, feeling virtuous but hungry. Initially, McDougal thought the private dining room at 21 for the two of them was wasteful, but as Rob clued him in on the proposed defection, McDougal wondered if there weren't a more private place.

Rob paused, waiting for some feedback. McDougal played with the chopped egg dusting his raw spinach.

"Rob, this isn't a simple issue. Will we or won't we accept them into the league? You've already made it clear that this is a highly classified matter. One wrong word, one leak, and the team could be recalled. How can I answer for all the teams and players' unions?" He took a deep sip of his third martini.

"First of all, we have to consider that the Players Association might resist the idea of Russian players competing for their spots if we set up a special draft midseason. And to start a new team franchise to make room . . ." He paused. "We can't have all the Russians playing on one team. They might sew up the Stanley Cup for the next five years and start a revolution! Of course, we could compromise, start a new team, scatter the Russians among the existing teams, and shift around other players to fill out the new roster. It's possible. We have a number of franchise requests we're considering. Charleston. Toledo. Others."

"But it's possible?"

"There is the language barrier to consider too."

"Most of them speak some English or French, and I'm sure the State Department will arrange crash courses." Rob carefully wiped a crumb from the left corner of his mouth. "All right, Mac, bottom line. And remember, crowds might be interested in coming out to watch our defectors from behind the iron curtain playing in freedom. Think what your press department could do with that! What can we tell them?"

McDougal lighted a cigarillo and inhaled, filling his lungs to capacity, exhaling slowly, measuring his reply. "We will do everything possible to integrate them into the NHL. I can't give absolute guarantees. And I certainly can't quote firm salary offers. But I can give you my personal assurance that I'll use every ounce of my influence to work out the best plan for them—and for the league."

Rob rang for the waiter. "I was hoping that would be your reaction. I know I don't have to tell you not to mention this to anyone—not your wife, not even your dog. Forget there's a Russian tour. Right now, Mac, we're in a position where one false word could be disastrous. Our actions can spell freedom for these young men, or great danger."

For whom? wondered MacDougal silently. He forgot to ask about Martha's Vineyard and the yacht.

# ANDOVER, MASSACHUSETTS
## February 14
## 1:00 p.m.

Mattie asked Ivan Malitinsky if he'd like more roast beef. She'd gone New England for the luncheon with Yorkshire pudding, brown gravy, succotash, and Indian pudding.

"No, thank you," protested Ivan with a grin. "If I eat another bite of your delicious food, I'll think you are trying to get me too fat to play hockey!" He dreaded the afternoon practice with such a full stomach.

Brian pushed his chair back from the table and invited Ivan to join him in the basement family room, giving the excuse that Ivan might like to see little B's air hockey game. It would give them an opportunity to talk privately. As Brian led the way down the polished stairs into the plush family room, he had a moment of fear. What if Yori had been fantasizing? What if Ivan and the others weren't part of it? He'd have to phrase it to be certain before he delivered the message. "I have news," Brian began. Why hadn't he asked Yori to give Ivan a code phrase or something?

"Yes?" Ivan asked eagerly. "Our conditions can be met?"

Brian's jaw unclenched. Brian hurried to give the report before Mattie finished clearing up and joined them. "Everything possible is being done to meet your conditions. The league cannot quote specific salary figures at this point. To do that, they'd have to call a meeting of all the team owners and have a special draw for you before you are available. That would be too risky. Too many people would have to know your intentions. But the commissioner had given his assurance he will personally help arrange your placements on teams."

"What about Vladistock's family and my mother? They will be brought here?" He knew he could talk the team into accepting promises on their placement on American teams. They were as good as any of the players they'd competed with, or better. But Vladimir would not accept asylum without Nadia and little Vladimir. "How will they do it?"

Brian shrugged his shoulders. "They didn't give me details. They said to tell you the wheels are in motion."

Ivan nodded as he realized the less, he or any of them knew about details, the better were their chances of success.

"Did they tell you when it can be done?"

"No," Brian said. "They promised to give you further directives as necessary. Your conditions aren't simple. They said they might not know until the last minute if they have brought your relatives safely out. You haven't given them much time, less than a week."

Ivan thought for a moment. "Tell them Vasili is back with the team. He is the only one not with us in our plans. Already he has criticized the coach for letting us be too free. Yori believes Vasili is on the KGB payroll, so we didn't include him. The coach listens to him. This is the last meal any of us shall have in the home of an American. I told the coach it would be an insult to cancel this lunch with the captain of the Bruin team." Vasili had also insisted that the meals with players be discontinued to tighten discipline. Western decadence, he told the coach, was bad for the morale of the younger players. Ivan felt had to maintain his party line image until the last moment.

Brian moved over to the air hockey table. The danger to the Wings suddenly felt very real to him. "Then you'll have to stay cool and let our . . ." He almost said State Department but realized he didn't know who was handling the operation. He finished lamely, "people contact you or arrange a phony hijacking or something. I don't know any more details yet. I'd counted on having Vladimir Vladistock over for dinner tomorrow and could give him any updates."

"That all has been changed. We leave for Philadelphia early." Ivan sat down heavily on the bottom step. "All we can do now is leave it in the hands of your people. Contact with one of us is contact with all. We are together in this. Perhaps we should establish a message system to use during tomorrow's game."

"I don't know," Brian said as he picked up the air hockey puck and examined it sightlessly. "They didn't give me instructions for that. They said they will find ways to contact you."

# Code Coral

Brian welcomed the interruption as little B, home from school early, clomped down the stairs and interrupted their conversation. Brian was aware that Rob had given him few specifics and equally aware that Ivan could have many questions.

"Hi!" B called to Ivan. "You're a captain of the Wings, aren't you? Are you waiting to play hockey with me?"

Ivan broke into his first heartfelt grin for the day. "Yes, I would like to play hockey with you."

B led him to the game table, explaining it was easy once you got used to it. "I hope so," Ivan responded seriously. "Now first you must explain to me the rules." He glanced up at Brian, raising his brows.

"To begin," Brian said, moving after them, "there are two sides."

"Dad, that's not always right, when there are four people, there are four sides!" objected little B.

"For purposes of explaining the game," Brian continued, "let's start with two sides."

K atya gave Peter a questioning look as she ladled the stew into bowls.

"I'll walk to the bakery with you after dinner, Mother," Peter said, smiling at her. She would help him make his decision just as she had in 1945. The mission had to be extremely critical for the United States to initiate Operation Contact. How could the three relatives of the hockey team members be so important? He'd been told in his orders that the timing was critical. Obviously, it was part of a team defection scheme, but he'd assisted numerous important defections in the past years, none of which affected his cover. The information called for on oil reserves and arms shipments were high priority, but he'd passed out other information before that was more urgent.

Operation Contact was reserved for the highest of crisis situations. It meant no measures barred. Blow cover, if necessary, kill, if necessary, but get it done. But the orders following Contact were stronger—come out, period. As far as he knew, American intelligence should have no knowledge of the search for a plant or leak within the KGB, but in the intelligence game, almost anything was possible. Conditioned by military training on both sides, Peter had a bad gut reaction to intentionally disobeying an order. Perhaps he could ride it out. Wait until he'd gotten the relatives and files out and then request further orders. Headquarters had no way of knowing Taikov had selected him as heir apparent of the KGB. Think what he could slip through the bars of the iron curtain in that position!

For decades, Peter had edited his tongue while allowing his mind to roam freely. He'd been lucky, avoiding interrogations under drugs. Through his private studies of Yoga and mental discipline, he could outwit their lie detectors, used for standard security and loyalty checks.

Silently, he enjoyed the rich stew and hungrily showed his appreciation of Katya's walnut cake, moist and flavorful.

"Where did you find the walnuts?" he asked. "They're scarce these days." He wanted to keep the conversation banal.

"A boy from the country was selling them on the streets." Katya smiled. "Remember how you used to climb the trees and get them for me by the school?"

The task of reinforcing the coached memories of his childhood had begun years before. Now it was part of the texture of their lives. Peter came close to actually remembering the incidents as part of an earlier life of his own; Katya had become as much his mother as his own. If he had to blow his cover, it would leave Katya vulnerable.

Nurtured by the State, his children were truly "Sergei's children," with an ideology like the original Sergei's. They were dedicated to the Soviet system, a process begun in their preschool day care center. And he had always pushed himself to keep up a wall against his heart, not let the children get too close, to consider them the children of his Soviet wife. For their safety. And for the safety of his own soul.

His daughter Sophie with her esoteric formulas! Tall and blond and brimming with confidence. A natural scientist reported her professors. Working on her doctorate so, like her mother, she could enter the mysterious world of chemical warfare. So intense and serious for a student.

His thoughts flashed back a lifetime and culture to his Harvard days with bright, restless girls from Radcliffe and Smith ready to kiss or discuss politics at the drop of a mug. It didn't matter which, as long as it was wholehearted.

Had those girls been so different from his gentle, serious wife? Yes. The Soviet system in the mid-fifties had little room for frivolity. So Serious. So little space for the mysticism and whimsy of his own American-Russian childhood. Take away the folklore and Mother Church and modern Russia's remains were often drab and serious, the artists and writers sad or angry.

There were times when Peter felt starved for wit, rapier wit not heavy-footed, barracks-style humor. He had steadily collected lighthearted incidents that he kept on file in his memory banks, which he would pull out for private mental leavening. He liked to remember an Allied assignment with an M-1 agent in Bonn before its liberation. They were holed up in a decaying rooming house when they heard the SS raging into the downstairs hall. His M-1 companion calmly turned to Peter and remarked with British aplomb, "I say, it's time for new roles. Let us recast as firefighters before we're playing lamp shades in Berlin." He'd placed an old shade on his head and led the way down the rickety fire escape. They'd "made it in the shade," Peter had quipped.

He searched his mind for a much-needed present-time chuckle. He relished the projected picture of Konstantine reacting to the revelation of Sergei Padov's true identity.

"Impossible!" he could visualize Konstantine protesting stiffly, insisting he had monitored the colonel's every move for a year. Peter was certain that would finally take some starch out of Konstantine's collars. He pulled back from the image; he would make every effort to assure it would not materialize.

Katya began clearing the dishes quietly, sensitive that Peter-Sergei was deep in thought. Peter noticed the motion and quickly helped clear the table. He dried the dishes as Katya washed. He wondered how Konstantine would view his cold colonel if he could see him now.

Dishes dried and put away, they walked through the dark streets toward the bakery. Katya's spritely pace matched Peter's. He marveled at her energy. "Sometimes, Mother, I think you grow younger as I grow older."

She hesitated, placing her mittened hand on his arm. "It has come, hasn't it, my Sergei-Peter?"

He nodded, noting no one was close to them. "Perhaps and perhaps not, but I must move quickly." He summarized his orders, explaining that he was still debating following the order to come out. "If I do," he added, "I may be able to take you with me?"

She paused, thinking of her dead son. "I have lived this long in this new Russia. I cannot leave now."

Peter suddenly wondered if the three Wings's relatives he was to bring out would echo her sentiments. Kidnapping would be an ironic way to get them to enter the Free World.

"Age is no consideration when it comes to KGB interrogation. And I wouldn't be here to protect you."

"What of the children then?" Fear caused her voice to quaver. "I have lived my life. Thanks to you, much has been good. I am not afraid to die, but you must protect the children." She grasped his arm.

His blood ran cold. Take the children and have them blow the whistle. Even if he asked them, it would give them the opportunity to interfere. They would not want to come even if they had the choice. "They would not question the children. They know I see them rarely."

"There are better fathers in Russia," Katya commented with little warmth. "Forgive me, Sergei. I know it has been a difficult situation for you. But I wish you had more concern for them."

The children would survive. This frail, yet strong old lady was his main concern—and the new truth serums the KGB was using.

"My needs are small, Sergei. I can get by."

"Shhh." An old man shuffled by, faced half buried in a ragged scarf. Peter sensed she was thinking about the jewels. He had built a dozen caches for them—behind a sink, in walls, hollow bookcase backs—a new one each time they had moved with his advancing career. The thought of them pulled him back to point A, the beginning of the marathon charade that began with a glimpse of emeralds.

"Take them," she urged. "Here, they are of no use to me. You may need them."

Remembering the affluence of his youth, Peter shook his head. "I doubt it. And they are your security. If necessary, you can sell them on the black market." He recognized his own hypocrisy, when he'd considered buying a summer cottage fifteen years before. Katya had begged him to sell some of the jewels. He'd refused, explaining they could possibly be traced back to her. Yet people did it every day undiscovered. He'd realized they were beautiful shards from another world whose memories he wanted unsullied as much as she did.

A light snow began to fall. Flakes caught on Katya's lashes and gave her an excuse for the welling tears. "You have given me the best thirty years of my life since the war."

Sergei knew the "war" for her would always be the White Russian battles against the Bolsheviks.

"And the odds are we shall continue as we are. But you deserve to know the possibilities. I couldn't have survived this life without you, Mother." Peter emphasized the last word as he entered the bakery.

Large eyes gleaming with tears that left dirty trails on his round cheeks, the little boy asked, "Momma, why are we here?"

The young mother wished fervently she had an answer for her own satisfaction. She reached out her firm hand and gently wiped her son's cheeks. "They say for our safety—and for Poppa's, I'd guess. Perhaps some people think by harming us, they can harm him. So, the police have taken us to safety." She believed the internment related to her husband, Vladimir Vladistock. He was with the Wings, thousands of miles away with strangers in the capitalistic world. Perhaps the KGB was afraid American agents would try to reach relatives of the team and threaten them to reveal secrets or cooperate or the Wings would be harmed. But she didn't know any secrets. But why else would they be taken away "for their safety"? Anything was possible. But whatever their motives, the KGB was neither questioning nor harming them. The damp smell of the small room was offensive to her hospital-trained nose, but there were no bugs or rats or corner urinals like she'd heard about.

She hugged her son tightly and glanced at the stout middle-aged woman beside them. She'd seemed friendly enough as they'd entered the cell, chatting about how rudely she'd been awakened by the police and brought here. Nadia recognized the type. The kind of woman who loved to complain. She had patients like that in the hospital often enough. Then the guard had ordered them to remain silent as he shut and barred the door. The woman had plopped herself down heavily on the wooden bench and stared mutely at the earthen floor.

Nadia took her son's small grimy hand and began humming an old Russian folk song. "On the steppes, the harvest is near," she crooned. "The moon shines bright when the yield is good . . ."

The older woman looked up in surprise and interrupted, "Where did you learn that?"

"From my grandmother." Nadia smiled. "She grew up in the country north of Moscow where there were many farms."

"So," the woman exclaimed bitterly, "there is still some family feeling left in Russia?"

"Of course!" Nadia was surprised at the rancor in the woman's tone.

The small door within a door creaked open as a tin tray laden with bowls of greasy bean soup and dry pieces of black bread were pushed through. "Eat. Take it and eat," growled the faceless guard on the other side.

The food looks revolting, but the nurse in Nadia knew her young son and the older woman should try to eat something. "Ah, hot bean soup for you, little Vladimir," she encouraged.

Karl looked at the fresh peach tart smothered in whipped cream. "I shouldn't," he said as he plunged his fork into the confection.

"Charles, I won't boggle you down with more questions which you won't or can't answer for me. It's getting tedious." He paused, his forkful of tart frozen midair, "Exactly what is and will be happening in Moscow?" He gave Charles a wide-eyed fishy stare.

"That's Rubin's area. And even if I knew, I wouldn't discuss it here." Charles quietly announced.

"Hogwash! You act like everyplace in Washington is under surveillance. You use it as an excuse to keep me uninformed. And I don't like the political ping-pong you and Rubin play. He says ask Charles and you say ask him!" Bollinger fumed as he resumed consuming his confection.

Charles, content with his Camembert and espresso, calmly explained, "I'm not paranoid, Mr. Secretary, but technology is very advanced, and detectors are fallible. There is no top security clearance in this restaurant for obvious reasons." He glanced around the room, spotting a top columnist and the head of the Kenyan delegation. "Look around. Even without electronic aids, simple eavesdropping is entirely too possible."

Bollinger grunted. It was difficult to tell if it was a grunt of agreement or disapproval.

"Right now, things are moving on my end and Rubin has the wheels in motion for his side of the operation. The less said anywhere, the better our chances for success."

Bollinger only liked cat-and-mouse games when he controlled the catnip and cheese. Too much of this operation was beyond his direct control to suit himv. "All right. We won't discuss Rubin's mystery man right now, but we'd better move on to some important ifs," he spoke caustically but lowered his voice as he summoned the waiter to order another brandy. "For instance, if Rubin's man doesn't make it . . ." He paused dramatically as the waiter approached and took their after-dinner orders.

Sometimes Mattimore wondered if the astute secretary of state held dual citizenship with the Third Reich, which might account for his cold maneuverings. To the public, he was the dove of all doves, but in policy meetings and personal communications, his claw prints showed.

The waiter brought the drinks and quickly retreated. Charles proceeded to quietly answer Karl, "In response to that 'if,' Mr. Secretary, it would depend upon the stage of the operation at the point of failure and how much information had been blown. There could be an instant recall and a diplomatic protest."

"Why a diplomatic protest? How could it involve the U.S.? In their eyes, isn't the mystery man one of them?"

Charles raised his hand palm up and frowned to quiet Bollinger. But Bollinger indiscreetly barreled on.

"It's his lone operation. We can deny involvement, can't we?"

Mattimore was well aware that every agent ran the risk of denial. Regardless, Bollinger sounded as human as an IBM calculator. Maybe he should reconsider the plum Soviet trade relations spot Westinghouse was still offering him.

Bollinger persisted, "The press might try to implicate the CIA as usual, but they'd come up empty, right?" He glared at Charles. "How deeply are they involved? They're so adept at inside leaks these days."

"As little as possible, with compartmentalized functions only." Charles lowered his voice, hoping Karl would do the same.

"Good," Karl smacked his lips, tasting the fine brandy.

Mattimore replaced his glasses, again becoming the ascetic owl. "So far this is strictly military, NSA and State. Our Classifieds don't show up in Paris newspapers."

"You better hope it stays that way," Bollinger snapped. "Now, next step. If Rubin's man succeeds . . ."

"It means the terms have been met, we can complete our U.S. operations, and the rest is up to the president," Charles replied quickly and quietly.

"And the secretary of state," added Karl unctuously. "To summarize, Charles, let it suffice that I expect to see you on the nineteenth with the proper three escapees."

"Only three?" Charles raised his brows.

"Number 4 is your problem, not mine. I'm only concerned with the critical three—and a whole team for leverage."

According to Rubin at their private meeting, his mystery man was a KGB heavyweight, ripe to defect. The thumbnail sketch convinced Charles of one thing. The Russians might bargain as hard for one of their top KGB colonels with a head full of classified information as they would for the Wings. He didn't share the thought with Bollinger.

"Perhaps," Karl chortled as he polished off the final sip of brandy, "we could make a deal for a lifetime supply of their finest vodka. They do make the world's best vodka." He pushed his forefinger hard into Mattimore's lapel, looking at his unfinished martini. "Aren't you going to drink to that?"

"If I had a better insight into your plans for what happens after we complete our parts of the operation successfully, I might."

"Sometimes," Karl chuckled maliciously, "I think you don't trust me, Charles."

"I wouldn't say that Mr. Secretary," protested Charles, conceding silently that he was free to think it.

Bollinger seemed to read his mind. "But you might think it, no? That could be unfortunate."

Karl's mock petulance made Charles want to vomit. He held his tongue, trying to keep his eyes free from hostility.

"Such distrust from an undersecretary could be unhealthy, very unhealthy, for you," Karl emphasized and paused for a moment, dramatically, then he continued, "Don't forget, Charles, there are a plethora of so-called Soviet experts floating around this town."

"I won't lose sleep over it this week, Karl. It's tricky to change your work horse in the middle of a fording!"

Bollinger pulled his brows together dramatically. "So, you consider yourself a work horse? All you're doing is sitting on your derriere worrying about some mystery man in Moscow. I admit I have a touch of concern about him myself."

Sans Souci, with its graciously dim French ambiance and its well-heeled international clientele, was no place for Mattimore to protest that it takes an inordinate amount of coordination to set all the backup units in position to cover all the potential exit routes. They had to be ready for any of seven escape plans until they received word. Old codes had been resurrected and communicated with absolute security. It all was contingent upon their Moscow man's next communication. He'd accepted the assignment, but the choice of method would be his.

Bollinger had to be aware of the complexity of the process. Or did he? Bollinger was at his best around conference tables or in high-level closed sessions, proposing treaties and power politics. He had no military background and minimal intelligence experience. Mattimore took a healthy sip of his vodka martini and reminded himself "Mine is not to question why," but he still had all the worries of the "how" in front of him. He emptied his glass.

"Happy Valentine's Day," he toasted. "I'm glad we're not in Chicago. I might really get nervous."

Konstantine would not be replaced. Taikov agreed that Sergei needed optimum autonomy in his search for the mole. "Know thyself," the right corner of Sergei's mouth curled up slightly with the irony of the thought. He would keep Taikov apprised of his whereabouts until the last moments, even using Taikov himself if necessary.

Andrejeski and his driver were standing by. The routes chosen. As he picked up the telephone, he skimmed the list of prisoners at KGB Headquarters and checked off two additional names. "Get me Colonel Alexis Brosheko." He waited for the connection. "Alexis. Sergei Padov. Very well, thank you. I'm transferring some citizens for detention to your facility. I'll telex full information. Expect Major Andrejeski. Code Amber, top priority. Very good." He quietly cut the connection, still holding the receiver, for the benefit of the omnipresent microphones. "I shall accompany them myself. I have other business to discuss with you. I expect we should arrive the day after tomorrow, the seventeenth. Until then, Colonel."

The facility controlled by Alexis was due north of Moscow. Control would be thrown off until the morning of the eighteenth. By then, if all went well, it would be too late.

He crossed his fingers for a superstitious second, slipped a sheet of specially treated paper out and coded his instructions, using a code he and Waterbury had determined fifteen years before. Only one other person knew the code, a man in Washington. Peter did not want to know his name. If there were any leak, he'd have to dream up some fast Nomad disguises to get them across the mountains. But that could never be pulled off in three days. The

U.S. Army must think he was a miracle worker. He was saying his prayers, if that counted.

He buzzed transport. "This is Colonel Padov. Have the limousine I ordered in front of the West entrance in exactly thirty minutes." It was unusual, but not unprecedented, for him to accompany prisoners with highly classified information. It was irregular for him to be involved with more benign citizens interned for secondary purposes. He was relieved Konstantine had been neatly dispatched.

Peter rang for an aide. "Send this telex to Colonel Brosheko." The telex would confirm officially the transfer of Berthe Malitinsky and Nadia Vladistock, period.

He next spent a few minutes encoding a message for General Taikov explaining that he was laying a trap for their "mole," instructing him to ignore Control's reports or concerns about his whereabouts. He would call Taikov's private number within forty-eight hours with a progress report. He sealed the message and left specific instructions for its hand-delivery the following morning.

Peter mentally checked his list; he was doing fine. Buzzing security, he requested the Vladistocks and Malitinsky be prepared for departure along with Natalovya and Breinkov.

Natalovya was a middle-aged woman suspected of running a black market operation in the southeast sector of Moscow. Suspected of adding classified information to her contraband commodities, she'd been pulled into KGB Headquarters for interrogation. Breinkov was a prostitute in her midtwenties who'd shown up in the Control logs of three members of the presidium. That alone made her suspect. Both women had been brought in the day before and were Padov's responsibility. Standard procedure in such matters is to let the prisoners stew in their own guilt in solitary cells for several weeks. The enforced silence often made them eager to chatter when the questioning began. Control's board would not expect action on either case for a while.

Opening his old leather briefcase, a present from General Taikov for Padov's making colonel, Peter filled it with heavy unmarked manila envelopes containing the critical files on the oil fields and arms shipments. He'd added Polish and Hungarian files on his own. Just in case, he told himself. They contained lists of suspected pro-Western diplomats and officials. Headquarters might be able to do something positive with them.

He snapped the case shut, thinking as he had many times before, what a fine piece of craftsmanship it was. Taikov had a strong sense of quality, which surfaced on rare occasions. The case, along with the vintage port kept concealed beneath his regulation uniforms in his bedroom closet, must have been purchased on the black market. Peter had tried to maintain a psychological distance from the old general, considering him part of a nefarious system. But when the system slipped down and the humanity showed, Peter would experience a shudder of distaste at having to work at cross purposes beneath the protective shadows of the general.

Peter walked into the outer office, nodded to the guard, and walked down the stairs to the subterranean prison. "Is everything in order?" he asked the supervisor.

"Yes, sir," he handed a sheaf of papers to Peter. "Here are their documents."

He ordered the prisoners brought out. As the guard buzzed the inner sanctums, Peter leafed through the documents, extracted two, and placed them in a manila envelope which he slid into his breast pocket.

The supervisor turned toward him, "Would you like an envelope for those, sir?"

Peter took out a second envelope from his pocket and placed the remaining documents into it. "I have an extra, Sergeant."

The supervisor snapped to attention as the prisoners were led out. He ticked off the names as they were prodded forward. "Vladistock, Nadia and Vladimir. Malitinsky, Natalovya, Breinov." The ill-assorted group eyed them with a mixture of fear, anger, and curiosity.

A strange harem thought Peter.

The sole male, a young boy, whined half-hidden in his mother's skirts, "I'm hungry."

"Weren't they fed?" demanded Peter. "Standard food," replied the supervisor.

Peter silently sympathized with the boy as they were herded up the stairs to the waiting limousine. He was familiar with standard fare.

They drove through the snowy streets of Moscow in a silence broken only by Peter's curt instructions to the driver. As they reached Peter's apartment building, he ordered the driver to stop and pull behind the KGB car parked nearby where his driver was waiting with Major Andrejeski on schedule.

# Code Coral

Andrejeski would take Breinkov and Natalovya north for internment, using Vladistock's and Malitinsky's papers. Peter would not reveal the switch to him. Once the group was safely out of the country with only the driver and himself as witnesses, he would silence the driver and let him be responsible for the switch and escape. Peter expected to be back in Moscow within four days, if all went well.

As Peter climbed out of the car, Andrejeski hurried over to him. Peter opened the rear door and pointed to Breinkov and Natalovya. "You and you, step outside."

As they fearfully climbed out, not knowing what to expect, Peter told they would be going with Major Andrejesky. Then he swiftly turned and walked back to his KGB car where he greeted his driver, reconfirming his instructions and placing him under Major Andrejeski's orders until further notice. Andrejeski followed with Breinkov and Natalovya in tow. Peter opened the rear door of his car as Andrejeski herded them inside. Peter handed the young major the envelope from his breast pocket. "Here are the papers and orders for Colonel Brosheko. He expects to meet with you the morning of the eighteenth."

"Very good, sir. And good hunting."

Peter had explained to his prize pupil the night before that he himself was working on the Code Koral assignment and needed the diversion for a couple of days. Andrejeski knew enough not to ask questions. Sergei was the master. He only felt strange about being back in uniform for the first time in five years. His cover on this assignment was his true rank and identity.

He waited until the major's car had turned the corner, then leaned toward the window of the limousine. "Wait here a few minutes." Quickly he walked through the lobby of the old apartment building adjacent to his. Perhaps an unnecessary precaution, but sometimes the middle echelons of Control had their own backup systems. He raced down the steps to the cellar oblivious to the dank odor and hurried across the earthen floor, through a door into his own cellar. He took the stairs to his flat two at a time, key ready. As he burst open the door, he came face-to-face with a startled Konstantine.

"Your mother told me you weren't expected," Konstantine gasped. "When I couldn't reach you at Headquarters, I came to leave you some information. I must speak to you privately."

There was no time. The electrician was due any moment. Peter grabbed Konstantine's arm and pulled him out of the flat and down the stairs, racing back toward the basement.

"Control has your apartment under surveillance. We could not speak there." Konstantine spoke as they hurried down the stairs. Why would Konstantine tell him that? Peter's mind jolted to a halt as they reached the foul cellar. He turned to his pale young lieutenant. "Well, what is so important that it could not wait?"

"After I gave you the list of current KGB members whose records had been destroyed, I went ahead and ran another cross-check of those in classified positions. I took that read-out and requested those with any association with projects BEARD, LIMEY, EAGLE 4, SANDSTONE, and COBRA. The read-out gave me one name. Taikov. General Taikov."

"Christ!" Peter exploded. "Of course, Taikov would have knowledge of all those projects. He's the director! So would I! So would the premier! We're on the list too."

"The premier isn't filled in on operations in detail. You didn't know about LIMEY until the British blew the cover." A little knowledge could be a dangerous thing, Peter decided, but the unrecorded chairmanship of the Control Committee prevented Konstantine from knowing his possible involvement with LIMEY. Otherwise, Konstantine might be standing before Taikov.

"You're insane. Taikov is no traitor," he glared.

"The computer missed one important thing. It failed to pull out the names of aides who would have had secondary contact with those projects. Taikov's aide Lubo was on the original list."

"So, you have found our mole, have you? Lubo!" he spat. "Lubo drives the general's car. Period. He comes nowhere close to anything classified."

"Somewhere in those lists there is the key."

"You overextend yourself. You are no longer involved with this search." Peter smiled cruelly, noting the contrast between the starched aide and the chaos of the basement. He would alert Control through Taikov that Konstantine was following a Code Koral track. It might hold, if Konstantine's Control supervisor didn't get overly curious.

He raced back up the stairs. He'd give Taikov a call on their way out of Moscow. Tasha! In the past twelve hours of planning, he'd forgotten about her. When he first formed his plans and considered coming out himself, he'd contemplated asking her to come with him. He believed her allegiance to him was stronger than to the State, but the clock had run out before the test could be applied. The Americans would consider it an unnecessary risk, but blowing his cover meant early retirement, a retirement that could be lonely.

He was worried about Aunt Katya. Once his disappearance was known, she'd be subjected to brutal interrogation. He wanted her out with him. They could handle an additional prisoner or so in the large limousine. He found her in the kitchen, sitting quietly with her knitting.

"I'm accompanying some prisoners to a facility north of Moscow. I thought you might like to ride along."

"That is irregular."

"A bit, but these aren't criminals, only citizens held for the safety of the state. I have other business with the colonel in charge."

Tears welled in her wise old eyes. She would never see him again. She thought of her high-spirited grandchildren she hadn't seen in two years. They had little reality for her at that moment as she mistily focused on her son- nephew with whom she had shared so many beliefs and years. "I must wait for the electrician."

He glanced at his watch. "He'll be here momentarily. If not, he can fix it another day." The alternative contact was in place. "Get ready. Put on a warm coat and bring along blankets."

She would come. Peter wanted her to come. With birdlike grace, she pattered into the rear bedroom and pulled out a specially fitted floorboard as the bell sounded.

"Who is it?" Peter asked the intercom.

"Tasha!" came the response. A surprised Peter buzzed her in as Aunt Katya emerged from the back, carrying a wicker basket and several dark wool blankets.

Peter held the door open for Tasha. "Sergei!" She ran up the steps to him. "I was worried last night when you didn't arrive. Finally, I broke the taboo and called Headquarters. They would tell me nothing. I thought maybe you were ill."

"Why didn't you call here?"

She laughed with relief. "I don't know. It didn't occur to me. I guess it would have been too simple. I'm only a few blocks away." She started to put her arms around him, then noticed Katya. "I'm sorry, Mrs. Padov. I didn't see you. Hello," she added limply.

Aunt Katya smiled gently. "It is all right. Young lovers must have their moments."

Peter realized Katya was thinking they were last moments. He tried to lighten the mood. "Even when they're half "old" lovers?"

The buzzer rang again. This time it was the electrician. "Why is the limousine parked in front?" asked Tasha.

"I must take some important citizens to an internment place."

She tossed her dark curls and grinned. "I'd like to be interned with you for a while. May I come along?"

"What about your translations?" "I'm free today. I could go."

"You act like this is a picnic!" Peter's dark blue eyes evaluated her as she shrugged and laughed. "We might never return, you never know. Flat tires, runaway drivers."

"So?" she challenged. "They have other translators. It wouldn't be life or death if we got tied up. Translating's not my life." She left "but you are" spoken only with her eyes as Katya calmly ushered in the electrician. Peter looked at Katya's calm old face. The strength of Mother Russia lies in her women, he thought.

Peter reached into his pocket. "We are going out. You'll have to finish the job another day. I still owe you twenty-seven rubles for the work you've done?"

"Only twenty-five."

"Ah! Good news for today. An honest electrician!" Response check. Peter handed him the money with the coded message. The electrician pocketed both without looking at them. "Thank you, sir."

"Thank you. The light is working well." He wouldn't need the backup contact. The electrician quickly left.

"We must hurry," Peter said. "The driver will get impatient." He wanted to avoid an unnecessary call to Headquarters.

"Let me come along," urged Tasha." You could say I was being interned also. Bring Mother Padov and we'll playact. It's a huge car." She stretched her arms to show Katya.

There was little time to explain why Katya was going and Natasha could not. Aunt Katya silently handed the blankets to Tasha, in tacit agreement that she could join them. The timing of her entrance was too providential to ignore.

# Code Coral

The superstition of old Mother Russia was implanted deep in his marrow and he vowed Operation Contact would succeed in spite of it—or perhaps because of it. Explanations and the choice would be given Tasha later. If she refused to come along, he could give her the car at the last moment and she could claim kidnapping. He believed that an operation that began too smoothly inevitably hit complications later. Peter hoped the reverse would also hold true.

# ISTANBUL
## February 15
### Noon

Faeuil Al Rabu had been through many spine-tingling moments in the months of political turmoil in his overt position as third undersecretary of the air force and his covert position as chief NSC representative for undercover operations in Istanbul. But as the weeks passed and no special agents appeared at his doorstep at midnight and his name remained off the most wanted lists, he realized through some fluke he had squeaked by the revenge and the political ravages of the revolutionary spasm that had overthrown the Shah.

This morning, he'd received a small piece of special gelatinous paper as he bought a sweet roll from a "beggar" on the street outside his office. He signaled his secretary-aide to hold all calls for ten minutes and went inside to read it, silently thanking his gods that he'd steered clear of CIA involvement when he was offered a job following his education at George Washington University and that he'd met Rubin Silverstein on a train heading for New York one weekend in 1968. All that seemed a thousand years ago.

Quickly he decoded the instructions:

PRIORITY. TURKISH F-111 SQUADRON TO CROSS TURKISH BORDER AT 43' 30' LONGITUDE, 40' 1' LATITUDE AT PRECISELY 0100 ZULU. FEBRUARY 18. CONTINUE INTO GEORGIA CLAIMING NAVIGATIONAL ERROR IN RESPONSE TO SOVIET GROUND CONTROL. SQUADRON TO RECROSS BORDER AT SAME POSITION, PRECISELY 0120 ZULU. CONFIRM IF RECEIVED REPORT IF POSSIBLE.

Faeuil thought quickly. The Turkish government had retained several "freelance" mercenaries in their armed forces whose loyalties were primarily the almighty "bullion," gold or silver. He smiled to himself. This was a perfect assignment for that old air-dog, Charlie Vickers. The fact that Charlie was ex-CIA, drummed out of the organization for private blackmail on the side during a few assignments, proved him eminently corruptible for all sides. The Turkish Air Force kept him on only because he was one of the best F- 111 instructors in the world. Charlie knew and loved those jets like he'd hatched them himself.

Vickers would do nicely. Faeuil coded his response, slipped it in his pocket, and buzzed his aide. Time to attack the work of the day.

Mattimore carefully reread the telex Rubin had forwarded by hand. Peter was on his way. The backup program was moving into position. Rubin remarked that the KGB information pool must run deep for Peter to add the Iranian air diversion to his escape plan. Evidently, he'd pulled the information from KGB files, regarding the U.S.-Iranian relationship. FYI, observation, Rubin had added. With luck, Rubin noted in the eyes-only memo, they'd be out by 0120 ZULU, 8:30 p.m. Philadelphia time. Rubin planned to have Nadia Vladistock on the phone from Turkey to assure Vladimir they were safely out. Then they'd have to move quickly. Rubin planned to oversee that part of the operation personally in Turkey. Charles was surprised Rubin was involving himself so directly. It wasn't his style.

Charles felt Rubin had the Russian operation well under control. He wished he felt as secure about their plans for Philadelphia. As he contemplated spiriting seventeen Wings out from under the eyes of their KGB guards and the press, he remembered to call Rob Carson and express his thanks for both his and Brian Earle's help. Charles assured Rob the United States was moving to meet the Wings's conditions. To avoid the outside possibility of a phone trace, Charles kept the conversation under twenty seconds. He didn't want Rob's name on the wrong lists. He wondered briefly if he should have postponed that courtesy call. Was the little he said too much? He should have told Rob the entire operation was classified at this point. He trusted Rob's discretion to a point, but . . .

His thoughts were interrupted by a noise in the outside corridor. He glanced up through the open door. He saw a figure pass but couldn't discern who. He remembered one of his aides had been wearing a navy shirt and white tie that morning. He'd caught a flash of the white tie and decided that's who it had been. At least it was an acceptable guess. The incident suddenly sparked a brainstorm.

Charles buzzed for his chief aide, Bob Moore, as he carefully reviewed the plans to date. As Bob walked in, Charles looked up at him through his glasses. "A few points," he began. "Sit down." He waited while Bob pulled up a chair. It made him nervous to have discussions staring up at people. "The bus in the alley," he began. "What kind?"

"A regular city transit bus," Bob noted. "If the KGB guards see it, they won't know it's unusual for it to be there."

"But the city police might spot it and inquire. I think you'd better go with delivery trucks—meat, bread, whatever. And forget about diversionary transfers. If there's a chase, it means we've blown it. Get them right to the airport and use private charters manned with agents. Keep that part simple, because the next part is tricky enough. We have to keep the guards from blowing the whistle to the press long enough for them to receive orders from Moscow."

"Sir?" interrupted Bob. "Yes?"

"I'd think as soon as they were headed for D.C., even before, you'd want the press to know. I'd thought there'd probably be a press conference right then and there."

"It's a good thing you don't act on what you think, Bob. Bollinger would transfer you to Puerto Rico. Karl wants the defection handled covertly. No one besides the team and the agents involved are to have the slightest suspicion about what's happening. The moment the team is out of the motel, the guards will receive their orders direct from Moscow. WHCA will have lines ready. There's no sense asking why it's being handled this way or what Karl has up his sleeve. Our job is to get them away from Philadelphia and coordinated with their relatives coming in from Russia. Period. End quote."

"Yes, sir." Bob's mind swarmed with unasked questions. "Now," Charles continued. "How's the CIA been?"

"Completely cooperative and tight lipped. Evidently Shields has read them the riot act about secrecy. They make a point of asking no questions, only if there is anything else we might need."

"Good, because we're going to lean heavily on them for some special agents with particular qualifications," Charles stated.

"What kind of qualifications?" Yale-trained, prematurely gray at thirty-one, Robin Chapin Moore pulled his chair closer to the desk and sat down, notebook in hand.

A half smile played on Charles's narrow lips. "How soon can you get us a master photo file of CIA agents?"

"If you call Shields yourself, sir, and request priority expediting, about twenty-five minutes with luck," Bob calculated. "Plus, the time it takes for them to drive in from Langley."

"Fine. I'll call Shields while you arrange for picking up the materials on the outside. I don't want unnecessary CIA-State Department contact inside our offices."

Bob hurried out, deciding Mattimore was bordering on paranoid, but he had to concede this would be one of the splashier defections if they pulled it off.

Mattimore removed his glasses and watched Bob hurry out the door. He smiled to himself as he doodled, eight twenty kitchen and drew in seventeen small circles. Seventeen waiters in the kitchen and seventeen diplomatic virgins in the dining room. Simple arithmetic, he thought as he dialed Shields's private number.

Ninety minutes later Bob reentered Charles's office, a fat bound book in his hands. "Just got back, sir. Here it is."

Mattimore reached for his own special pile of photos lying on his desk. Everything was falling into place. He'd asked Shields to have his agents do some special wardrobe checking in Philadelphia, but he wanted to handle this part of the plan personally.

"What's it all about, sir?" asked Bob as he pulled his chair up and placed the CIA photo file on the desk.

"If you're ready for some light entertainment, Bob, I'll show you how we play the CIA match game." He wondered how long it would take Bob to catch on.

"Sir?" Bob felt in the dark. Mattimore didn't usually play games with him. Charles pulled a picture of Vladimir Vladistock from the top of his pile.

"Focus on Contestant Number 1!" he ordered.

Bob stared at his boss for a moment, light dawning. "It just might work, sir, but you know it's insane."

# Code Coral

"Perfectly appropriate for this operation," Charles dryly responded. "Now let's get to work."

# PENN CENTER INN, PHILADELPHIA
## February 15
## 11:00 a.m.

Vladimir Vladistock pulled shut the geometric print draw curtains and turned to Ivan. "We've heard nothing since yesterday! This waiting drives me crazy. We'll be landing in Moscow, and nothing will have happened. Why don't they tell us something?"

"They have promised to act when they have met our special conditions. We should be grateful the rest of the team agreed to those conditions. We ask a lot—perhaps the impossible."

"What if they can't do it?"

"First we shall wait to hear if they can. Be patient."

"Patient! Our whole lives are changing, our world's about to turn around, and you say be patient."

"If they cannot meet our personal conditions, I shall offer to stay anyway," Ivan said.

"I won't leave Nadia and . . ." Vladimir's powerful fist slammed down on the windowsill. "I won't."

"That's a decision you don't have to make yet. There is still the possibility that they will meet the conditions in full."

"I know. It's this infernal waiting!" He rubbed his head. "With my luck, there'll be a mix-up and I'll be on my way back to Moscow while Nadia and little Vladimir head for Washington."

"Always the pessimist. Wait and see." The phone rang. Ivan answered. "Yes?" He listened for a brief moment. "Be right there." He hung up and rummaged through his suitcase, explaining, "Yori wants to borrow some tape."

"What's wrong with his own tape?" grumbled Vladimir.

"I suspect he has more to trade for it than a thank-you." Ivan walked out, wishing Vladimir was less dense, controlled. He returned in less than three minutes. "He didn't want to tell us on the phone. He thinks the KGB have taps on them. They told him they are moving to meet all our conditions. There will be special arrangements made at the final banquet here at the restaurant on Thursday. He wanted us to be the first to know, because of our families."

"How did they give him the message if the phones are tapped?"

"The chambermaid." Ivan put his suitcase back in order. "Yori will keep Vasili occupied while I alert the rest of the team during practice."

"How are they getting them out so quickly? Exactly what will happen Thursday night?"

"There is no need for any of us to know the details. The less we know, the better . . . in case something goes wrong."

Vladimir's brow wrinkled. "What could go wrong?"

Ivan sighed. "Get ready for practice and don't think about it, and if you must think about it, don't talk about it, not a word or you'll be responsible for Nadia and little Vladimir being stuck here while we're back in Moscow!"

President Dodge leaned forward, chin in hand, elbow resting firmly on his desk, frowning slightly as he listened to Mattimore.

"I can assure you, Mr. President, that the U.S. backup forces for Operation Contact are in position, and if all goes well, we can expect to see our man with the defectors' families here on the nineteenth." Mattimore's normally pale face looked ashen and drawn. It had been a long night with more to come.

"Exactly how is our man bringing them out and what is the role of the backup forces?" Dodge was growing impatient with having to pull out particulars.

Mattimore looked pained. "Mr. President, I'd rather give you a detailed report after the mission is accomplished. The plan is our man in Russia's. The CIA and military intelligence are cooperating as needed."

Dodge straightened. "Am I or am I not the commander in chief of all military forces, responsible for NSA, CIA, the military, and the State Department? I'm only requesting an in-depth report."

"Mr. President, as Secretary of State, perhaps I should remind you that there have been many times in the history of our country that it serves the Commander-in-Chief best to maintain a distance from details." Bollinger turned up the edges of his mouth slightly.

# RUSSIA
## 225 miles north of Volgograd
## February 15
## 6:50 p.m.

The limousine kept a steady pace, the sullen driver's eyes fixed on the regulation highway. Thank God for a few good highways, thought Peter as he calculated time. Right on schedule. They'd pass through Volgograd about 11:00 p.m. He debated stopping at KGB facilities there for the night but decided his old friend at the installation twenty miles outside town, and twenty miles closer to Contact Point, would be safer. "Code Koral" was all it

would take to keep their names out of official reports and prevent unnecessary questions. He glanced into the backseat. Berthe Malitinsky, despite her proximity to the KGB, was criticizing the State's supply operations and everything that was contemporary, if not modern, Russia. The old lady had nerve. She might relish her no-choice exodus.

Everything was moving along well. He'd made the coded call to Taikov, verifying Konstantine's temporary assignment to Operation Koral, and even made a fast call to Tasha's supervisor, notifying him she was being borrowed for a minor but classified KGB affair until next week. That should keep him quiet.

Tasha, sitting beside Nadia and little Vladimir in the rear seat, facing forward, caught his eye and cleared her throat. For the first hours, through the hurried lunch stop at a small grocery for cheese, sausages, and bread, she'd been quietly amused with her role of state prisoner. Now she sent questions with her eyes. He knew he was short hours away from having to face her with the devastating choice. He avoided asking himself whether she would resist. He didn't want to face that possibility. He still had to make the final decision of when and how to take out the driver. One at a time.

Little Vladimir awoke from a nap, sweaty and curious. "Momma, are we there yet?" Where are we going?"

"We are in the country, away from Moscow," Nadia replied vaguely. "Here, have some cheese. Pretend it is a picnic."

"It is not like a picnic. We are in a car with policemen. I want to go home." Tears filled his large, dark eyes.

"Hush. There is nothing we can do. You aren't being hurt and your father would want you to be brave."

The boy sat up very seriously and looked at Nadia. "I promised him to take care of you. Are you afraid?"

"How could I be afraid with my brave son beside me?" She smiled. "Now share some cheese with me, please."

They sat in silence as they watched the wintry landscape pass by them, Vladimir munching contentedly on the cheese.

"You are very good with him," Tasha said to Nadia. "Like a psychologist.

I'm afraid I would be more direct."

With a gentle pat of her son's cowlick, Nadia chuckled. "When it is your own child, you have more patience, sometimes. And today we need all the patience we can summon." She shifted on the seat. "I'm getting numb from sitting."

Tasha raised her voice so it would carry to the front seat. "I think some heads are getting numb! How far are we going?"

"There's no point in asking," Nadia sighed. "I would like to know why they have taken us. They tell us nothing."

Peter restrained a chuckle. Tasha thinks she knows why. They'll all have the where's and why's soon enough. Aunt Katya and her knitting were holding up well. Perhaps older women had more experience dealing with minor frustration. Berthe happily philosophized while Katya knitted and purled.

The driver spoke for the first time in hours. "Do we go much farther, sir?" "About four more hours, south of Stalingrad. You are still alert?"

"Yes, but I thought we were to head north."

Lord, the man was slow, thought Peter. It had taken him all day to compute the change in plans. "The orders were changed. The northern facility was overcrowded." Peter spoke casually, then caught himself. KGB officers do not explain themselves to their drivers. He was softening too early in the game. In forty-eight hours, he could be as gracious as he pleased, if they made it. And, he told himself, they weren't going to make it by being gracious. "You are doing well, Sergeant. When we reach the station to rest overnight, I shall commend you to Headquarters and make certain your superior is clear on your assignment."

"Thank you, sir." He was content for the moment.

Peter was grateful the driver had brought up the issue. A fast call to the man's supervisor would allay suspicion when he did not return tomorrow as anticipated. Peter mentally kicked himself for letting that detail slide. He'd have to review his plans more carefully.

From the backseat, the sound of Tasha's fingernails tapping on the back window caught his attention. He paused to listen. She was incorrigible! She was tapping in Morse code "What the hell is going on?" in Russian. Peter glanced at the driver. He seemed oblivious, but Peter was certain the man had been trained in it. It was part of standard training.

Peter swung his head around and glared into the backseat. "Silence. You're distracting the driver."

# PHILADELPHIA THE SPECTRUM
## February 15
## 1:30 p.m.

Malitinsky retied his shoelace as Vladimir approached. "Ivan!"

Slowly, Ivan looked up. He was all too aware that Vladimir was edgy, and they still had more than forty-eight hours to go. "Yes?"

"Have you talked to Yori again?" "Only to say hello."

Vladimir moved closer, leaning over Ivan. "How are they going to get us out of the restaurant?"

"I told you that's not our problem. The less we worry about it, the better." Vladimir persisted.

"What about Nadia and little Vladimir? Are they still in Russia? Do you know?"

"Not a thing." Ivan rose, testing the new lace. "Don't talk about it here. The walls may not have ears, but others do."

Vladimir glanced around. "No one's here but us. Then everything's OK?"

Ivan picked up his hockey stick and checked the tape.

"As far as I know. If I hear anything different, I'll let you know."

Vladimir paled. "You don't think anything will go wrong, do you?"

Ivan held up his hand for silence as he froze, listening. He shook his head. He was hearing things. Vladimir tapped his hockey stick on the bench.

"My stomach is killing me. How can we play in this condition?"

"We're professionals," stated Ivan flatly. "This afternoon's session is only

89

an exhibition for school children. Use it to loosen up for tomorrow's game."

"I hope someday my son can watch me play hockey here."

Ivan brandished his hockey stick above Vladimir's head. One wrong eavesdropper and Vladimir could destroy all their plans. Didn't Vladimir realize that at this point he could be endangering Nadia and his son as well as all of them? The thoughts raced through Ivan's mind as he waved his hockey stick in warning. This was not the place to lay out the reasons for Vladimir. "Vladimir! Enough! I mean it. Enough!" was the best that he could do.

"All right. Let's go practice. I just hope . . ."

Ivan hissed "shut up" between his teeth as he saw the door move. He shot Vladimir a warning look and forced himself to relax as Vasili hobbled through the door.

"They're all waiting for you," accused Vasili, leaning on his crutch. "What's taking you so long?"

Ivan tried to read the injured player's impassive face. Had he been listening? What had he heard? Vasili's face didn't look friendly, but there was little love lost between them in the best of times, and the ankle incident in Montreal had increased the freeze between them. "I needed a new lace," Ivan explained as he hurried out the door Vasili held open. "Vladimir had an extra." Vladimir had already rushed out and joined the others on the ice.

# RUSSIAN FACILITY
## Twenty miles south of Volgograd
## February 15
## 11:20 p.m.

"Lead the way," Peter instructed the driver. "I'll guard the flank."

As Peter stepped aside for his bizarre harem to follow the driver, Tasha stepped out of line and moved toward him.

"Sergei!" she hissed. "What's going on?"

He frowned, pushing her to follow as he muttered, "Trust me. I'll explain tomorrow."

"But they'll miss me at work!"

"Shhh, it's taken care of." He gave her an extra push and said coldly in his full voice. "Get a move on!"

Tasha, angry with the rebuff raced ahead, passing Aunt Katya who lagged a few steps behind the others. Katya tripped on the step leading to the main door. Peter lengthened his stride to help her.

As he grasped her elbow, she whispered without turning toward him, "I forgot. The papers Konstantine brought for you are still on the table." Spoken quickly, quietly, it could have been wind blowing through icy branches. He released her arm at the top of the steps. It might not matter, depending on what was in the papers. Computer lists? His cover stories only had to hold another forty-eight hours. They couldn't go back. A coded telex to KGB Liepzig could relay instructions back to the Americans in Moscow to get it out, but every communication had possibilities of leaks, or questions. He would let it ride.

In the reception area, the guard was asking the driver questions. "Is there perhaps a mistake? I have no listing." He was shuffling through his papers." He rose and crisply saluted as Peter entered, KGB insignia in full view.

"Get me Colonel Popov. I must speak with him immediately." He added, "And privately."

The guard dialed a number and gestured to the side room, where the door stood ajar. "Use the phone in there, sir," he said. Tasha stared after Peter as he shut the door. Overnight in a strange prison hundreds of miles from Moscow were far from an afternoon picnic. Berthe, Nadia, the boy? A strange threesome to warrant all this. She could think of nothing to do that would not openly challenge Sergei and create problems for him. Pushing aside her disquiet, she patted Nadia's shoulder. "You must be exhausted. You held Vladimir for half the trip."

"That's not tiring. It's the unknown that's exhausting." She gave Tasha a hollow-eyed smile. "Last night this time I was getting in from a late shift at the hospital. Everything was normal. My cousin who babysits was full of idle gossip. Vladimir was asleep like an angel on his pillow. I remember thinking that in less than a week my husband will be home. I can't believe that was only a day ago. This is like a nightmare." "Where is your husband?"

"He is in the United States. He is one of the stars of the . . ."

Peter, reentering the room, caught Nadia's response and interrupted, "You shall have beds for the night." He turned to the guard. "Colonel Popov is on the phone to give you your instructions."

Tasha's eyes narrowed in thought. The puzzle pieces were falling off the board and she wasn't certain whose board. Why did the driver indicate the mission had changed? What was Nadia's husband doing in the United States?

The guard pushed a buzzer and another guard entered. "Take these prisoners to number 17." He turned to Peter. "Your driver can sleep in the guards' quarters. We also have a VIP guest room . . ."

"Not necessary," interrupted Peter. "I'll be staying with Colonel Popov." He glanced at the driver. "I'll place the report to Headquarters from there." The driver nodded stolidly.

Nadia grunted as she picked up little Vladimir. He was falling asleep on his feet.

Tasha's eyes were fastened to Sergei as he gave orders for the prisoners to be ready for an 8:00 a.m. departure. Every muscle in her body, from her temples to her calves, was tense. She wanted to scream, to somehow break out of the nightmare, but she didn't want to disturb the authorities. It struck her that Sergei was one of the authorities. She'd never thought of him as part of her image of the cold, ruthless KGB. Was he using her for some subversive purpose? How could it be a setup when she'd spontaneously suggested to come along herself? It occurred to her he could have spontaneously involved her in a twisted scheme.

Fear flowed through her. She held her breath. Then she felt Katya's gentle touch on her arm, urging her to follow the guard. She tried to take strength from Katya's calm acceptance. Sergei would not place his own mother in jeopardy. Or would he?

The guard led the weary quintet from the reception room through a long, dingy corridor to a room with seven cots, each with a worn woolen blanket. A solitary bare bulb glared from the ceiling. "The bathroom?" asked Tasha.

The guard gestured toward a large bucket in the corner.

Nadia slid her tongue over her travel-parched lips. "Water?" He pointed at the corner to an old sink.

Vladimir roused as she placed him on a cot. "I'm thirsty." "Come." She led the groggy boy toward the sink.

"The light will be turned out in five minutes," monotoned the guard. He left, bolting the heavy door behind him.

Nadia used her remaining strength to turn the rusty faucet. "Momma!" protested Vladimir, "it's yellow."

"Let it run a bit. Perhaps it will become clearer."

Nadia's words echoed in Tasha's mind. "Perhaps it will become clearer." Meanwhile it was time to visit the bucket before the lights went out.

# PHILADELPHIA PENN CENTER INN
## February 15
## 5:30 p.m.

Ivan stepped out of the steamy shower and rubbed himself briskly with a towel. He whistled as he whisked the towel behind his knees.

From his position beside the window, Vladimir called, "What are you so happy about?"

Ivan grinned as he appeared towel-clad, an apparition emerging from the mists. "I have a feeling in my bones everything is going to turn out fine. Vasili is busy writing his impressions of American teams for Pravda."

"I thought you already took a shower in the locker room after the exhibition."

"I did," answered Ivan cheerfully as he reached in his suitcase to pull out a turtleneck. "but I love the showers here. The hot water runs forever!" He froze, looking down into his suitcase.

"What's wrong?" Vladimir strode over to him.

"This suitcase has been tampered with. I had the blue sweater on top. I distinctly remember. Now it's underneath the gray one."

"And you accuse me of being paranoid! Are you certain?"

"When I got out my shaving things this morning, I saw it on top. It made me plan to wear it this evening. And I haven't touched the suitcase since."

"Is anything missing? I've read there are many thieves in American hotels."

They both carefully checked their belongings. "Nothing missing. How about you?"

"Everything's here except a couple of socks," reported Vladimir. "And I always lose socks. I can't remember what was on top or how things were placed. But everything seems to be here." Vladimir stirred through his suitcase.

Ivan nodded. Vladimir's suitcases normally looked as though they were packed by a tornado; he'd never notice a disarrangement of his chaos. Ivan snapped his own suitcase shut. "Who could have been messing with our things?"

Vladimir worried a small hangnail on his right thumb. "Do you think it was our guards? Do they suspect something?

Ivan shrugged. "I don't know. It's not a simple thing for seventeen men to guard their tongues. I've been worried that Vasili might have overheard us before practice in the locker room. All it takes is one simple slip . . ." Ivan drummed on his suitcase, thinking. If they'd been overheard and the KGB was suspicious, it wasn't their style to search for evidence before saying something. They would call them in for questioning and search them personally. Unless they weren't certain, he thought. Unless they weren't looking for something but adding a surveillance device. He stared at Vasili and whispered, "Unless they planted a . . ." He silently mouthed the last word microphone. A shared fear ran through them.

"I feel sick," groaned Vladimir.

Ivan rose, feeling miserable himself. If there were a bug, he'd already been indiscreet, talking about seventeen men guarding their tongues. There was nothing he could do for the moment except say no more. "Let's get ready for dinner. I probably made a mistake about the turtlenecks and slipped the gray one on top."

Vladimir wasn't consoled. Ivan rarely made mistakes, especially in matters of observation.

Ivan pointed at Vladimir's casual slacks and turtleneck. "Are you going to dinner like that?"

Vladimir nodded. "I'm saving my suit for the official dinner tomorrow night. But you"—he looked at Ivan's towel—"better not come to dinner like that!"

Ivan pulled off his towel and snapped it at Vladimir. "Why not? I'll give the American girls a Russian thrill!"

"I've seen better," Vladimir retorted, smiling in spite of himself.

"Hmmf! A fine thing to say about your captain," grumbled Ivan as he quickly dressed, glad to note that Vladimir was improving in his ability to relax a bit. Ivan hoped it would last. He also hoped they were wrong about the surveillance.

# GAITHERSBURG, MARYLAND
## February 15
## 8:00 p.m.

Major J. L. Rhodes pulled an icy Budweiser from the refrigerator and pulled the metal tab. Two deep sips later, he let out a breath of relief. What a day. To begin with, his secretary had called in sick. Then the ordinance officer insisted on using an emergency requisition form to buy some nonemergency mikes, claiming GSA was playing games with them and the prices were 30 percent lower at the local store. J. L. knew the man was trying to save their company money, but the number of emergency requisitions were getting embarrassing. It looked like they didn't plan ahead. That put him in a perfect frame of mind to chew out Sergeant Bixler for scheduling an important WHCA softball game on a weekend that both the president and vice president were scheduled for trips. Half their best players would be out of town on assignments! "Why am I being punished?" He performed for his own and Bixler's benefit. "Why must I work with idiots?"

The irritants hadn't stopped there. The day ended with a top priority order for immediately dispatching a double team to Philadelphia to install a battery of phone lines in the kitchen of a restaurant in Philadelphia—an undercover operation for a vice presidential trip. That was a new one. Watson's security and communications backup were kept minimal usually. The only threats against his life, even rumored, came from Watson's wife after he drank too much at White House receptions. It didn't make sense.

When he finally got around to checking the Oval Room recordings and the meeting between Dodge and Mattimore, he'd discovered Mattimore had turned on a scrambler early in the discussions. He wasn't worried about the NSA unscrambling; Mattimore was using U.S. equipment, but his curiosity on the progression of the defection plans went unsatisfied. He added a note to make sure Rubin had it unscrambled before taking it home to listen to. J. L. knew Rubin often took them home to "eavesdrop in peace," as he phrased it.

J. L. grumbled to himself. The extra operation was bad enough, but to insist that it be a totally covert trip added a number of big, fat hassles on top of it all. Then the general told him it was all for a possible visit by Watson on the eighteenth. They wouldn't have their final orders until the seventeenth, but all the lines had to be there on standby. He started asking the usual "whys and wherefores" but the general was unresponsive. A straight directive, allowing for no additional questions or answers. They were to establish top security lines with Bollinger's office, another State Department Office, and to install two special transatlantic lines—one to Moscow and one to Turkey. All within less than thirty-six hours. That wasn't much time to work out bugs, let alone worry about putting in special ones for NSA.

J. L. had already sent eight men to Philadelphia to begin working on the logistics. They'd call him if they ran into problems. He could relax for the night as long as his beeper remained silent. He stared at the innocent-looking black rectangle as he unclipped it from his belt and placed it on the bookshelf. He grabbed a second Bud and returned to the living room, flipping on the TV and picking up the paper to skim the headlines.

As he sank down into his soft couch, he realized with irritation he hadn't turned up the sound. "Shit! One of these days I'm going to get myself a remote control," he muttered aloud as he walked back to the TV. A promotional slide caught his eye. "PHILADELPHIA FLIERS VS. WINGS OF THE SOVIETS. 8:30 P.M. FEBRUARY 16TH." As it registered, a bell went off in the back of his head. He ignored it as he thought about the way the Wings were leaving American teams sprawled on the ice in cold defeat. He'd watched them play the Capitals; the Wings deserved to win that one— they outplayed the Washington team. They were tough. Then he wondered how their defection plans were progressing and again regretted Charles using the scrambler that afternoon.

A shadowy question formed in his mind but was chased away by the sound of his beeper. The garbled "Rhodes, call Signal Board" sent him to the telephone.

"J. L. Rhodes, what's up?" he asked.

"One moment, I'll connect you with General Bonekemper."

"Ruby," J. L. protested to the Signal Corps operator, "why do you always get so formal when the general calls?"

She giggled. "He's the general and he's always in a hurry." "Then put him on!"

Fifteen seconds of static later, "J. L.?" "Yes, sir!"

"I've just returned from a session with State. No delays. Get your tail to Philadelphia on the first flight tomorrow. We don't want a fuck up on this! Top priority all the way."

"No, sir." The general must have had some briefing! Tail and fuck up were normally reserved for late-night bull sessions at the Keg in Anacostia.

"We have State, Military Intelligence, and the CIA all cooperating in case you hit any snags. This operation must be kept under deep cover. Tell none of our men anything more than they must know to perform their jobs. The Com Center will be completely scrambled."

"How can I tell our men anything? You've told me nothing. Will I get an in-depth briefing?" He paused. "If I must say so, sir, I doubt if it's possible to have State, MI, and CIA in bed together."

"NSA is also cooperating. You'll be briefed by State."

His curiosity was more than whetted, but he'd gotten the message that no more questions would be answered until Philadelphia. "Fine, sir. How long shall I plan to stay?"

"You'll break down the setup on the nineteenth and head back." The general paused. "The men can disassemble the systems without you. I want you to personally make certain everything is in working order by noon the eighteenth. It has to be perfect. Plan to fly back early the nineteenth."

"Yes, sir. I'll get right on it."

"You'll be working with State Department Deputy Robert Moore. The operation is under the direction of Charles Mattimore of State. He has the final word for operations, and he'll get you instant CIA backup if you think you'll need it. Moore will brief you fully when you get there. Even I don't know what this is all about."

"Very good, sir. I'll check with Moore first thing."

"Good. Then we're all set. I hope I didn't ruin your night."

"Oh, never, sir," J. L. added sarcastically. "You know me, sir, just planning another night in."

Bonekemper chuckled. "Sure, J. L."

He added as he hung up the phone, "With a nice quiet poker game at the Legion." He consoled himself, "I'm probably saving money by missing it."

He called in his apologies and headed for the laundry room to throw a load of dirty wash in the washing machine. I knew I should have taken it to the base last week, he thought. But I'll need clean underwear—even in Philadelphia.

# COLONEL POPIV'S HOME
## Twenty miles south of Volgograd
## February 16
## 3:30 a.m.

Peter tossed on the soft mattress. Popov's spare room was comfortable, but Peter needed more than creature comforts to still his turbulent thoughts.

He reviewed the day. Except for Tasha's perceptibly mounting tension, he almost believed the cover. Aunt Katya had been a superb supportive influence. He didn't like the loose end of Konstantine's delivery, lying like a mine waiting to explode on the hall table.

He had a well-deserved reputation for luck. Perhaps it would hold.

Tomorrow would be the tough day—confronting Tasha, taking out the driver. They were covered until they reached Tbilisi. Anywhere before that he could show papers giving their destination as that facility. But Tbilisi was 125 miles and three checkpoints from Contact. They had 575 miles to cover tomorrow on secondary roads in the worst season. The minimum time was fifteen hours, getting them there around 11:00 p.m. the sixteenth, with Contact Time 3:00 a.m. the eighteenth. He'd debated giving them the extra day, but he needed some cushion time. They could break down or hit a blizzard. If they had to alter the route under chase, they'd need every extra minute. It was a toss-up between having one less day to worry about the time for handling emergencies.

He'd discarded the idea of sending an electronic signal from Contact Point to indicate their arrival. It could be monitored. Much of his operation was based on faith. Faith that the instructions had gotten through and could be carried out. He'd breathe easier when he had confirmation from the American contact in Tbilisi.

He'd also discarded the part of his original plan in which he ditched the car and walked the last five miles through the forests. His original plan hadn't included two old women and a child, let alone his mistress. None of them were properly dressed for the cold. They would make many stops tomorrow and pick up warmer clothing in Tbilisi. There was no reason to rush just to have to wait. He would not change the schedule when he spoke to his contact. All the necessary personnel and equipment should be set by now. Any change might get confused in transmission. Everything was moving on schedule. He should feel more confident. He commanded his muscles to relax and his thoughts to quiet.

His eyes sprang open. He stared at the dim outlines of his rumpled blanket. He must have dozed off momentarily. He wondered how Tasha and Katya were faring in their cell. He rolled over on his right side and hugged the pillow to his stomach. Tasha's presence beside him might have helped.

# INTERNMENT ROOM

## Same Time

Tasha inhaled deeply, craving a cigarette. The odor in the cell was rank. The guard had not touched the bucket. She dug her fingernails into her palm. It was not a bizarre dream from which she'd awaken. It was a bizarre reality. Her supervisor would miss her in the morning. Perhaps Sergei would let her call in sick. If they tried her flat, no one would answer. In twenty-four hours, they'd issue a missing person report. How could Sergei explain? Where were they going? Even the driver didn't seem to know their destination. Her warm and passionate lover had turned into a cold, unresponsive monster.

Mother Padov was the only one who seemed calm. Even Sergei was tense in comparison. She had to know something Tasha and the others didn't. She wasn't surprised when the afternoon adventure turned into an overnight horror in a locked and guarded room. What did it all mean? They were hundreds of miles south of Moscow, heading farther south with every mile. Soon they would reach the Black Sea or Turkey, the edge of the iron curtain.

The thought froze her thoughts. She felt her hands grow clammy with cold sweat. Sergei was a KGB colonel. They were in a KGB limousine with a KGB driver. It was ludicrous to think for a second that they could be headed out of Russia—ridiculous. Her mind searched frantically for another explanation.

Perhaps he needed her as a translator for an interrogation and her absence would be officially explained to her office. But then he would have told her openly. No, that couldn't be the answer. If he was on such secret business, why were they allowed to come along? Or had the operation, as well as the destination, changed midstream?

# Code Coral

The thought that they were headed for Turkey kept tugging at her, but she wasn't prepared to cope with the consequences if Sergei was planning to leave Russia. What did that make him? She wished fervently he'd stop playing his strange game. She couldn't get through to this cold KGB colonel who had a wall over her Sergei's eyes and explained nothing. The threadbare blanket and rancid air in the cramped room held no comfort. She fought back tears. Tears would solve nothing, but they flowed freely, bringing their own kind of release from frustration.

Little Vladimir moaned in his sleep. Nadia whispered, "Hush, love, hush." Nadia was having trouble sleeping too.

Tasha fought back her sobs. She didn't want Nadia to hear. Berthe Malitinsky snored shamelessly while Mother Padov slept quietly. Everyone was accounted for, but everything wasn't accounted for. The answer to her questions was like the extra cot beside her—nothing there. Nothing made sense. She could wake Mother Padov and demand explanations, but the old woman had to be exhausted. Compassion stayed her actions but did not ease her curiosity. She tossed restlessly, trying to find a comfortable position.

# WASHINGTON, D.C. NATIONAL AIRPORT
## February 16
## 6:30 a.m.

Dressed in a conservative three-piece business suit, J. L. Rhodes waited impatiently at the Quik Snak Bar as the woman behind the counter spilled coffee on his Danish.

"Little early for you?" He grinned.

"I'll get you another one." The old woman shuffled her excess weight to the pastry tray behind her and returned with a dry Danish. "A dollar six."

"A dollar six!" he echoed indignantly. "Did you charge me for both Danishes?"

"Sixty cents for the Danish, forty for the coffee, six for tax," she droned. "That coffee must be Columbian gold!" he commented as he reached for

the exact change, juggling his briefcase and coat as he paid. He carried his tray to a round plastic table. The fluorescent lights glared in his eyes. "First flight of the day just like the old man said," he grumbled to himself. Dragging himself out of bed at four forty-five in the morning wasn't doing his disposition any good. He believed that in his twenty-two years of military service, eleven with WHCA, he'd paid his early morning dues, but the old man kept scheduling early morning departures no matter how much he'd protest. The old man had sounded uptight about the Philadelphia operation. He'd decided the sooner he got there and made sure everything was under control, the better the general's state of mind would be. And the better the general's state of mind, the better J. L.'s. His favorite axiom. His men had heard it many times.

# Code Coral

He dipped his dry Danish in the coffee, finished it, and considered buying another. Too sweet and gummy. He'd pass and go buy a paper. Twenty minutes to kill. He could read the paper and do the crossword by the gate.

"Six fifty-nine," he commented with good-humored gruffness to the girl at the newsstand. "What kind of a commuter leaves at six fifty-nine?"

"Allegheny," she replied seriously, handing him the change.

"At least you still charge 15¢ for a paper," he said, thinking of the Danish and coffee prices. She made no comment. And he wasn't energetic enough to pursue the conversation. Normally, he enjoyed chatting with waitresses and clerks, collecting opinions and reactions. Today, he didn't bother explaining his remark.

He checked in at the gate and sat down to read the Post. Nothing very exciting. A feature on the Sports Page caught his eye. It led with a three- column photo of Ivan Malitinsky, captain of the Wings of the Soviets, rifling a slap shot at the net. Nice-looking guy, but his name must be fun for the fast- paced sportscasters. He skimmed the article. It was a nice puff piece, making the team sound like decent men with a quote from forward Vladimir Vladistock about his little boy's interest in hockey. The TV promo had been accurate. They had a game scheduled with the Fliers in Philadelphia that night. J. L.'s radar tuned in, remembering the conversations in the Oval Office regarding the Wings's proposed defection. It was planned for Philadelphia. He could feel it in his bones. The thought had been nagging at him in the back of his mind since the night before.

The article didn't mention which hotel the Wings were in, probably for security reasons. There were too many nuts running around the country, even in Philadelphia.

The plane was being announced. "Time to head for Philadelphia, cradle of liberty." He grinned at the stewardess, adding to himself, "A perfect city for a defection." If he was guessing correctly, this assignment wouldn't be routine.

# STATION RHO TURKEY
## February 16
## 11:30 a.m.

Sergeant Jim Blaire crossed his arms in front of his chest and stomped his feet to stimulate circulation as the icy wind blew across the airfield. "Damn, it's cold. A few years ago, I was skiing in Vermont this time of year, between semesters. It was mild compared to this. I thought Turkey was supposed to be a Mediterranean paradise!" At twenty-seven, with ten years as a navigator under his belt and a bloody beginning in Vietnam, Blaire was considered an old pro.

"Is that why you failed out of school second semester?" laughed First Lieutenant Pat McLaughlin, a redheaded prankster who'd been assigned to the twelfth helicopter unit six months before. McLaughlin had finished the intensive ten-week pilot's course with high honors. A natural flier, he was already considered the best at Station RHO.

RHO was easy duty. The most excitement either man had so far was the twenty seconds when the main rotor of their Huey helicopter jammed during a patrol mission. Once assigned to RHO, the base became your total world. No leave, no contact with the locals. Practically, as well as officially, Station RHO was nonexistent in Turkey and Code X in U.S. military and CIA files.

Pat approached the drab ten-passenger Huey silhouetted against the gray, overcast sky like a giant prehistoric insect. He patted the sliding door. "Feeling OK, baby? Engine like that new high-grade oil?"

"Yeeow!" whopped Jim. "It's finally happened, sir. You've lost your marbles and you're coming down with that dreaded disease indigenous to these parts, helicopter-itis!"

"One of these days, Sergeant Blaire, you may hope this baby can hear us." He glanced at the complex of metal buildings to the northwest. "I hear some interesting visitors have mysteriously appeared in RHO occasionally, eager for an old Huey to quietly take them to the next hop. You must admit our location is intriguing since we don't even exist."

"I wouldn't go around repeating rumors like that, sir." Blaire looked serious. "Even on base."

"Speaking of visitors, did you see the new guys who flew in this morning?" McLaughlin grinned his special brand of freckled mischief at Blaire. "They sure did look important, especially to themselves."

"I didn't catch them," Jim replied.

"If they weren't State Department or CIA, I'll give up my beer rations for a week!" Pat exclaimed.

"In this place, sir, that would be real hardship duty. They looked that heavy?" Sergeant Blaire, despite his counseling against rumor, was curious.

Lieutenant McLaughlin had felt their official airs from a hundred feet away. "Briefcases soldered to their wrists. Steely eyes. All business and in a hurry. I wonder what they're here for. Maybe the major will give me a clue."

Blaire had taken the orders for maximum security on base at all times to heart. He didn't like open expressions of curiosity.

"One of these days, sir," Jim worried, "your curiosity is going to get you in a heap of trouble. If they're who you think, you'd better stop thinking about it. If we're supposed to know, we'll be told."

What a real army man Blaire is, McLaughlin thought. Blaire was a hell-raiser with the best of them. He could outdrink and outshout anyone on base. But when it came to policy and procedures, his manual was a holy book. "Sarge," he told Blaire, "relax. The appearance of these official types intrigues me. We've put in enough duty hours that we own a piece of this place by now, and I think we have a right to know who's tramping across our territory—and why."

Blaire shook his head, knowing the base commander wouldn't share Pat's views. "Save your energy. It's one to a million we'll never know. They're probably comptrollers from stateside checking on why we use Charmin instead of PX no-name tissue!"

"We use Charmin in the heads?" McLaughlin looked disbelieving. "I never noticed."

"You worry about the wrong things, sir. You're missing the basics."

Pat laughed. "Now you have me curious about who's running the Charmin smuggling operations! Come on, Sarge, what do we have to do around here except try to guess what everyone else is doing?" He walked back over to the Huey. "Boy, would I like to take a spin today. I haven't had my hands on a throttle in almost a week!"

"I thought regulations where you have to take it up twice a week for routine checks," said Sergeant Blaire.

Trust Blaire to know the regulations for pilots. "Right, Sergeant," Pat acknowledged. "But big Huey here, the old duck, had a little transmission trouble this week. Wasn't getting enough loving, I guess."

"Now if you want to do some worrying and guessing about something with real impact on this base, Lieutenant," Jim smiled, "put your mind to that base-wide concern—not enough loving!" He patted the young lieutenant lightly on the shoulder.

"It's not my mind I'd like to apply to that problem," laughed Pat. "Sarge," he said growing more serious, "do you think they really put salt peter into our food?"

"From the taste of it, they could put carbon tetrachloride in it for all I know," joked Blaire.

Laughing, with no more thoughts of the visitors interfering with their good humor, they headed for the canteen, neither one intending to sacrifice any beer rations.

Within the hour, both men were sitting in a secure room inside the base headquarters, learning why the strangers had arrived, if not who they were. The briefing, handled by a cool stranger they called Adams, was precise and to the point.

There wasn't a hint of a twinkle in Lieutenant Pat McLaughlin's blue eyes as he cleared his throat, rubbed his eyes, and slowly looked from his friend and navigator Jim Blaire to the colonel and the stranger called Adams and back to Jim. "All we have to do is set our Huey down in a field in the mountains outside some town called Kirovakan in the middle of the night, pick up some people, and come on in, right?"

The colonel coughed briefly and nodded.

"And," Pat continued, "it happens to be a field in Russia."

Clearing his throat again, the colonel nodded. "That's about it. There are some diversions planned for the Soviet radar system. You shouldn't have much trouble with them."

"Can you get us up-to-date aerial maps, nighttime ones? It might be tough to find the right airfield." Jim would navigate.

"It is technically a real airfield. You'll be going primarily by compass points, Jim, until the landing itself. Remember, this will happen at two in the morning our time—three Moscow time. There won't be any lights to speak of."

"I'd still like to study the aerials." "You'll have them."

Adams added, "You'll be carrying additional medical supplies and blankets and food. We have no idea what shape your passengers will be in when you reach them."

"How many passengers?" Jim asked. "Three or four as far as we know."

"The smallest 'copter we have on base is a ten-passenger. A six-passenger would take up less airspace, create a smaller blip on a radar screen," Jim noted.

"There is no time to requisition a smaller one and check out its condition. The mission is two nights away. Besides, with both of you and extra supplies, a small bird could get crowded. I'd vote for the ten-seater even if we had a smaller one on hand."

Sure, thought Jim. You'll be following the mission from the ground.

Adams glanced down at his notes, eyes narrowed in thought. "There will be no radio contact of any kind once you are airborne."

"No radio contact!" Pat's baby blues opened wide.

"You'd spill our hands to the Russians' directional finders. We expect to keep their radios and radar busy from another direction. We want you in and out as quietly as possible. A sneak play 'round end. Keep your receivers tuned to us. We'll let you know if there's trouble brewing."

The line between Jim Blaire's brows deepened as he asked, "Is the source of this diversion too classified for us to know?"

The colonel glanced at Adams for permission. Adams nodded, explaining, "I suppose not. Everything said in this room today is classified. The diversion will be a squadron of Turkish F-111's crossing into the Soviet Union at exactly the same time, if everyone stays on schedule, and leaving at the same time. That's why your timing is so critical."

The colonel added, "Don't discuss this among yourselves in unsecured areas. Our directives come from the Secretary of State and the president himself."

Jim wondered who the passengers were to cause such VIP concern.

Obviously, defectors.

Adams returned to his notes. "One passenger will be a male child, about five years old. Two will be women and the possible fourth a middle-aged man. He is scheduled to see them off if not come along. His code recognition will be 'Peter' and your response 'pumpkin' and your final response 'shell.' His final response will be 'Koral,' hopefully."

Blaire looked at Adams. "I wish you wouldn't use hopefully so often."

For the first time in the session, a glint of humor softened Adams' eyes. "I wish I'd stop thinking it," he retorted as he snapped shut his briefcase, told them he'd check back with them later, and followed the colonel from the room.

Silently they pored over the aerial maps and photos. After an hour or so of concentrated study, Pat looked up from the map he was trying to etch in his mind. "Sarge?"

Blaire was studying the aerial of Yerevan, hoping they'd never see it since it was thirty miles west of Contact Point, but he wanted to recognize it, just in case. There would be more lights there than in the open countryside. He glanced up, distracted for a second. "Yes?"

"What do we do if we see some Russian fighter plane barreling down on us?"

"Pray and reach for a machine gun. Cuss them out in Turkish. I don't know."

"Shit, Sarge, I'm serious." Pat's young forehead wrinkled with concern. "If they have anyone halfway decent manning the radar, they'll notice our little blip despite the squadron."

"I imagine," replied Jim more calmly than he felt, "that the theory is the squadron will sufficiently upset them and they won't watch for the little blips . . . like us. Look at it this way, sir. This is a top-priority operation, from the president's mouth to our ears. They're pulling out all the stops. They must have confidence in the plan."

Pat's freckles stood out on his white face. Station RHO was no place to pick up extra color in February. A touch of fear didn't help. He didn't like the risks.

"Pat, all we have to do is get to the right location, make a fast pickup, and hightail it out of there. That's all we have to worry about."

"In the middle of the night in an area we've never scouted," Pat added pessimistically.

"Hey, you're the officer. You're supposed to bolster my morale. I'm the poor NCO navigating. You do have supreme confidence in my unfailing sense of direction, don't you?" He stared into Pat's worried blue eyes. "Well, don't you?"

"You're the best of the best, Sarge," Pat conceded. "And you're our best pilot, sir. So how can we miss?"

Pat's native humor sparked. "Oh, by five miles—maybe ten."

"No way!" protested Blaire. "We're going to set down right on target, jump out, and dance a mazurka. If the police arrive, we'll say we're having a Russian festival at RHO and need some local color. We'll invite them all to fly back with us!"

Lieutenant McLaughlin remembered how to smile.

# RUSSIA
## Two Hundred Miles South of Volgograd
## February 16
## 3:00 pm

They sat in the limousine outside the small market eating bread, cheese, and Polish ham. The canned ham had been a pleasant surprise to find in the country market. Peter studied the map, calculating: two hundred miles in seven hours. Good. He glanced at the hulky driver's stony face as he bit off a chunk of bread. The man had shown no emotion so far. Did he even taste what he ate? He was like a robot. Just as well, Peter thought, it would make it easier when his time came.

"Momma, I'm thirsty," little Vladimir piped up.

Peter was brought back to his passengers. In a child's world, he thought, the important things are water to drink, food to eat, and Momma close at hand.

Nadia tried to calm the child, gently explaining there was no water, urging him to have more cheese. "It's moist," she said.

Tasha sympathized with the boy. "We're all thirsty! Why can't we have water?"

Why not? Peter echoed to himself. The charade would be over soon. Even if the guard thought Peter was being too soft on the "prisoners," there was little he could do at this point.

He realized he was already moving to the "other perspective" in his mind, regarding the KGB guard as the enemy. Deep in his role of Colonel Sergei Padov, Peter was 90 percent with them, completely submerged in the life of the KGB for weeks without thinking of those around him as anything but comrades and coworkers. He handed the driver some rubles. "Go inside and buy bottled water. And bring back chocolate, at least two pounds."

"Yes, Colonel," the guard replied flatly.

Did Peter detect disapproval in his tone? He watched the straight-backed driver march stolidly into the grocery.

As he disappeared, Tasha leaned forward and hissed, "Sergei, what is going on?"

Peter took a deep breath, turned toward the back, and addressed them all, "I want everyone to relax. This trip is not what it seems. You'll all be joining the one you love best soon. The driver will return momentarily so there isn't time to explain it all. Trust me. I promise there is no harm intended for any of you."

Nadia gasped, "Vladimir. This has something to do with him. Is he all right?"

"He's fine. It's nothing like that." Peter glanced at the market door. The driver was still inside. "I must continue to play the role of KGB colonel for our driver until we are past the checkpoint near Tbilisi."

"But you are a KGB colonel," protested Tasha.

Aunt Katya patted her hand. "Yes and no, my child." "I don't understand!" Tasha cried.

"The driver is returning. No more questions now. But remember, no matter how it seems, I am your friend, not your jailer." Peter's face grew stern as he nodded sharply and barked, "No more questions!" The driver opened the door, carrying bottles of water and a bag. He looked awkward. Peter handed the bottles into the backseat and peered inside the bag, "Good. This will come in handy for later when there will be few places to stop."

"Momma! Is that the chocolate? May I have some?" "The colonel says it is for later."

"A little piece?" begged the boy.

"You must obey the colonel," Nadia said emphatically.

"Have some water, darling." Smiled Tasha, her mind dancing with one echoing phrase—the one you love best. For Mother Padov and herself, the answer was Sergei. For the others? She remembered Nadia saying her husband was in the United States. A cold certainty filled her; they were headed out of Russia. But did she want to go?

The driver impatiently cleared his throat. Peter glanced at him. Was the man showing emotion?

"Shall we move on, sir?" he asked stonily.

"We've been on the road over seven hours. I think everyone should get out and stretch their legs."

"What is our projected time of arrival?"

"When we arrive," briskly answered Peter. "It is not your concern."

The driver's lips tightened. "Yes, sir."

"All right!" barked the colonel. "Everyone out."

Berthe pulled her coat tightly around her. "It is so cold."

"No excuses. Better to be cold than lose your circulation." He had to continue his role. He did not want to waste unnecessary energy driving before it became necessary.

The exercise was needed, he thought, and it would kill another twenty minutes.

# WASHINGTON D.C. STATE DEPARTMENT
## February 16
## 9:30 p.m.

Mattimore looked up from the six-inch high pile of files on his desk and shook his head in amazement as Bollinger padded in and gingerly placed his weight on the straight-backed chair.

"This is a surprise. I didn't know you went slumming."

"Let us dispense with your so-called humor. I came to find out if you have everything set."

"Almost." Mattimore couldn't resist baiting him. "Almost?"

"We still have nearly forty-eight hours, Karl. We're having minor problems with rounding up the right kind of delivery trucks."

"Delivery trucks," snorted Karl. "I only want verification of the precise timing. We shall know by 8:30 p.m. the eighteenth if the families are out of Russia?"

"If all stays on schedule, we'll know by 3:20 a.m. Moscow time. 0120 ZULU time. Here, we should know by 8:30 at least."

"Good. The second we have word, I want that Moscow line open and the premier himself on the phone." His small marble-round eyes gleamed with the anticipation of manipulation.

Mattimore lowered his head to massage the tension building on the bridge of his nose. "What are you going to say to the premier, Karl?"

"You have your secrets, Mr. Soviet Expert. I'll have mine." He changed the subject back to details of the operation. "It is absolutely vital that the KGB guards are given instructions from Moscow before they sound the slightest alarm, destroying the entire operation. Above all, we must keep the meddling press at bay."

A leak to the press, thought Mattimore, would guarantee the team their defection. If my directives weren't from Dodge himself to follow Karl's lead, I'd help blow the whistle. But conscious disregard of a presidential order would be treasonable.

Bollinger's small eyes coldly probed Mattimore. "One slip, Charles, could be considered treason."

Charles was too tired to analyze the relationship between morality, national or personal, and treason. He'd had less than two hours sleep, one on the couch and one right in his chair, the previous night. "You'd better revise your timing on this, Karl. The team has to be out and away before we put the KGB on the phone. Your call, if all goes smoothly, should be placed at eight forty-five."

"But if the team is already gone, the KGB will have a chance to blow the whistle."

Mattimore's fatigue was obvious as he clipped, "You have your clandestine strategies, I have mine. I assure you it will be safe to call then."

Bollinger sat relaxed, watching his undersecretary with tolerance. "You'll be in Philadelphia?"

"I'll be right here. My top aide, Bob Moore, will be with Major Rhodes of WHCA on the scene in Philadelphia. Rhodes used to be with Silverstein at NSA. He's got top security clearance."

Karl nodded. "I know him."

Charles heard himself rattling on. "We're well covered. I hope not too well. Philadelphia is like a haystack filled with undercover bodies. Cross your fingers that the KGB doesn't start searching for needles!"

"That's your problem, Charles. All I want is your absolute guarantee that the KGB won't blow the whistle before Moscow has time to issue proper directives. Remember, Charles, our greatest enemy in this operation is our own press."

Charles looked drained. "An absolute guarantee, Mr. Secretary? This operation is fast and dirty. Controls are minimum. We've selected agents for their track records, but we have a potpourri from several agencies." Charles felt his pique at Bollinger's smugness grow into rage. He fought for control as he snapped, "Don't ask for guarantees, Mr. Secretary. Say your prayers."

Bollinger smiled nastily. "God helps those who help themselves, Charles. I'd hold your prayers for this one. If you blow it, you'll need them for yourself. Your best bet is to make sure your plan is perfect, no leaks, no mistakes." Bollinger pulled his girth out of the chair. "I'll be running along. I have to meet Jeanne at Leon D'Or." His exit line was "I trust you'll be here most of the night if I need you?"

Charles's forty-three years of upbringing deserted him; he could not bring himself to utter a polite "good night."

# PHILADELPHIA
## Penn Center Inn February 16
## 10 p.m.

J. L. Rhodes looked up from his notebook and watched Bob Moore pacing. "OK, Bob, let me see if I have this straight. We need a direct, secure tie line with Mattimore at State. Another to Bollinger and one to Dodge at the Oval Office so he can listen in. Scramblers, the works. We need transatlantic lines cleared and held open, one kept open to Station RHO in Turkey for Silverstein and the relatives and another line open and ready for connection to the Kremlin from eight o'clock on. Right?"

Bob nodded, without interrupting his pacing.

"Of course, that's on top of interagency connections with CIA, State, and WHCA. Plus five secured delivery trucks, scrambled wirelesses, and secure communications for the transport plane. Right?"

Another nod. "Affirmative."

"Are you sure you don't want anything else? A marine marching band playing Stars and Stripes in the alley with dancing bears?" J. L. asked.

Bob stopped in his tracks, ignoring the quip. "You can do it, can't you? If you need more men or equipment . . ."

"We can do it. We prefer a lot more notice and we've never had to put all of this in for one job. I've already called for more men."

"This place is already crawling with more agents and State Department men than the White House itself. What a clandestine operation! We have the cooperation of the hotel management, but the staff is supposed to be kept in the dark. Many more of us and they'd have to be blind and deaf not to pick up on something. And the odds are there's a KGB plant or two around."

"You want the communications system in and working, right?" "That's top priority." Bob reached for a cigarette.

"You still have one burning," noted J. L.

"Three hours sleep in two days . . . sorry." Bob put the cigarette back in the pack and reached for his burning one.

"Listen, I'm not chewing you out personally. It's not your fault Bonekemper only had a piece of the story before we arrived. But it's a damn good thing I got here early to pick up the pieces. Believe me, three more of my men won't blow the cover. Most of them look like plumbers or schoolteachers. We don't go for body types like the FBI or Secret Service. They'll be all decked out in Bell Telephone of Pennsylvania uniforms, putting a nice intercom system for the hotel in the kitchen. The kitchen staff will be told it won't be operational until next week. How long would you say the kitchen operation will take?"

"Smoothly, fifteen minutes." Bob stared at J. L. "You don't want to put Moscow on the kitchen line, do you?"

"Why not?" grinned J. L. "The CIA will have the kitchen staff cleared out by eight."

"True. And all but the head chefs in the back kitchen will be agents from six thirty on." Bob checked his notebook. "The waiters change shifts at six and our men take over. They'll cue the players from the floor."

J. L. chuckled. "And I thought the CIA wasn't involved in domestic operations."

"But this is internation—" Bob caught himself and laughed. "You're too fast for me today."

"Why don't you go catch a catnap?" suggested J. L. "You're going to need to be alert for this one. Meanwhile, I'll get on the horn and check our reinforcements."

"After I give the boss a call, I'll see." Bob gave a tired smile. "Where will you be when the operation comes off?"

"Right in the kitchen. I've always wondered if the CIA would be better for KP duty than the military. Seriously, I want to be certain those lines are open and ready. We'll put in a backup system if we have time." Bob still didn't move. "How 'bout your?"

"I have KP duty too. Mattimore will call the second we have word they, the relatives, are on their way out," said Bob. "It will give us our standby cues. Anticipated time is eight twenty."

"If he doesn't hear by then?" asked J. L. He wanted an alternative plan ready.

Bob leaned on the door. "He'll call and keep us posted. We'll be on a holding pattern until he gives us other instructions."

"Like, tell everyone at Henry's to have a wonderful dinner and be sure to drop us a card from Moscow?" J. L. raised his pale brows.

Bob's thoughts moved out of his own safety zones. What if Rubin's mystery man didn't make it out? Would Bollinger trigger the defection anyway? Then, when the Wings discovered the truth, would they retract the defection? It could get messy. Political kidnapping. And someone would have to convince Vladimir that his wife was out without his hearing her voice on the phone.

What if Charles asked him to tell that lie? What would he do? And if they did convince the team to defect without the relatives, no one would know Bollinger pulled a fast one. They'd be in safe houses tucked away before they discovered the truth. Bollinger would have time to wheel and deal. Bob's blood ran cold. With the defection taking place under wraps, away from the press, Karl had time to wheel and deal anyway. Maybe the exodus of the relatives was a total sham. Charles seemed to have great respect for Rubin Silverstein. Would he be party to such a political charade? Bob rubbed the back of his hand across his eyes.

"Are you OK?" J. L. asked with concern.

"What do you know about Rubin Silverstein?" Bob asked J. L. "Why do you ask?" J. L. inquired cautiously.

"He's running the Russian end of the operations, bringing out the relatives.

Is he competent?"

J. L. grinned. No wonder Rubin had been so interested in the presidential briefings with Mattimore. "If Silverstein's involved, I'd say we have a 99 percent shot of it coming off well. I used to work for him at NSA as his military consultant. There's no one better."

J. L.'s assurance eased Bob's mind. He decided his fatigue was making him paranoid. "I'm going to try to catch a catnap, J. L. Call me if you need me."

# Code Coral

J. L. dialed the signal board as Bob left. He had a list for backup supplies he wanted flown in. There was no room for a walkie talkie battery to go dead-during this assignment.

Brian munched his whole wheat toast and absentmindedly drank his Postum as he read the Sports Page. "Mattie!" he called between paragraphs. "If you're making eggs, do it fast! I have to get to practice!"

She stuck her head around the corner and silently looked at him. When he didn't hear a reply, Brian glanced up and looked back at her. "Well?"

"Well," she echoed. "I was waiting to see if you were talking to column 2, page 7, or to me. Now that I know it's me, I can report that your three eggs, over easy, are on their way." She grinned and disappeared back into the kitchen.

"Listen to this," Brian called. "The Wings are playing the Fliers tonight.

Their next to last game."

Mattie walked into the dining room with a tray, stopped behind him to peer over his shoulder at the article, and placed the eggs in front of him with a flourish.

"Aren't you eating?" he asked.

"I had my eggs with our chickens an hour ago, but I'll have a cup of coffee with you." She sat down, poured herself a cup of coffee, and helped herself to a piece of Brian's toast and added jelly.

Brian looked puzzled. "I didn't realize their tour was nearly over. It's their last game."

"You already said that."

Ignoring her remark, he continued, "It says there's going to be an official dinner for them tomorrow night and they're heading back for Moscow the next day."

"So?" Mattie responded indifferently. "All good tours come to an end.

They were sweet." "Sweet?!"

"Yori was shy for such a big brute and Ivan could steal the heart of many a young girl. They had a fantastic tour and won a lot of games. They did their country proud!" She saluted with her toast. "I toast them!"

Maybe it couldn't be done, thought Brian. Maybe they changed their minds, but Rob said they were moving on with it. There was no Bruins game on the eighteenth. He could fly to Philly for the game and talk with Ivan and Yori. Maybe even attend the banquet. Who was setting it up? The paper didn't say. He decided to give Rob a call and see what could be arranged. He'd done his part and was out of it, but his curiosity was running high.

"What're you thinking about?" asked Mattie. "What?"

"When your eyes glaze and you stop flipping pages, I know you're thinking. It always shows."

"I'm thinking about how great you look this morning," he recovered. "If I didn't have to run to practice, I'd stay and have you for dessert."

Mattie dimpled and offered him the last half piece of his toast. "No thanks, I have to watch my figure!"

"I thought you were watching my figure!" She added jelly and wrinkled her nose at him.

"Got to run," said Brian, planting a kiss on the top of her head as he headed out of the room and up the stairs two at a time. He hurried to the bedroom telephone.

Mattie piled the dishes as she finished her toast. Maybe Cecily would like to explore the new sweater outlet she'd heard about. She carried the dishes to the sink and picked up the wall phone to call Cecily. Brian was on the phone. As she started to hang up, she heard Rob's voice. "Did you hear a click?" he asked Brian.

"Don't get paranoid. These small-town phones are full of clicks and static." Now that his part seemed complete, Brian was relaxed. "Don't worry, my phone's not bugged."

"I'm not so sure about mine these days," Rob countered.

"I thought you were just a high-class courier, a cut above me." Brian laughed.

"You have no idea how highly classified this operation is! The State Department practically uses code when I talk with them."

"I'm only curious. Are they, or isn't they? They only have two more days."

Rob was getting nervous. "We shouldn't talk like this. Maybe one of these days I'll get to Boston and we can let it all hang out, but not on the phone!"

"OK. New subject. There's going to be a special banquet for the team in Philadelphia tomorrow night."

"I thought you said new subject," protested Rob.

"The banquet is the new subject. I have off tomorrow, no game, and whatever happens, I'd like to wish them well."

Rob sighed audibly. "You never let up, do you?" "Without me, all this might never have happened." "You're like a dog with a big bone!"

Brian chuckled. "That's why not many pucks get by me!"

"All right. You win. I'll see what I can do. I can't guarantee anything, but I promise to give it a good try."

"Thanks, Rob. When should I check back?"

"This may take a few calls. Is tomorrow morning around nine good for you? It'll give me all day."

"I'll call you at home tonight."

"OK, but be discreet for God's sake."

Mattie kept waiting for a moment to break in with a "Hi, Rob," but as she listened, she decided it would only get her in trouble. She held her breath and tried to figure out what was going on. The banquet had to be the one for the Wings. What was supposed to happen? What was so highly classified? It was obvious Brian didn't want her to know what he was doing. What was the phrase? A high-class courier. What was that about? He didn't have any secrets she knew of. Maybe that nice Ivan Malitinsky wanted to defect. Or Yori. And Brian was helping. Don't let yourself get carried away, she chided herself, putting down her imagination. It was probably some dumb team merger or franchise sale. She hung up moments after Brian. "I've got to stop reading so many spy novels," she lectured herself.

Brian bounded down the stairs. "See you later!"

"Brian!" she called after him. He was already out the door.

# PHILADELPHIA PENN CENTER INN
## February 17
## 12:30 p.m.

In the lobby, Ivan Malitinsky turned to the KGB agent standing to his left. "Want some gum?"

The burly KGB guard, conspicuous in his ill-fitting suit and overcoat, was startled. The team members generally made a point of ignoring their keepers.

"No, thanks," he grunted, moving another foot to Ivan's left and staring out the window. He remained fixed as the other Wings players entered the lobby and headed for their rooms.

J. L. was buying his third pack of cigarettes for the day, Lucky filters. "'Cause we can use all the luck we can get," he silently added to himself. Five minutes before, he'd discovered they needed to run an extra main cable into the kitchen for the open transatlantic line. The phone company was screaming at the twenty-four-hour deadline. For a while he thought he'd have to request that Dodge himself call the area supervisors.

As he made a ninety-degree turn to leave the newsstand, he nearly crashed into Ivan. He stared into friendly, dark eyes. "Excuse, please," came the heavy accent.

Impetuously, J. L. spoke, "You're Ivan Malitinsky, captain of the Wings!" The role of a fan was as good as any.

Ivan grinned. "Yes, I am Ivan. Tonight, we play here in Philadelphia. You come to the game?"

"You're too popular. The game's sold out, but I can wish you luck." J. L. found himself wishing Ivan luck on many levels. He instinctively liked this strong stranger who wanted to join his lot with the United States.

J. L. reached out his hand to Ivan.

Ivan looked at it for a moment then firmly grasped J. L.'s hand. "Thank you."

"Again, good luck."

Ivan caught the KGB guard taking a step toward them. He quickly released

J. L.'s hand. "Please excuse me. I have to buy some things."

"Have a great game," J. L. said as he pocketed his cigarettes and moved toward the elevator, his thoughts still on the Wings's captain. The personal contact added a sudden reality to the risks of the mission. What if the transatlantic cable broke down or the radio backup failed? The whole setup was crazy. Why should a defection require all this direct-to-Moscow stuff?

They'd find out soon enough in the Kremlin. Let them call us. Save money, he thought.

His afternoon was a series of interviews. Twenty men to brief, giving each the minimum information required. Some of them had been on the job for two days, others had only arrived. It was time to get progress reports, give directives, solve the minor conflicts, and coordinate schedules so tomorrow would be a piece of cake, providing they got the new cable in on time.

He visualized headlines as he rode up in the elevator. "SOVIET TEAM PUTS RUSSIA ON ICE." Ouch, he critiqued himself. Those were worthy of the Daily News. The newscasts should be exciting. TV, radio, papers—he'd catch them all.

Icy roads proliferated with potholes facilitated nothing but a snail's pace. The winter was severe, but the forecast didn't call for snow until the weekend. The gods were still on their side. Peter noted that they were making perfect time, very slow. Now he had to make some critical choices. There was a KGB installation outside Grozny. They could stay there for the night, driver included, or they could continue, keeping the driver until past Tbilisi. At their present speed, they'd reach Tbilisi at 1:00 a.m., which would bring them to Contact Point around two thirty or three a.m. That would leave them a cold twenty-four-hour wait. They couldn't keep the car running that long.

The passengers were quiet. The only sounds came from the limousine on the bumpy road and Aunt Katya's knitting needles. Peter glanced back into the shadows of the backseat. How could she see to knit? He frowned, then remembered she often knitted in dark rooms. "The German method," she'd told him. "You do it by feel, not sight. It's that way with many things. You trust your feelings rather than what you see."

His current feelings were that they'd fare better with a good night's sleep, even in a risky facility.

Berthe Malitinsky burped and excused herself.

"Don't worry," Tasha assured her. "None of our stomachs feel very solid." Nadia looked pale in the shadows while Vladimir slept on her lap.

"We shall stop at the installation outside Grozny," Peter directed the driver.

The driver nodded, staring straight ahead at the road. He spoke with a touch of hostility. "When we arrive, I must call my commanding officer."

"It has been taken care of."

"It is customary for me to report directly."

"You are under my command," Peter spoke authoritatively. "I will handle all communications."

"Even when I drive generals, sir, I report to my commander personally. In Grozny, I shall place the call myself."

Tasha, sensing the tension mounting in the front seat, leaned forward to catch the conversation.

"As your superior officer, I am ordering you to handle no communications. If you continue to exhibit such insubordination, I shall place you under arrest."

As though for emphasis, the limousine lurched as the front wheels sank into a deep pothole. The driver jammed on the brakes, throwing everyone forward and sending adrenaline shooting through all of them.

The driver stared at Peter without attempting to restart the vehicle. "I do not like the feeling of this whole assignment. It is irregular. I was told we were going north. We head south. It is also irregular for a colonel to accompany such insignificant passengers. You are too nice to them. You do not treat them like prisoners."

"Enough!" Peter knew the driver's time had come. "You push too far."

"I shall call my commander and find out what to do. Until then, you will drive."

"Nonsense," Peter paused as he saw the gun in the driver's hand. "Put that away," he spoke softly but threateningly. "You are requesting many years of hard labor in Siberia."

"I'll take my chances. We will get out now so we can change positions.

Get out on your side. I shall follow."

Hearts fluttered in the backseat. Katya stopped knitting and started praying. Tasha edged forward on her seat. Nadia had never liked the surly driver. She feared for Peter. Berthe hoped both of them would disappear. She knew how to drive.

Peter slowly slid across the seat and opened the door. The driver carefully slid toward him, gun aimed at him steadily.

The gunshot blasted in the quiet night. The driver howled, reaching for his hand. Peter dived down and came up with the gun, which had flown out of the driver's hand and landed below the seat. Shattered glass was sprinkled across the front seat. Peter held the gun on the driver who was holding his bloody right hand.

"Thanks, Tasha," he said without taking his eyes off the driver. From the corner of his eye, he'd caught the glint of the water bottle as she'd leaned forward and smashed the bottle at the gun.

"Are you OK?" she breathlessly asked. In that split second, she'd made her first step toward commitment.

"Thanks to you, my love."

Nadia, catching the endearment, touched Tasha's arm. "What's going on? You are . . .?"

Tasha turned to Nadia. "Colonel Padov will have to explain . . . or perhaps Mother Padov."

"Mother Padov?" gasped Nadia.

Peter concentrated on the driver glaring at him. "Get out of the car."

Peter carefully followed the driver from the car, hoping Berthe and Nadia had no sympathy for the driver that would inspire another attack from the rear.

"You must take me to a doctor. My hand needs attention." Peter held the gun levelly, silently, not responding.

"If I am under arrest, I demand to contact my supervisor." The driver was not giving in gracefully.

"You have no rights anymore." The words didn't come easily. On the brink of exodus, he wanted the old ways to end. There had been too much death in the past thirty years. He was weary of it. He didn't want to add this nameless driver to the growing list. "Open the trunk."

The driver walked to the trunk and unlocked it.

"Throw me the keys," Peter coldly ordered. They rattled on the gravel. Peter didn't bother picking them up; it could throw him off guard for a second.

"Get the rope."

The driver rummaged in the trunk and came up with a coil of thick hemp rope. "Good. Now walk toward the forest."

The driver stared fixedly as Peter's intention sank into his stolid mind. Then he turned, walking heavily toward the trees. He stopped at the edge of the forest. "Keep moving," Peter ordered, gun barrel pressed against the driver's back. Peter scanned the forest for a tree he liked, strong but not too thick. "Stop here," he ordered. "Turn around."

Breathing noisily in the silent forest, the driver turned slowly, searching for his moment to resist.

"Back up against that tree behind you."

The driver took a shuffle backward and growled, "You can't leave me in the woods to freeze to death."

"I should, but no. When we've reached our destination, I'll send word for them to find you. If the wolves don't first."

The driver lunged left and thrashed through the woods. "Stop!" ordered Peter. "Stop!"

He fired a shot into the woods as he ran, following the noise the driver was making. He thought he was gaining ground when the sounds stopped. He could hear only his own panting. He moved forward cautiously, stopping to listen. Nothing. Then the dark heavy form of the driver was on his back. They rolled on the frozen ground, twigs and stones pressing into exposed flesh in their struggle. The gun cracked. Peter felt the full weight of the driver press him into the snowy ground. For a moment, he thought he'd been shot. His head cleared and he pushed the leaden body off and rose unsteadily. He rolled the driver on his back and felt for a pulse. Blood was soaking through the driver's coat. Peter could feel the sticky warmth as he probed for the wound. It was in the man's chest. He was unconscious, but alive. Peter reached for his gun, which had fallen to the ground. He aimed carefully and shot the driver between the eyes. No more room for compassion. The momentary lapse had almost been a fatal mistake. He felt empty. A childhood scene at his uncle's farm in Upstate New York flashed in his mind. A roan had broken a leg trying to jump a fence. The vet had shot her. Peter at eleven had felt more emotion for the horse. It was long past time to go home.

Tasha stood near the car, half-lighted by the headlights as Peter stumbled into the clearing. She hesitated as she saw him, not knowing which man it was.

"Sergei?" she hesitated until he reached the pool of light from the headlights then ran to him, hugging him to her. "Thank God. We heard shots. I didn't know if you were . . ." She stopped as she felt the sticky blood on his coat. She drew back, looking at her bloody palm in the light. "Are you hurt?"

"No, it's not my blood." He wanted to forget it. He looked toward the front wheels. "How badly are we stuck?"

"Sergei, what happened? Why did the driver pull a gun?" There was so much she didn't know. "You have to tell me what's going on!"

"Yes." He sighed as he checked the safety on his gun and placed it in his overcoat pocket. He put his arm around Tasha. "You must be cold."

"I am too confused to be cold. And afraid." She hesitated. "Did you . . . kill him?" A shudder ran through her.

"He tried to run away." He didn't want to dwell on it. He pushed her toward the car. "I must see about getting us out of that hole."

She stopped and turned around, moving closer to him. "Careful," he warned. "You'll get blood on you."

Tears, a mixture of relief and alarm, streamed down her cheeks. "I don't care. But I have to know. Are you acting in an official capacity? Was the driver wrong?"

He measured his words. He would explain things as they continued. First, he had to make certain the car was all right. "Yes, I am acting in an official capacity."

"Then where are we going? Why did you bring your mother and let me come? Why . . ."

Gently, he wiped her wet cheek with his hand. "Hush, Tasha. Get inside while I check the wheels. When I rejoin you, I'll tell you our destination—at least my destination."

"What does that mean?"

"But I want your solemn word that wherever or whatever it is, you will not try to stop or hinder me." He gripped her shoulder.

Slowly, looking at the lean outline of his stern face framed in the glow of the headlights, she responded, "I give you my solemn word."

Peter lightened his grip and released a tense breath.

"But if I disagree," she added quickly, "I shall tell you and try to change your mind if I can."

"It's far too late for that. I have already dealt the cards. Now, lady luck and skill of play shall determine who wins the game."

"And what is the game, Sergei?"

"We must help our passengers out of Russia." "What have they done?"

"Nothing. They have relatives who wish to defect." He pushed her toward the limousine purposefully. "Inside for any more explanations." The February night blew a cold gust.

Inside the car, little Vladimir chattered, "Momma, see? The colonel's OK. Can we go home now? Do you think he shot the driver? Did he have a real gun?"

There was no space between Vladimir's comments for Nadia to answer so she nodded and shrugged and stared out the window watching Tasha and Peter in the headlights.

Needles clicking in the dark, Aunt Katya added, "This journey is not all it seems."

As Tasha entered the car, Nadia turned to Katya. "He called you Mother Padov. Are you his mother?"

"I was his official mother for nearly thirty years. His mother is my sister." Her knitting needles were silent.

Tasha, catching the statement, turned in surprise. "You're his aunt! He never told me!"

"Never told you what?" asked Peter, getting in the driver's side. "That she isn't your mother."

"She's been the best mother in the world to me." He turned the key he'd retrieved from the road, hoping the lights hadn't drained the battery too much.

"Is your real mother dead?" Tasha asked.

"I don't know." The engine sputtered and caught. "Hold your questions until we're out of here and running again."

The car lurched forward and caught on the front edge of the pothole. He backed up a few feet and tried again, revving the engine and creating a greater jolt. Again, he backed, then inched forward slowly. The car caught once more on the front edge, back wheels spinning.

"I'll have to fill the hole with some brush. Ask my mother all the questions. What she can't answer, I'll answer later." He got out, commending himself on his escape from the carful of curious women.

Tasha began. "Mother Padov or Aunt Padov, where are we going?"

"That much is easy, child. We are headed for the free world outside of Russia, a world I haven't seen since the summer of 1915." She sighed.

"My husband, Vladimir, is in the United States with the Wings hockey team. Does it involve him?" Nadia asked.

Berthe Malitinsky gripped Nadia's arm. "So is my son, Ivan. He is their captain!"

"Ivan Malitinsky!" Nadia's eyes lighted up. "They are friends!"

"Defect," Tasha said, "Sergei said defect. Your husband and son must be defecting."

The women stopped short at the thought. Nadia was the first to speak. "Where Vladimir is is where I want to be," she said slowly, "but I find it hard to believe."

A strange small smile lifted the corners of Berthe's mouth. "It is come full circle." She shook her head slowly. "After my husband died in prison, some friends, some of the few alive after the futile Hungarian attempt at freedom, wanted me to escape from Russia with them. I refused, fearing there would be reprisals on Ivan, my son, fearing they would use him to force me to come back. How many times have I wished I could have escaped with him?"

Katya interrupted gently, "Why didn't you take him with you back then?"

"They already had taken him away to a State boarding school, away from my corrupting influence. But I could see him on special holidays, and that was something." She sat back against the seat, her thoughts swarming. Could Ivan have remembered things he heard when he was three and four? She'd seen so little of him since they'd put him on the Wings. But whatever happened, she knew a greater peace of mind than she had for years. Somehow, her son had not subscribed to the totalitarian values, and he loved her enough to want her with him. If she died in the attempt, it wouldn't lessen her joy.

Each sat lost in their own thoughts, until little Vladimir became edgy. "I'm hungry," announced Vladimir.

Tasha felt under the dashboard for the bag of chocolate while she rolled Katya's words around in her mind. "Here." She handed him the whole bag.

If Katya had the choice of coming along, then Sergei must be leaving Russia forever. Where did that leave her? She trembled, closing her eyes as the possibilities tumbled through her mind.

"Careful," Nadia cautioned little Vladimir. "You'll get all of us messy."

"We're already all messy," observed Berthe. "A good hot bath would go a long way toward improving life right now."

Tasha entered the conversation, finding relief in commonplace thoughts.

"I'd settle for a bowl of hot water and a nice clean cloth!"

Nadia added seriously. "Will Colonel Padov tell us what is going to happen next?"

"Patience," counseled Katya. "He'll be back soon. Meanwhile, it might help if I told you a story about his mother and me that began in 1917."

Katya put down her knitting and reached for her basket. She rummaged through the bags and boxes until she found the box she wanted. She pulled it out and opened it, revealing the emerald necklace Peter had discovered that November night in 1945. She handed it to Tasha.

"It's beautiful!" exclaimed Tasha, fascinated. "Where are they from?"

"They're all part of the story. The war in the north was being fought by White Russians and we were White Russians."

As Katya told the story to her fascinated listeners, Peter struggled with the pothole. He dragged dead branches from the forest and packed them into the cavernous hole with snow and gravel. Finally, he decided to try again.

As he slid behind the steering wheel, Tasha said, "I don't know what to call you now, Sergei or Peter."

He replied in English. "Just call me darling."

She responded in English, "And all this time I thought you couldn't understand English. When I think of the times I've sworn at you, thinking you didn't understand."

"I usually was being a 'goddamn son of a bitch' when you did," he chuckled.

Tasha relaxed. Her Sergei, or Peter or whatever he was called, was back.

The KGB colonel had melted away again. The atmosphere in the car was rarified.

"Here we go," Peter said in Russian, turning the ignition. The motor quickly caught. There was a slight bump as the front wheels hit the edge of the hole, but then they were clear.

"Tasha, keep your eyes on the road and help watch for more bad potholes.

I don't want to take up general road repairs on our way out."

"How much longer?" asked Tasha. Everyone strained to hear his reply.

"We're fairly close, but we have twenty-four hours plus. We have to kill some time. There's an installation a few miles west of Grozny where we can put up for the night, but you'll have to be my prisoners again."

"Ugh," Tasha wrinkled her nose. "Do you have any idea what those beds are like? You slept in the officers' quarters!"

"I know what it's like," answered Peter curtly, "but the alternative was to sleep in the car. At least it's warmer and there are beds."

"It will only be for one more night," added Aunt Katya. "I think it's best as long as the child doesn't say the wrong thing at the wrong time."

"Yes, we need rest, all of us," agreed Nadia, "and Vladimir will be quiet as a mouse. You won't say a word, right?" She hugged the boy tightly. "You will speak only when Momma says it's all right. It's very, very important."

"Yes, Momma."

Peter watched the road, wary of potholes. He would be taking an additional risk by going to the Grozny facility. Any of them could blow the whistle. He still wasn't certain where Tasha stood. He hadn't pushed her for a decision or offered substantial explanations. "What time is it?" he asked her.

"Nine thirty."

"We'll be at the Grozny outpost by eleven. I'll instruct the guards to have you ready to leave by eight a.m. Then we'll head for a market to find the makings of a leisurely breakfast."

"What about your coat?" "My coat?"

"The blood."

Peter felt a wave of relief. She is thinking about my safety, he thought. "If they ask, I'll say we had an accident on the road. I cut my arm while fixing a fender. I doubt if they'll ask. I should be dry by then." He felt the front of his coat. It was damp. In English he continued. "Tomorrow you must make your decision."

"My decision?"

"Whether you come to America with me or return to Moscow?" "But . . . how would I get back?"

"I can give you the limousine. You can say I kidnapped you, forced you to drive us . . . or you could say you escaped at the last minute. Remember, I'm old enough to be your father."

Tasha remained silent for a full minute. "I love you," she whispered. "That's not the issue."

"I am still married," she voiced carefully.

"That can be taken care of by American attorneys. The only question relevant right now is whether you want to come with me."

They drove in silence, broken by Nadia's question. "Are you taking us to my husband?"

"Yes," Peter flatly replied. "He is defecting, but his conditions include you and little Vladimir being brought out of Russia. It's the same with your son, Mrs. Malitinsky."

He stopped as he realized he'd handed each of them the information to destroy the mission. They'd have the opportunity to blow the whistle at Grozny. At Grozny, the destruction of Operation Contact would be as close as the nearest guard.

"Vladimir! You ate all the chocolate! I shall tell your father!" Nadia chided.

"He's not here," came the smug response. "We'll see him soon."

"Is he coming home soon? Will we be home to see him?" "Hush, we'll see him soon. Now try to sleep."

None of them seemed ripe for rebellion. He glanced at Tasha again and sighed deeply, continuing to peer ahead into the blackness. Each person was now deep in his or her own thoughts.

Bob Rhodes had stepped outside for a breath of fresh air. The patterned drapes, bedspreads, even the shower curtains were beginning to dance before him like the field of marigolds in the Wizard of Oz. There were three exits from the main lobby. Four, counting the main entrance to Henry's that had a corridor leading through the coffee shop into the main lobby. One man could handle the main lobby. If they positioned a man at the back entrance, he thought as he paused by that door, he couldn't see the kitchen door, especially blocked by the delivery trucks. To be safe, a KGB guard there would have to be silenced. He made a note.

He continued walking down the alley toward the kitchen door. The parking garage entrance could be a problem if cars backed up, waiting to get in. They'll need a contingency plan, maybe a police van on call to demand clearance. He'd rather avoid unnecessary confusion, but they had to be covered. He jotted it down in his notebook. Thank God it was a one-way alley.

He turned right into the kitchen entrance where a military-looking dumpster spewed sodden paper bags and rotten lettuce on the macadam. It covered half the entrance. He made a note. The dumpster should stay. It was good cover. Nobody would believe they'd make the defecting star hockey team crawl over garbage to get out. The dumpster did mean that only one delivery truck could pull up to the entrance at a time. That shouldn't be a major problem. Six men each in three trucks. If one truck is in position by eight fifteen,

139

the others can be parked on the sidewalk. He'd check with the CIA. That was their problem. They were working on using fewer trucks, anyway, removing pie racks or something.

In front of the building, J. L. was returning from a short walk. He noticed the Wings's bus parked beside the front entrance and spotted the KGB guard he'd seen earlier beside the bus door. He hurried in the door, nearly crashing into Ivan Malitinsky.

"Sorry," recovered J. L. "we keep running into one another."

Ivan gave J. L. a searching look, suddenly wondering if he were part of their special arrangements. "That's OK. I was hurrying too fast. We must go to the stadium."

As Ivan continued out the door and into the bus, he decided his imagination was working overtime. He saw spies everywhere. Just because the man bumped into him twice didn't mean anything. He was probably a salesman. The coach had said a lot of salesmen stayed at the hotel.

J. L. lighted a cigarette as he waited for the elevator, watching other Wings players cross the lobby. They all looked very serious. American players wisecrack their way in and out of hotel lobbies. He conceded that the Wings must have a lot on their minds right now. But then, he added to himself, so do we. And there are more of us than them. The numbers were growing alarmingly. Some agents were booked at the Sheraton. He half expected General Bonekemper himself to walk through the door to double-check their last-minute plans.

The elevator door opened. He followed an elderly lady inside and pushed the button. "Young man," she chided, "can't you read? Don't you know our government is trying to protect us from ourselves?"

He looked at her, startled, as she pointed toward the No Smoking sign. A hassle a minute.

"Sorry, ma'am." The elevator stopped at his floor. As he headed for Bob Moore's room, he hoped the "Veep" would stay put. They didn't need him to add to their worries. He was beginning to understand the old W. C. Fields line, "First prize, one week in Philadelphia; second prize, two weeks in Philadelphia."

"I'll take the call." Mattimore reached for the phone. "Rob. How are things?"

"That's what I called you to find out. How's the operation going?"
"Complicated as all get out. Haven't slept in days—"

"Great," interrupted Rob. "I have a favor to ask. Brian Earle, the Boston Bruin, the first contact—"

"I know," Charles broke in. "Go ahead."

"He'd like to attend the Wings's banquet tomorrow night. He read about it in the paper."

"Sorry, impossible." It occurred to Mattimore that Brian could become a problem. "Rob, this operation has become top priority classified. As far as you and Earle," he stressed, "are concerned, you never heard a thing about it."

"Wait a minute, Charles. Don't go official on me. Remember, Brian's been in on this since day 1."

There were already too many elements in Philadelphia to worry about. "Rob, I must repeat, you are to forget about the entire thing. And make certain you get the message to Carson and Earle immediately and discreetly." He tried to soften the blow. "Tell him he has our deepest gratitude for his patriotism and loyalty, but for national security reasons, he must forget the whole thing!"

"Charles?!"

Charles thought quickly. He didn't know what was up Bollinger's sleeve, but he had to keep Rob and company under control. "If you don't see anything in the press, don't be concerned. It's a delicate situation."

"I'd think you'd want every headline in the world."

"Don't think, Rob. I'll fill you in when I can." He made a concerted effort to lighten his tone, "Rob, I have 304 things to do. Come to Washington soon and we'll have a long lunch."

Rob tried to regroup his thoughts. "Charles, I'm still puzzled. Why . . . ?"
"I can't answer any questions now. Sorry, but I have to go. Give my love to Nancy. I'll get back to you next week, I promise."

Rob frowned as he hung up the receiver. Brian wasn't going to like this.

And he didn't like the brush-off Charles had just given him.

No use delaying it. He picked up the phone and called Brian, repeating Charles's conversation. He agreed with Brian that they were being strange and mysterious, but there was nothing either of them could do but stay away.

As Brian replaced the phone in the cradle, Mattie entered the bedroom and caught his puzzled expression. "What's wrong?" she asked.

Brian tried to brush it off. "That was Rob." She waited for a fuller explanation. "I was hoping he could swing a couple of seats for the Wings's banquet tomorrow night. After all, we did wine and dine them. He says the State Department says there's no way."

"That's crummy," Mattie said as she leaned over to pick up a piece of lint from the floor.

"That's an understatement!" Brian exclaimed. He didn't understand why he couldn't attend and Rob had no good answer. "Highly classified" was bunk. He'd been in on it from the beginning. If they were defecting, he'd be glad to help. If not, all he wanted to do was wish the Russians good-bye and good luck. Brian tried to tell himself the State Department must have their reasons. Rob had been firm. Stay away and let the government take care of it. A move like this had to be kept under wraps until it happened.

"Brian. Brian!" Mattie stood, arms akimbo, shouting at him. "You must be getting old." She laughed when she'd gotten his attention. "Your hearing's gone!"

"I was trying to figure out who'd be at the Wings's banquet." "Are players from other teams going?" she asked.

"I don't know. I guess some of the Fliers."

"So who else will be there?" she prodded his thinking.

"The paper said the vice president. And I'd guess that reporters will be there." Rob had told him not to worry if they didn't see anything in the news right away. That was peculiar too.

Mattie folded her arms determinedly. "Let's have some of the other Bruins and their wives over and have our own banquet. We'll fix those old snobs in Philadelphia."

"Sure. That's a great way to fix them," chuckled Brian as he pulled her into a hug.

"Colonel Omnarsky, Padov will be checking with me tomorrow. I'll question him on it."

Omnarsky leaned forward and slapped his hand flat on the general's desk. He looked as though he'd been an athlete who had traded the training table for vodka and fine food ten years earlier. He was still a strong man.

"General," he persisted, "I don't like the smell of it. Konstantine's best quality is his attention to detail. He said I'd receive a copy of his information in the morning."

"The same information he was taking Padov?" Omnarsky nodded, "Yes, sir."

The general thoughtfully responded, "Padov specifically told me he was taking Konstantine with him. He sounded as though they were on to something important. He may have decided the information was safer away from official channels."

"Regardless, sir. Konstantine would have followed procedures. He would have at least sent me a summary report, sealed—to be opened only if the mission failed or he was terminated." Omnarsky had an innate distrust of Padov that went beyond the normal competition of officers on their way up. He recognized that Padov was the general's fair-haired boy and that galled. He'd never caught Padov in a mistake or suspicious situation. It was a gut feeling.

"I trust Padov will explain it to our satisfaction," the general spoke calmly as his sparrowlike hand darted to the telephone on its first ring. He looked searchingly at Omnarsky. "You're overly concerned, Colonel. Are you afraid of what might be in the document?

"General Taikov speaking." It was after hours; his aides had been sent home. "Yes, Colonel." As he listened, the web of wrinkles on his old face deepened.

Omnarsky let his attention drift until he heard the general mention Padov's name.

"You were correct to contact me. Colonel Padov is on a highly classified assignment and cannot be reached. The women have both confirmed their identities. We shall investigate and get back to you. I understand your embarrassment at the situation, but we are all human, Brosheko, subject to the passions of the flesh." The general replaced the receiver and sat lost in thought for a moment.

Omnarsky brought him back to the present. "Well? What did that have to do with Padov?"

"Two prisoners were delivered to Brosheko at Syktyvkar a few hours ago, along with their papers and a memo from Padov. Padov indicated they were being detained as relatives of Wings of the Soviets and would be released and returned to Moscow the twentieth."

"So?"

The general emitted a dry chuckle. "Brosheko, quite apart from his new delivery, decided to make the rounds of his facility, to keep his men alert. He encountered the new prisoners as they were being issued their standard supplies. One of them, the younger one, recognized Brosheko." He paused to give full drama to his story. "A bit embarrassing since it turns out she is a prostitute he had 'encountered' some months before in Moscow."

"I don't understand," Omnarsky ignored the ironies. "I thought you said they were relatives of the Wings."

"Padov's memo stated that," Taikov flatly noted. "He had switched the papers."

"But why?" asked Omnarsky.

Taikov wordlessly shook his head. "If Brosheko had not fortuitously stumbled across his former playmate, the switch in papers would have gone unnoticed for days."

"I say we put an alert out for Padov and Konstantine." Suddenly Omnarsky rose. "My control report indicated Padov was accompanying Andrejeski to Syktyvkar!"

"Brosheko was trying to track Padov down to explain the papers."
"Then I say we should immediately pull in Padov for questioning."

Taikov looked levelly at Omnarsky. "You say? Remember who is in command here. Padov is my lone wolf. You were not involved during his years in the field. His methods were unorthodox, but his results extraordinary. I do not wish to jeopardize his mission."

"Then let me make some preliminary checks here in Moscow to be certain nothing happened to them."

"I spoke to Padov this morning. He indicated no problems."

"I will only check with his mother. If the mole suspected Padov is on his trail, he might try to reach Padov through her. And I shall also check with Konstantine's family. It will be unofficial, sir. A precaution."

"Very well, Colonel. I hope it will all be meaningless as I expect to speak to Padov tomorrow."

"I shall attend to it immediately and report back to you in the morning." Omnarsky walked to the door then turned back to Taikov. "I consider Sergei Padov one of my few friends. I respect him. My concern is that he might be in jeopardy. I wish to be able to give him optimum backup."

Taikov did not respond. Perhaps the man was protesting too much. Omnarsky waited then saluted. "I'll report back in the morning."

# TURKEY STATION RHO
## February 18
## 12:30 a.m.

Jim Blaire heard machine guns firing below him. "Fly lower," he instructed. They took a nosedive down toward the lush jungles. The gunfire grew louder. Sweat ran down his neck onto his clammy chest. The eerie whir of a bomb echoed inside his ears. He looked down in time to see the jungle explode into flames, moments before it dissolved into icy mountains. He heard Pat McLaughlin shout, "We're off course! Check your coordinates!"

Jim tried to answer but froze as another bomb burst to their right. Pat was shouting, "The radio's dead!" He heard a child crying, "Momma." It sounded foreign. Another bomb exploded, flashing on the mountains. "Sarge!" Pat screamed. "What the fuck should we . . ."

Red. Pain. Metal tearing. Black.

Jim sat up, instantly awake, hyperventilating. He wasn't in Vietnam. He wasn't heading into Russia. He thought for a second, he was dead. He grabbed for the wet sheet sticking to him like a shroud. We're all dead, he thought. He reoriented. Only a dream, but too vivid for comfort. The dream had those same mountains he'd been studying all day. He couldn't escape them even in his sleep. He told himself he was only tired and nervous, but he was shaken. He wouldn't recount the dream to Pat. Pat's Irish superstition would take it as a bad omen.

Peeling off the wet sheet, he grabbed the blanket from the foot of the bed and pulled it over his damp body. A girl told him once that Germans go directly from their baths to bed and cover themselves with blankets. The dampness and warmth were supposed to awaken the fetal memories and bring on sleep. He tucked the blanket around him and tried consciously to relax his muscles. As his eyelids began to droop, he wondered if Pat was also dreaming about grinding gears, exploding bombs, and missing latitudes.

A building away, Lieutenant Patrick McLaughlin was sleeping dreamlessly, a slight smile on his lips. He'd done his worrying in the daylight hours.

# RUSSIA
## Prison near Grozny February 18
## 2:00 a.m.

Peter's room shared a wall with the reception area. He slept restlessly, one ear literally to the wall, the voices of the guards always on his threshold of consciousness. He rolled, groaned, and came awake, listening to the voices in the next room.

The guards were discussing him and his strange party.

"He came in without a driver?" asked a deep-voiced guard.

The second guard answered in a nasal voice, "Yes, but his identification was genuine. And he had the proper papers. I'm certain he is who he says he is."

"He looked rumpled, you said?" asked the deep voice.

"Tired. He said they had driven from south of Moscow and had to reach Baku tomorrow," the nasal voice answered. "Should I call the commander and report it?"

"It does seem irregular," the deep voice noted. "The commander will be here before these strangers are scheduled to leave. He'll be here by seven." The tone of the deep voice lightened. "Now, would you like to play cards?"

"Only to pass the time. You cleaned me out last week," the nasal voice replied.

"We'll play for sport, not money," promised the deep voice.

Peter buried his head in his pillow to avoid the harsh laughter. He knew he needed rest.

A long corridor away, Tasha twisted on her lumpy cot. She wanted to scream for Sergei and beg him to stop this masquerade. Go back to Moscow. Pretend the past two days had never happened. She could tell the guard Sergei was acting strange and call for the commanding officer. They would investigate. Sergei would have to make up a cover story for them and they'd miss arriving at Contact Point. The players couldn't defect. Everyone would come home. But Sergei's cover story might not hold. He would be imprisoned. She shivered and sat up, stretching her neck hard first right and then left. It cracked.

Everything was happening too fast. Two days ago she was sitting in her cubicle, translating English newspapers into Russian, knowing she would see Sergei the next day. She wanted to be with him all the time. She wanted him to ask her to get the divorce over Andre's objections. But that dream was for Russia. What would it be like in the United States? Where would they live? What if the KGB kept searching for them there?

The bedsprings creaked as she dropped back on her cot.

Katya asked softly from the adjacent cot, "Having trouble sleeping?"
"Yes," whispered Tasha. "These cots are like bean bags."

"It is not easy to follow your heart," Katya whispered back. An odd statement, thought Tasha, but oddly reassuring.

# GEORGETOWN
## Bollinger's townhouse February 17
## 8:00 p.m.

Bollinger's hand tightened on the receiver. "You're certain they'll arrive on schedule?"

On the other end of the phone, in his office, Mattimore shrugged. "Evidently everything is moving like clockwork. All forces are in position. The Philadelphia reports are fine. We've only minor problems to resolve in the next few hours. A few team members seem edgy, but I think they'll make it through."

"Good. Good," Bollinger jumped over Charles' last few words. "Then it appears we'll pull this off with style."

Unseen by Mattimore, Charles gritted his teeth at the we. "So far. We won't know until tomorrow. All we can do is move a step at a time, trying to cover all eventualities." He hesitated. "Karl, once we have them in the air, what next?"

"You take them to the safe houses as scheduled."

"That I know, I arranged it." Charles's irritation could be heard. "But how long will they remain there? What do we tell them?"

"As little as possible. Make up something about some procedures . . . yes, procedures . . . to take care of." A slight smile crossed his lips.

"But you're planning to talk to the Soviets immediately."

"Not in detail. I shall only demand that they immediately calm their KGB unit and have them return to their embassy. Once they know we might be open to special negotiations, I'm sure they will agree. They won't want the KGB talking to our press if there's a chance of bargaining."

"What are your terms, Karl?"

"We're working on the alternatives. You'll know soon enough."

"Mr. Secretary," Charles became formal, "as an expert on Soviet affairs, I'd like to have the opportunity to comment on those determinations. I believe I could render helpful projections on Soviet reaction."

"I would think they'd give us nearly anything we request. Right now, the Wings are their greatest international PR tool. Surely, they don't want to lose that." Bollinger's voice became icy. "If I need your advice, Charles, I'll ask for it. Meanwhile, you would do better to concern yourself with getting them out without incident."

"You thrive on mystery games," Mattimore commented caustically.

"You play a few yourself with your mysterious man in Moscow, not to mention the request for eighteen additional CIA agents. I didn't push you on your mystery." Charles didn't respond. "Incidentally, we're sending the vice president as the U.S. representative to the banquet. Your men can brief him there."

"Christ!" exploded Mattimore. "Why didn't you wait until tomorrow to drop that bomb? Thank god Rhodes is already there."

"Who is Rhodes?"

"Number 2 man in WHCA. You've seen him around, I'm sure. The vice president requires his own special communications set up, but a signal board and Com Center is already in. But Watson is going to increase the number of reporters and photographers with more requests for audio feeds, equipment . . . more hassles. Besides, Watson is dense!"

Bollinger snorted impatiently. "I don't care about all that nonsense. Do what you have to, but Watson will give the official farewell."

Mattimore's mind was swimming with this new development. "The press could upset this whole operation."

"That's your problem. Keep them clear of it."

"WHCA usually has two days, minimum, to set up for the VP."
"You said yourself half the equipment's already in. They have a day." "Less than twenty-four hours. At this time tomorrow, the Wings should be heading for Andrews."

"And we'll get down to the negotiations in earnest." Bollinger rubbed his round stomach beneath his plush maroon smoking jacket. "We're meeting on it first thing in the morning." "You and the president?"

"No, me and my aides. I'm meeting President Dodge in the late afternoon.

I suppose, you should be there too," he added grudgingly.

"So, if something goes wrong, you can point the fickle finger of fate in my direction?"

"My, you are in a sour mood. You shouldn't work so hard. It's ruining your disposition." Bollinger laughed nastily.

It took all the self-control Charles could muster to prevent himself from slamming the receiver down full force, hoping to irritate Bollinger's eardrum, at the least. Instead, he took a second for a deep breath and replied, "Let me know when and where. I've a lot to do tonight and tomorrow. With your latest news, I have to call my man in Philadelphia."

"Yes," chuckled Bollinger. "We wouldn't want anything to go wrong with your end of things. Have a good night, my boy. You know where to reach me if something comes up you can't handle yourself."

The sarcasm wasn't lost on Mattimore.

The small smile remained on Bollinger's face as he replaced the receiver. Mattimore acted as though every minor change was a national disaster. Bollinger had personally asked the president to send Horace Watson. Whoever heard of a state dinner without a proper dignitary? Horace Watson, VP, fine grass roots person that he was, would be a splendid representative. It might even get him some good press for a change. In the eventuality that something went wrong, Bollinger preferred to do his grandstanding in Washington.

"Darling!" he called from his manicured leather and lemon-oiled oak den.

Within a minute, a tall, willowy brunette in a flowing red silk lounging robe appeared in the doorway.

"You called?"

"I shall wring your beautiful neck if you don't find another martini for my empty glass."

"Empty threats," she scoffed.

"Empty glass," he insisted.

"When I married you, Karl Bollinger, lousy jokes weren't part of the contract."

Karl pulled himself out of his chair with unaccustomed speed, if lacking in grace, and put his arms around her, lifting his chin to rest on her shoulder. "It's one of the fringe benefits. I could name a few others if you like."

She stepped back, picked up his empty glass, and headed for the living room bar. Karl tagged along. "In fact, I'll give you a demonstration of what a superb mixologist I am." He took the glass from her. "Shall I make one for you too?"

"Please."

"Watch." He first filled the glasses with ice then added a capful of vermouth to each. He drained the vermouth from the glasses, leaving a slight film on the ice cubes. He grinned as he filled the glasses with Grey Goose vodka.

"Voila!" He handed her a glass.

"I've known for a long time you like to mix things up!'

"Others might agree, pet. But all I do is try my best to do my job in the best manner humanly possible."

"You're sounding like a Boy Scout."

Sinking into the decorator beige velvet couch, he saluted. "On my honor, I will try to do my duty, beauty." He noisily took a large sip of his martini and raised his eyebrows at Jeanne. "You like?"

She took a sample sip. "Hmmm," she responded without enthusiasm. "It certainly is dry."

He rose and took her glass, reaching for the vermouth. "I can remedy that. Old Karl can remedy anything!"

Vladimir watched Ivan getting undressed. "Ivan?"

Ivan stopped in the middle of pulling off his turtleneck and peered at his friend. "Yes?"

"Are you certain everything is OK?"

Ivan gestured toward the suitcase. "Closed subject."

"Vasili's making me nervous. He came up behind you when you were talking to Yori."

"Then all he heard was me congratulating Yori on a great game—better than you did. You spent more time in the penalty box than on ice!"

"I wasn't trying to start a fight out there."

"You were doing stupid things, tripping over feet and sticks."

"My mind wasn't on the game," protested Vladimir. "It was on tomorrow night and—"

"Vladimir! We aren't discussing it!" He threw his dirty turtleneck at Ivan. "Don't even think about it!" GROUND FLOOR

Bob Moore and J. L. Rhodes were quietly "walking it through" one more time from the alley behind the kitchen.

"I'll be stationed here in the kitchen right beside the transatlantic phone." J.

L. turned to Bob. "And you'll be?"

"The latest revision has me at a table near the Veep. That way I can play State Department Representative and keep my eye on the KGB goons at the same time."

J. L. worried the cuticle on his left thumb. "With the vice president coming in last minute, I've called for four more reserves to get the lines working in his suite. We may give Bell Tel of PA a permanent headache."

Bob laughed humorlessly, "That should be the least of our worries." "Which one of twenty things I can think of offhand are you worried about now?"

"For openers, the CIA agents keep insisting on checking everything with Langley. I've insisted this is a closed operation, that they can only check in and confirm the operation is moving on schedule without a detailed report, but I wouldn't bet that they're not running it all down for their supervisors' benefits." He sighed. "It's that many more opportunities for leaks. We know the KGB has insiders at Langley."

"Not much more you can do about that except remind them that they report only to you according to their directives." J. L. was getting edgy himself. "There're too many bodies involved, Bob. It'll be the miracle of Market Street if we pull it off."

"And maybe the end of some careers if we don't," glumly replied Bob. "I don't even like to contemplate what could happen if one of the players changes his mind."

"Then don't." J. L. scratched his nose nervously. "We have enough to do worrying about what we know is going to happen."

"Let's hope serendipity's on our side tomorrow!" Bob shivered in the dim lights of the parking garage and stared into the dark alley at the shadowy backs of buildings. "Could be an alley in Berlin, over the wall."

"And out to freedom," finished J. L.

"I hope it's freedom," Bob muttered, his mind jumping to Mattimore's implications that Bollinger was plotting behind the scenes. The thought disturbed him. He didn't share it with J. L. The present operation was concern enough.

# MOSCOW
# KGB HEADQUARTERS
# February 18
# 3:00 a.m.

Geneneral Taikov stormed into Omnarsky's office, leaving his aide, Lubo, on guard in the hall. "This had better be good, Colonel!"

Omnarsky rose until the general sat down. He handed the general a sheaf of documents and began, "We found these documents and that memo to Padov in Padov's flat. His mother is missing. So is his mistress. The manager of the building, Padov's building," Omnarsky explained, "reports that a young man of Konstantine's description entered the building the morning of the fifteenth. The manager was in the front hall until noon. He did not see the young man leave."

Taikov looked up from the computer printouts. "Padov called me before ten a.m. Could the manager have missed them?"

"Perhaps, but that doesn't explain his missing mother and mistress. I've called for an all-out search of the building. Everyone is being questioned." He paused. "The memo and printouts regarding the search for the mole were lying openly on the hall table at Padov's. That in itself is strange. Konstantine's memo indicates that he requested regular military files on those suspects that had re-cords destroyed in the KGB fire who had been transferred in from the army."

"Yes? What does that prove?"

"Konstantine believed that an irregularity in those files—or a missing file —would point a finger at a possible plant." "Get to the point."

"The requested army files had been delivered to Konstantine's desk. He did not appear to come back for them or to even call and check. Most unusual if he was working with Padov on this secret assignment."

"Don't play cat and mouse with me, Colonel." Taikov's patience was running low. "What are you getting at?"

"There was only one file the army archives couldn't find." He paused, looking at Taikov, anticipating a reaction. "Padov's."

The phone rang. Omnarsky noticed the general's face whiten as he answered, "Omnarsky here."

He listened for several minutes. "The identification is certain? His gun? Continue as directed." Omnarsky replaced the receiver. His eyes had never wavered from Taikov. "We have found Konstantine's body in the coal bin in the basement of Padov's apartment. His own gun had not been fired."

Taikov rose, without energy. He seemed to have withered in the past minutes. "Very well, Colonel. We shall put out a Red Alert for Padov."

# RUSSIA
# GROZNY INSTALLATION
## February 18
## 6:00 a.m.

"I'm going to make rounds. I'll be back in an hour, before the commander arrives."

"I'll stay by the phones."

Peter heard the first guard close the outside door. Time to get moving. He rose quickly, slipping into his clothes. The term rumpled would have been complimentary. The dried blood felt rough on his overcoat. He checked for money, papers, and keys. Everything in place. He quietly opened the door to the reception area. The guard whirled around and came to attention. "Good morning, sir. You startled me."

"Get the prisoners ready. I wish to leave." "So early?"

"I awoke early and there is no reason to delay." His voice became cold and authoritative. "Get the prisoners immediately."

Pavlovian response to authority won. "You must wait for the commander" remained unspoken as the guard hurried down the hall to the room where the "prisoners" still shivered in their sleep.

Peter waited at the guard's station, fingers tapping impatiently. He glanced at his watch, calculating time and distance. A hundred and twenty-five miles or so to Tbilisi over mountainous roads. Conservatively, they would arrive close to noon. When he'd mapped this route years before, he'd discovered some small roads, practically cattle paths, in the mountains surrounding the small city. If they took the direct route by Yerevan, they'd have to pass a small checkpoint. He preferred taking the mountain roads if the weather held and the car could navigate the rocky, twisted gravel trail.

The guard returned with the "prisoners," holding his left wrist, looking fierce. Little Vladimir, face white with anger, finger marks clearly outlined on his cheek, followed the guard, Nadia's hand firmly gripping his shoulder, restraining him.

"The little devil bit my wrist," reported the guard.

"He grabbed me! I'm going to tell my father as soon as . . ." "Prisoners are to remain silent!" ordered Peter. Nadia's hand dug into Vladimir's shoulder. The boy winced.

Peter gestured toward the door. "Unlock the door," he ordered as the phone rang.

"Excuse me, sir. I'm alone on duty." He picked up the phone. "Station 17. Kaminsky." He stiffened. "Yes, sir. A red alert . . . for a Colonel Padov." His eyes widened. "Sir!" he began, then stopped short as he felt Peter's gun pressing into his side and felt his own gun being pulled out of his belt. He glanced at Peter, fear pouring through him. Peter glared at him, finger to his lips for silence.

"Very good, sir. I'll see you then." The guard hung up the phone and blurted, "Colonel Gregory! What does this mean?"

As a precaution, Peter had used false documents for himself, but the women were checked in under their own papers, with the exception of Berthe and Nadia, whose papers identified them as Natalovya and Breinkov. Something has gone wrong in Moscow. Konstantine's papers? His body? A slip in Syktyvkar? A leak by the Americans? It didn't matter; the alert was on. Perhaps he could get Taikov to call off the dogs, depending on how serious the leak. He needed to buy time. He calmly pulled the trigger of his gun, aiming up toward the guard's heart. The concussion of the shot sent the guard sprawling across his desk. Peter's hand burned. Despite the silencer, the noise echoed in Peter's ears. "Get in the car," he ordered the women. "We have no time." He rifled through the papers on the desk, pushing the guard's body on the floor.

In shock, the women turned and hurried out the door, no one saying a word.

Peter found the evening log from the night before and pocketed it. The second guard would not be back for another forty-five minutes. He might not remember the prisoners' names. The commander would not be there until seven. They'd have their description from the other guard, but there would still be a shadow of question. He grunted as he straightened the desk, removing blood-splattered papers and stuffing them in his overcoat pocket. He leaned down and picked up the dead weight of the guard, placing him over his shoulder.

He awkwardly picked up his briefcase as Tasha came back in the door. "I told you to get in the car."

"I thought I could help."

"Take my briefcase and those keys on the desk. See if one of them fits the door. Then lock it and head for the car."

He laboriously walked down the front steps, looking for a place to stash the body. In the predawn winter morning, in the single bulb burning beside the door, he looked like a grim reaper with his bloody burden. Tasha struggled with the keys, glad to have a task to divert her chaotic thoughts.

As Peter began crossing the small parking lot toward the woods, the guard dogs behind their wire mesh walls barked furiously, banging against the walls, trying to reach him, smelling blood, ready for a kill of their own. They won't let up, thought Peter. If the second guard is anywhere near . . . He changed direction, carrying the body to the edge of the mesh fence. Summoning his strength, he catapulted the body up and almost over the fence. It caught grotesquely on the barbed top, dangling over. The dogs leaped in fury below. Peter stretched then jumped up to give the heavy boot on the dangling guard a shove. The ghoulish fulcrum shifted, and the body dropped inside the wall, then disappeared under a swarm of Dobermans. Peter did not stay and watch. The dogs were silenced. He hurried back to the limousine. There was no question of route. They had to make it through the mountain roads, stopping only at the edge of Tbilisi for gas and a call to Taikov to see how serious the alert was.

# TURKEY
## Airfield near Istanbul West February 18
## 7:00 a.m.

Charlie Vickers, ex-U.S. Air Force and former CIA operative, present consultant to the Turkish Air Force, leaned his large, square frame across the table, staring at the map. "We have five birds, men, so we'll have to stay in touch."

Perplexed, the translator shook his head.

Charlie glanced at him. "You don't understand?" "No, sir, I don't know how to translate that."

"OK, we'll try again." He paused. "We're flying F-111's in formation for a very special training mission. It is vital that we keep information. If we are contacted for any reason, I am the only person who can respond, through my pilot. Understand?"

The translator repeated the statements in Turkish. Nine serious young faces nodded. Charlie's Turkish was adequate, but stilted. He preferred using translators wherever possible.

The men as a whole needed to know no more. He'd need one crew briefed to take command in case something happened to his plane. He'd do that separately. The Turkish government had given its covert sanction, planes, and men. The logistics were his problem. Charlie had quickly accepted Faeuil's assignment. Ten grand for a night's flight wasn't bad—five up front and five when the mission was completed. It would be a little tricky. They'd have to fly north, but circle in formation to hit the border at 0100 ZULU. Tough, but possible.

He wished he'd have old George Rannilucci navigating. George was in Angola. Lousy grounds for a good mercenary these days, thought Charlie, when things were easier and money freer in the Arab world. And the women were fine stuff once you got under those veils. At fifty-one, Charlie's interest in what went on behind the veils remained strong.

Charlie addressed the young Turks, hopefully. "Do any of you speak English?" No one responded. He tried again. "Parlez-vous francais?" His French wasn't great, but it was better than his Turkish. No response. In frustration, he turned to his translator, "Doesn't anyone on this base speak English?"

The slightly insulted reply, "I do, sir."

"But you can't fly an F-111 while I navigate! Ask the men if anyone on the base—any pilot, that is—speaks English."

The translator posed the question. Several of the men chattered back, excitedly. The translator turned to Charlie. "The men are upset that you will not be piloting one of the planes. They know you are a great pilot and will feel safer with you leading the squadron."

"Tell them they'll feel safer if I navigate, keep us on course, and get us back safely!"

A comparatively light-skinned young man stepped forward hesitantly. "I speak some English, sir."

"Well, why the hell didn't you say so?"

"I wanted to know why you needed someone to speak English."

"It helps if the pilot can understand the navigator! Now you know. You will pilot the lead plane with me."

"Yes, sir." The young pilot looked like a chastised child, eyes dropped. Charlie felt like an old man as he continued, "We have until two tomorrow morning to get our act together, but we take off at one a.m." He wanted plenty of time to get into position. "We'll have a full briefing of your entire crews at nine this morning. After that, take a nap and be sure you eat well. I don't want you tired or hungry at midnight. You are dismissed until nine."

The English-speaking pilot waited beside him. Charlie turned to leave, noticed him, and said, "You might as well join me for breakfast. We'd do well to get to know each other quickly."

# ANDOVER, MASSACHUSETTS
## February 18
## 3 a.m.

Mattie stood in front of the stove scrambling eggs as she had done for the past ten years whenever Brian couldn't sleep. She put rye bread in the toaster as she listened to Brian's tale of intended defection. Despite his resolve not to tell her, after four sleepless hours and dozens of questions, his resistance had broken. He decided sharing his concerns might help.

"That's exciting! The whole team!" She smiled sleepily. "Is it going to happen tomorrow night? I mean tonight."

"They're scheduled to fly home the nineteenth. If it comes off, it has to happen soon."

"No wonder you want to go to the banquet—it could be then!"

"Who knows? It's up to the State Department. I'd only like to say 'welcome' or good-bye and good luck'—one way or the other."

Mattie placed the early breakfast in front of him and perched on a kitchen stool, chin in hand, searching for an idea. "How's this? We take a historical trip to Philadelphia. And we just happen to stay at the same hotel and you 'accidentally' bump into Ivan and Yori. It's dumb luck."

"Or meddling. It might create an incident. Rob was absolutely firm on my staying away. Orders from Washington. National security."

"What could they do?" she asked, eyes twinkling. "Put you in the penalty box?"

"No, love. This isn't a game. I don't know their plan, but if they don't want a stray Bruin around, I'd better stay put."

"You're so straight." She planted a kiss on his cheek. "Would you like more toast?"

"One piece. No jelly. Maybe I could give Yori a call tomorrow night. Discreetly, without saying anything other than good-bye and good luck. See what he says. They may have officially defected by then or be planning to do it in the morning."

"That has a nice ring to it." Mattie was getting tired and punchy. "Defecting in the morning, fast without a warning . . . it could be a song."

"I'm not going to tell you another thing! Either you come up with cock-eyed notions or treat the whole thing like Saturday Night Live."

"I can only take so much of being dead serious. Here's your toast."

"And I want your sacred word that you will not repeat any of this to anyone—and that includes your canary bird friend, Cecily. Not until it's over."

"Yes, sir!" She stood at attention.

"I could forgive you for almost anything, but not that!" He tried lightening the conversation. "Even though you're sensational in the kitchen."

"What about the bedroom?" She grinned.

"The two rooms where women should be good . . . and you're the best!"

She hugged him from behind. "That's awfully chauvinistic, but I love you anyway."

"Seriously," he added earnestly. "No local scoops for anyone."

"I know this is serious," she protested. "I wouldn't say anything." "Do we have any milk?"

"Sorry, I forgot." She went to the refrigerator for milk.

"It's hard to believe that Yori was first here less than a week ago." He couldn't get the Wings out of his mind. "Mattie," he hesitated. "Would you hate me if I went to Philadelphia alone? I could slip into the banquet more easily by myself."

She returned, milk in hand. "You really have an itch, don't you?" She knew her hardheaded husband. "You won't be satisfied unless you know."

"I'll take an afternoon flight and be back on the first plane Friday morning. But if anyone calls, even Rob—especially Rob or James—say I'm out playing with the kids or something logical. Don't tell anyone I'm out of town."

Peter lightened his foot on the accelerator. He'd been driving for more than four hours, climbing higher and higher into the Caucasus Mountains. Everyone's ears were popping with the change in altitudes. The ride had been tensed and quiet, the memory of the guard's death too fresh in the women's minds; the question of how much they knew in Moscow weighty in Peter's.

He turned slightly toward Tasha, who was riding shotgun. "We should be about twenty-five miles north of Tbilisi. We're about to hit a turn for Gori on our right. If we stay on this road, we might meet a patrol out of Tbilisi." Normally, that was unlikely, but the alarm should be out by now. They were skating on thin ice until they reached Contact, he thought. Then he revised his thought; they were in danger until they were out of Russia.

The road narrowed and followed a deep ravine. "Beautiful!" Tasha clapped her hands. "Look at that." At the bottom of the wide ravine was a crystal forest, trees gleaming with ice.

Little Vladimir peered out the window. "Momma! What if we fall?"
"Don't worry, the colonel won't let that happen."

Hardly a colonel anymore, thought Peter, wondering if he still had his American rank of captain.

In English, his eyes still on the road, Peter asked, "Tasha, I have to know if you're coming out with us. It will affect my plans for all of us."

"I wouldn't have chosen this way to be with you," she haltingly replied, trying to collect her thoughts, "but I am here."

"Momma, are they talking in English?" asked Vladimir.

"I believe so," answered Nadia. "We shall have to learn to speak English also when we join Poppa. Everyone will speak it there."

"Is it hard?"

Aunt Katya laughed. "You'll learn quickly. I could speak English when I was a girl. I'd visit my English cousins in the summers. In a few short months, I was chattering away. So shall you be." The passengers were finding their tongues again.

"Do you still speak English?" asked Nadia.

"Very little, but perhaps my old memory can be rattled."

Berthe laughed. "I was always terrible at languages. My husband could not even get me to speak Hungarian. My son will have to act as my translator since he is bringing me out!"

"That might be difficult," Aunt Katya noted. "If he plays hockey, he won't be able to excuse himself from games or practice to translate for his mother at the store!"

"I'm sure the government will send you all to school to learn English— current slang and all," Peter added from the front.

"How do you know?" challenged Berthe. "You haven't been there for thirty years."

"I know they treat defectors well, make certain they are well settled."
"We shall see," sighed Berthe. "If we get there, we shall see."

Tasha felt a sudden chill. "Of course, we'll get there. We're nearly there already! Right, Peter-Sergei?"

"Less than a day away."

As they reached a plateau, the road smoothed and widened. Peter didn't pick up speed.

"I feel like we're crawling," said Tasha.

"We have lots of time, too much. I'd rather not reach Gori before noon.

We can stop at a market, pick up food, find gas, and fill some of our extra hours. Taking the Gori route not only avoids the Tbilisi checkpoint but adds fifty kilometers to the trip."

"Oh dear," Tasha sighed.

"At this moment, we have over fifteen hours until Contact. Would you rather sit in a cold car for twelve hours?" he asked.

"Of course not!" As they turned a corner, Tasha gasped, "A checkpoint!"

A guard house was positioned on the side of the road. There was no easy way to turn on the narrow road. Peter's hand tightened on the steering wheel as he approached. "It looks deserted." He slowed as they passed it. "I wonder why no one's around." Then he saw the notice. Checkpoint closed. Next station fifteen kilometers. Everyone visibly relaxed. "That next checkpoint is the one I anticipated. This is a new one that perhaps is only used in the summer. Not much traffic off-season."

Tasha ran her hands through her dark, shoulder-length curls. "I would give a week's salary for some soap and hot water."

"That's not much when for all practical purposes you are unemployed." "I can find a job anywhere—even in the United States!"

"That's good, because you make a lousy navigator. We're at the turn-off to Gori and you missed it!" Peter laughed as he made the turn.

"If I had anything to throw, I'd throw it right at your head!" "Momma, are they fighting?" little Vladimir asked.

"No," chuckled Nadia. "It's called a lovers' squabble." "I heard that," laughed Tasha from the front seat.

The empty guard house was a good omen for the passengers. They had experienced fear, discomfort, and death together. Now they shared relief and humor. Even Berthe joined in the repartee. The sun was breaking through the cloud cover, shining on the rutted road leading to Gori. Tasha broke the silence. "Peter, I prefer Peter."

Peter agreed. It was time to finally bury Sergei Padov. He hoped he'd never have to answer to that name again. "Are we past all checkpoints?" she wondered aloud.

"I hope so."

"Mmm. I wish you knew so."

# TURKEY
## Station RHO Dining Room

Pat McLaughlin ignored his hams and eggs. "Sarge, you're sure— absolutely sure—that if we take off at exactly twenty-seven minutes before, we'll cross at 0200."

"0100 ZULU, sir. Another five to Contact, five to load, five for safety, and five out at 0120."

"Not much margin for error."

"We don't have time for error, sir." "We signal at 0120, right?"

"We signal as we cross the border, back in."

Lieutenant Ray Kensington rattled his tray down on the table beside Pat.

"What are you two whispering about? What's the big mystery?"

"A fixed poker game, Ray," Pat quipped, realizing they were violating security precautions talking in the mess hall. Pat had cleaned Ray out the week before.

"Sore subject, buddy, and you know it. From now on I'm limiting my betting to the 50¢ pool on how many times the colonel pulls his mustache during inspection."

Jim picked up his tray. "I'm leaving you two young troublemaking officers. Some of us have work to do."

"Thanks, Sarge," called Pat.

"Thanks for what?" asked Ray. "These NCO's around here are all alike. Trying to get us to do their work for them." He watched Jim's compact form return the tray to the dirty dish window. "Blaire's better than most, I guess. What are you two up to?"

"A special test flight. He's playing navigator to my pilot." "He's the best . . . even if he's a little weird."

"What do you mean weird. This whole army's weird, especially RHO!" "Takes one to know one!"

Pat attacked his hash although his stomach was churning. He'd be glad when take-off time arrived. The waiting was the worst part. As soon as he finished eating, he'd go recheck the Huey. It seemed fine when he'd taken it up yesterday, but . . .

"Pat! Pat! You're daydreaming. Don't tell me you've fallen in love with the cook again."

"I have to confess. I love that fag like he was my sister! Adds a little incest."

"You really were daydreaming."

"I do that sometimes over corned beef hash. It affects the mind." "Not while you're flying, I hope."

"Never eat corned beef hash in the air."

# WASHINGTON, D.C.
## State Department February 18
## 8:00 a.m.

"They're connecting the cable now? The vice president's team is there? Everyone coordinated? Good. No trouble getting the restaurant closed to the general public? OK, Bob. Keep me posted. I won't have any new information from this end until they've arrived in Turkey. It's a waiting game. It sounds like you're doing fine."

Mattimore leaned back in his chair, mentally reviewing plans, searching for any small detail they might have missed. So much could go wrong. The press would be all over the place with the vice president there. Horace Watson's appearance was a Bollinger brainchild.

Twelve hours and twenty minutes until they knew if the families were out, and they could trigger the defection scheme. Then what? Keep the team on ice while Bollinger plays his cat and mouse with the Russians.

The intercom buzzed. "Yes?" "The secretary of state."

"What's precipitated this momentous call, Karl?" Mattimore asked.

Ignoring the sarcasm, Bollinger said, "We're meeting to discuss this hockey thing with the president at ten this morning."

Charles appreciated the "advance notice" Bollinger always gave him. He suspected the man intentionally waited until the last moment. "Have you decided on the terms?"

"That's on the agenda to discuss." "How about running them by me first?" "At the meeting. See you then, Charles."

173

# Code Coral

Although Charles's role of coordinating the dual defections, east and west, with Rubin et al, was well defined, he resented Bollinger's high-handed manner. It stuck in his twelfth-generation American throat that Bollinger intended to sell the Wings down the river, but Bollinger's ignoring him in the development of terms burned like acid. He rationalized that his conscience might feel better if he knew the terms of barter that might validate the monumental double-cross.

He reached for his coffee. Cold. He'd been at his desk since 5:30 a.m. He buzzed his secretary to request hot coffee. The operation was now in the hands of too many people. He felt out of control.

# PHILADELPHIA
## Penn Center Inn "Henry's"
## February 18
## 9:00 a.m.

The waiter brought Vladimir scrambled eggs and sausage and placed a steaming pile of hotcakes in front of Ivan.

"Ivan," Vladimir choked, "I think I'm going to be sick."

"Relax. You don't want to miss the banquet tonight." Ivan said quietly. "Have they told you how it's going to take place?"

"Why don't you scream at the top of your lungs?" Ivan hissed angrily. "No details but I think it will happen at the banquet. Now change the subject." He spoke quietly, pouring syrup on his hotcakes. "Eat your breakfast and stop staring at me. Vasili or one of our watchdogs will wonder what you're so excited about!"

Several tables away, J. L. noticed Vladimir's nervousness. I hope he calms down, he thought. All we need is him cracking up in the middle of this. His stomach churned. All it would take is one false move and the whole plan could explode with Network cameras rolling. He finished his coffee and dug into his eggs over easy.

It had been 3:37 a.m. before he and Bob were satisfied that their plans were solid. Bob was either still sleeping or eating in his room. According to their "lie low" policy, he should be eating upstairs, too, but the flowered curtains had begun closing in on him again. He glanced at the entrance. Watchdogs in position. They liked it by doors and windows. He munched his bacon and signaled the waiter for more coffee.

Ivan looked around, his gaze fastening on J. L. for a second. "There's the man who bumped into me. I wonder who he is."

Vladimir jerked upright and began searching the room, swiveling his neck, "Where? Which one?"

"Hey, relax. Forget it. Probably some salesman here on business. Stop looking around. You're being too obvious."

Time to get out of here, J. L. decided, waving for his check. He handed the waiter a five and three one's as he arrived with the check. "Keep the change," he muttered as he headed past the KGB guards and into the lobby. The waiter made no comment other than a pleased smile. The tab for J. L.'s breakfast was $4.38.

"I think I chased him out—or you did—by looking at him," Ivan quietly commented. "But I'll bet he's a good guy."

"I wonder if any of them are good guys," dourly replied to Vladimir between bites.

"Keep the faith," comforted Ivan. "By this time tomorrow, you'll be a new man."

"I still feel sick."

"We're being given a bus tour of historic Philadelphia this morning. If you're going to be sick, do it before we get on the bus."

"That's what's so great about you, Ivan. You may not know what's going on, but you're full of practical advice. I didn't say I was going to vomit, just that I felt sick."

Yori stopped by their table on his way to the bus. "Come on, get moving, we're about to get a Philadelphia Freedom Tour."

"What?" asked Vladimir.

"That's what they call it, the Freedom Tour of Philadelphia, birthplace of freedom. The place where the American Revolution got itself organized."

"I thought that was Washington, D.C.," said Vladimir.

"Guess it's time for a history of the U.S. lesson. You can get it on the bus." Yori smiled.

"You're in a good mood today." Vladimir burped. "Excuse me." "Today is the day! See you on the bus." He headed for the door.

"See?" Ivan reassured Vladimir. "Nothing to worry about. Relax. Enjoy the Freedom tour and please, stay calm."

Vladimir stood up and knocked his knife off the table with a clatter. "Damn!"

"That's what I mean," nodded Ivan. "Relax."

# RUSSIA
## Fifty miles northeast of Yerevan
## February 18
## 4:00 p.m.

"**W**e have moved slowly and cautiously like a wise old snail," stated Peter. "But we still have ten hours and less than a hundred miles to travel."

"My old bones have had enough traveling," Aunt Katya commented.

"This is the hardest part of this trip, but we still have many thousands of miles to go."

"Not in this car, thank goodness." Aunt Katya looked out the window at the dented fender. "I can see it age before my eyes."

The once-shiny limousine was now coated with mud and dust. Stones and potholes had chipped paint and dented the fenders. The KGB markings were gone. "It's served us well so far. We could go ten miles an hour from now on and arrive on time."

Vladimir stirred from his nest on Nadia's lap. "Are we there yet?" "Not yet, sweet lamb, go back to sleep." Nadia rubbed his head gently.

The road continued its wind around the mountains. Peter glanced at the gas gauge. It was getting dangerously low. "I'm going to cut off soon and head for the outskirts of Leninakan. I'll drop Berthe and Aunt Katya at a market for food and I'll get gas."

"If there is an alert out for you," Tasha spoke in English to prevent worrying the others unduly, "is it safe?"

"We'll run out of gas otherwise. I don't think we'd make it on foot, not with the boy. It will pass some time—and we have lots of that." He also wanted to place a call to Taikov to see how far the alert had gone. Perhaps there were only questions he could field and give them some breathing room. He had to take the risk. Without gas, they'd never reach Contact Point on schedule.

He turned at a weathered old sign pointing to Leninakan. The road was narrow and pitted, covered with ice. He decelerated. He concentrated on his driving as dusk quickly covered their path, making it difficult to see the ice and potholes. Peter felt a combination of relief and apprehension as he saw signs of civilization. Scattered houses, an old horse in a field, a car parked beside a barn. Soon there were more houses and street signs.

"There!" Tasha pointed. "A market."

Following her finger, Peter saw a general market ahead of them. There was a line, but it was short. "They will be looking for a man with five passengers by this time," Peter thought. "A man with his wife and child will attract less attention at a gas station." He gave Tasha money and stopped around the corner from the market. "You, Berthe and Aunt Katya shop for food. Buy what you like but keep it ordinary to avoid suspicion. Bring Vladimir in front, Nadia." He would meet them back at the same corner as soon as possible.

"What if?" Tasha hesitated.

"I will be here," he replied. There was no time for a contingency plan. They drove on toward the city, searching for gasoline. Peter spotted it first.

A small wooden station, sadly in need of paint, with one gas pump and no line.

"Is it open?" asked Nadia breathlessly.

"We shall see." Peter turned into the drive and pulled up beside the pump. He didn't see any lights on, but he got out of the car to inspect the pump. Perhaps he could unlock it if the owner was not around. An old man hurried from behind the small station. He explained the station was only open mornings. "Come back tomorrow," he cheerfully suggested. There was no time for complicated stories. Sergei pulled out his KGB ID and ordered the man to fill the tank. Nervously, he complied. Peter next asked if the station had a telephone. Despite his nervousness, the old man proudly replied he did. When the tank was filled, Peter demanded that the old man take him to the phone. He handed him fifty rubles to cover the cost of the call and gasoline.

The old man stared at the money. "It is too much," he gasped.

"You are also to tell no one that anyone has stopped here for gas today. That is an order!" The old man stammered his promise to remain silent. "Now attend to the windshield while I make my call." He watched the old man shuffle rapidly back to the car and start vigorously wiping the windows. The fear is strong in the old, he thought as he placed his call to Moscow, to General Taikov's private number.

Taikov answered the line himself.

"Koral 37," Peter replied. There was a pregnant pause. Then Taikov cleared his throat. "Colonel Padov, you are under arrest. Turn yourself in to the nearest KGB Headquarters. The charges are treason. If there are explanations, you may make them directly to me in Moscow."

"What?" Peter pretended astonishment.

"All borders are under full alert. There will be no escape." Taikov waited.

Peter watched the second hand of his watch. There was a computer tracer on the General's line. He had ten seconds to avoid a trace.

"I protest, sir! There has been a terrible mistake! I'll report in directly." He hung up the phone. It was serious. They had to move quickly.

Padov hurried back to the car. Taikov must still have some doubts. "If you have an explanation . . ." he'd said. If there had been time, Peter might have offered some, providing Taikov told him what needed explaining. He pushed the questions from his mind. He'd confirmed that the chase was on, and he knew, from innumerable times on the other side of the chase, that close checks would be made fifty miles from all borders. The net would be tight from Grozny to the Black Sea and across to the Turkish border. Their only hope was to stay in the mountains, within the icy cover of the forests.

He quickly slid into the driver's seat as a solitary car turned in to the station. Peter turned on the ignition, watching warily in the rearview mirror as the other driver stopped and got out of his car. Without turning his head, he casually pulled out and onto the road.

It was Rudolph Boliskya, KGB. The last Peter had heard, he'd been transferred to Leningrad. He was a good field officer, too good for Peter to feel comfortable as they drove away, although Rudolph seemed to only casually glance after their car. He was still waiting for the old attendant as Peter took a road to the left.

"This is not the same way," Nadia protested.

"I want to check something out," Peter said. He drove a block, made a U- turn and pulled up by a large old pine, a hundred feet from the main road. Within ten minutes, they watched Rudolph's car race past them. Peter noted it had a radio antenna. Boliskya was almost out of range of the Tbilisi headquarters north of the city. Almost wasn't good enough. He would report in. Peter waited a few minutes and headed back toward the market, resisting the urge to speed. He regretted his decision to stop at the Grozny KGB facility then dismissed the guilt. Wallowing in mistakes only compounded them. As they reached the appointed corner, they saw the three women huddled close, carrying bags. It was well below zero.

"What took so long?" demanded Tasha as they handed in the bags. "Quickly," Peter urged them.

"They are looking for us," Nadia added. "It is good it is nearly dark."

"Was there any trouble in the market?" Peter turned the corner onto the road leading past the market. There was no other way out of town. With half his attention, he listened to Tasha's story of the market owner questioning her accent. She'd finally admitted she was from Moscow, visiting a cousin. Aunt Katya, in line behind her, complained she and the owner were slowing down the line. The three women had agreed to pretend to be strangers to each other. The simple ruse worked. The store owner turned his attention to his long line of customers and Tasha quickly left.

He said nothing to the women as he noticed Rudolph's car parked in front of the grocery, nor did he change his speed or expression as he saw his former comrade talking to the shoppers in line on the sidewalk. As the miniature scene receded in his rearview mirror, he thought he saw Rudolph's chin lift and his eyes follow them. He accelerated slightly, driving with his attention half on the rearview mirror, looking for headlights behind them.

"It gets dark so early in the winters," Berthe noted.

"The darkness is our friend," Nadia responded. "There is less to see of us in the dark."

Tasha was watching Peter's eyes darting between the road and the rearview mirror. "What are you looking at?" She glanced behind them as they turned a corner. The road was quickly resuming its narrow, rutted mountain characteristics.

"I saw a man I know at the station. KGB. I believe he is looking for us," Peter spoke in English.

"But how?" Tasha began.

"It does not matter. Watch out the back while I pay attention to the road." He stepped on the accelerator, and they jounced forward. Tasha's eyes caught a glimpse of light as they turned another corner. "I thought I saw something," she gasped. There was a straight stretch in front of them. Peter looked into the rearview mirror and saw the headlights turn the corner toward them.

"Hold on," Peter stepped on the accelerator and maneuvered the narrow gravel road.

"He's still behind us," reported Tasha. "Is he gaining?"

"I don't think so."

It had been years since Peter had driven this road, and never in the winter. Dusk had melted into night. He felt for his revolver. He could stop and wait for Rudolph, or he could watch for a good side road and try to lose him. He skidded around a corner.

"Count how long before he turns the corner," he said.

"One, two, three, four, five, six, seven, eight . . . here he comes," she counted as they skidded into another corner with a screech. "It doesn't matter. We're going to crash before he catches up."

"Quiet," Peter concentrated on his driving. There it was. A small road off to the left. He didn't know where it led, but it was worth a try. He floored the accelerator and skidded into the turn, hurtling his passengers into the sides of the limousine and each other. He ignored the yells and grunts as he followed the narrow path in front of him. Behind him, he heard the squeal of brakes and the screech of a slide. Then a shattering crash and silence. He slowed then stopped and listened. More silence.

"What happened?" asked Nadia.

"Sounded like he crashed." Tasha turned to Peter. "What shall we do?

Turn around, and see?"

"Wait a minute. Let's see if he can still follow us."

No one said a word as they stared out the back window. Vladimir clung to Nadia's hand in quiet fear. There was a faint glow glimmering through the forest behind them. It could be headlights, Peter decided. He waited a few more minutes. They sat in silence. "Shall we turn around?" asked Tasha.

Peter looked at the brambled rocky land beside the road. The trees were thick. There was no room to turn around. He carefully backed the car toward the turnoff.

As they neared the main road, he took his foot from the accelerator as they drifted to a stop, staring silently at what was left of Rudolph's car. He'd missed the turn and hit a large pine dead center. The front of the car literally wrapped around the tree.

"I guess he won't follow us anymore," observed Tasha quietly. "He was a good man," said Peter curtly. "One of our best."

All eyes were glued to the wreckage as Peter backed carefully onto the main road, keeping the maximum distance from the accident. He maneuvered so his headlights shone fully on the left side of the wreckage. They could see Rudolph's body flung forward on the dashboard. The window was shattered, forming a glittering spider web where Rudolph must have hit it. Peter shut off the motor, leaving the lights on and opened the car door.

"Where are you going?" asked Tasha.

"I must finish the job," he said flatly. Cautiously, he moved around the shattered vehicle. As he forced open the right door, he heard a voice. Startled, he froze, then realized it was coming from the two-way radio. "Major Boliskaya. Come in, please. Come in, over." With luck, Rudolph had kept his call numbers. With the instinct for survival strong, he reached across the seat and took the microphone from Rudolph's stiff fingers. He must have been calling in as he crashed. Remembering the unusual high pitch of Rudolph's voice, Peter pushed the Callback button and spoke in a falsetto imitation, "K- 417 reporting in. False alarm. Repeat. False alarm. Heading in with full report. Over." The box was silent for a long moment. Then "Message received. Over. Report expected. Over."

He'd bought them some time, but he didn't know how much. He looked at Rudolph, head bowed into the dashboard. No pulse. Peter quickly got out of the car, noticing the gasoline seeping into the ground from the damaged gasoline tank. He moved away, reaching into his pocket for the papers he'd stuffed there at Grozny. He wadded one tightly around a small rock, lighted it and threw it at the gas-soaked ground. An explosion shook the air, hurling Peter to the ground and shaking the limousine. Flames engulfed the wreckage, lighting the sky and threatening the surrounding woods. Peter got to his feet; branches nearby were beginning to flame. As he thought he smelled burning flesh, he felt hollow and nauseous. His eyes teared, from the smoke and the sadness. He hoped the defections would be worth the sacrifice.

Silently, he turned his back on the flames and staggered to the car. Tasha and the others stared at him, afraid to speak to this suddenly stony-faced man. Finally, as Peter started the engine and headed away from Leninakan, Tanya spoke, "All is well?"

Peter closed his eyes for a long second to ease the sting. The KGB headquarters was several miles northeast of the town. The woods were dense, but the fire would not spread in the wet, snowy woods. There was hope, if not certainty.

"Are you all right?" asked Tasha timorously. "Shall I drive?"

He shook his head negatively in response as he continued toward Contact Point, trying to ignore his mental images of long-gone vodka-filled card games and nights of carousing with Rudolph.

# PHILADELPHIA PENN CENTER INN
## February 18
## 12:00 noon

J. L. watched Sally Garnette, the vice president's press liaison, flit through the dining room, the manager at her heels.

Eating up the scene, J. L. observed. Dressed in a bright orange pants suit, with a red scarf around her neck, she could stop traffic with the glare. She was explaining the "Veep's" traveling press conference style to the manager. The vice president liked to answer questions as he entered and left banquets. She explained he wanted to maintain his reputation of being "fast on his feet and hard to hit." J. L. silently believed that was the last phrase in the world that could be applied to the slow-paced Watson. The man was a lame duck in his first term.

The banquet would be held in the rear dining room, which would be closed to the general public. Special guests and the press would be cleared via a list at the door. The press would be given the tables on the outer rim of the dining room so that they would create less confusion when they rushed to follow Horace Watson out and through the lobby to his waiting limousine. It would be the first time that Watson's affectations would serve them well. His traveling press conferences—"when you have nothing to say, it's better to keep moving," Bonekemper observed—were the joke of WHCA.

The vice president would not be briefed on the defection operation. Mattimore had been adamant. He would play the role better if he were totally innocent of the plan.

Sally raised her left arm with a flourish, gesturing toward the door. J. L. had watched her confuse numerous press conferences with "general dumbness."

He was glad he'd be meeting privately with the manager later in the day.

Sally whirled her extra twenty pounds around and tottered over to J. L. on her spike heels. "There!" she puffed. "Everything's under control!"

"Great," he replied without corresponding enthusiasm.

"Want to take me to lunch?" She flirted, batting her plastic lashes. "I have the ear of the vice president," she added for incentive.

"So have it for lunch," he retorted, giving a wink at the manager before heading toward the elevator.

"Well!" she sniffed, staring after him.

"Please," consoled the short, round manager. "Have lunch with me. We have a Mediterranean salad you'll love."

"I hate salads," Sally said.

"Then have our prime ribs or eggs benedict."

"Those military types are a pain anyway." She followed the manager across the plush room to a corner table, thinking he might have, at the least, chosen one in the center of things. But she was hungry, and it was on the house. She picked up the menu with interest.

While Sally Garnette and the manager buttered their rolls, J. L. and Bob fine-combed their notes, double-checking everyone's roles and positions.

By the time Sally had eaten her way through a five-course lunch, they were satisfied they had everything under control.

"We have one bread truck that holds ten and they've cleared out a milk truck, shelves and all that holds ten, plus drivers and agents. That will cut down the transportation problem in the alley. It won't be comfortable, but it's only twenty minutes to the airport."

"Sounds good." "J. L.?"

"Yeah?"

"I have put together an in-depth contingency plan if the KGB catches on early."

"What does the CIA say?" J. L. asked.

"They're following, not issuing orders on this caper. And I'm not certain what the orders should be. We have enough men to take out the guards, but it requires a special contingency plan."

"We'll have total control of the hotel switchboard from four on, with a blackout on all unauthorized transatlantic calls—in or out. We should know if they try to scream Uncle Sam!" J. L. grinned.

"Good. That could help." Bob chewed on the tip of his pen. "I'm also uncomfortable about the press." Bob dropped his clipboard on the desk. "There are so damn many things that could blow."

"Then you'd better keep your nose deep in this one. I have to check if the transatlantic's in. Then I have to see the manager. I want to make sure the cooks stay away from the special lines, starting now! This kitchen caper could turn into a stew," J. L. said.

"Speaking of stew, do you want to order some lunch?" "No, go ahead. I'll catch something later." J. L. left.

Bob picked up the phone to call room service, then changed his mind and dialed Mattimore.

J. L. cheerfully whistled his way to the elevator. No sense in worrying about things that hadn't happened yet. There'd be enough to worry about later if and when they did.

# ISTANBUL
## February 18
## 7:30 p.m.

Charlie Vickers idly picked a piece of lamb from his rear molar and thought about their mission. He reached for his map. They were flying instruments so it shouldn't be necessary, but he liked the backup of knowing the area cold. He thought about catching a nap, but there wasn't time. He might oversleep. Best thing to do was consider this a regular training mission. What was the difference if the destination was in Turkey or Russia? Sure, he thought. Try believing that when some Russian fighter planes show up and don't ask questions. He opened his bottom desk drawer and pulled out a fifth of Bombay gin, opened it, and took a deep swig. And another. He began to feel easier. It was very simple. Fly to destination. If questioned, answer "navigational error." In Turkey. His Turkish wasn't bad. Ha, he thought, his Turkish was a turkey's. He'd have the kid say it. What if the Russians didn't understand Turkish? He'd try French or English. But Turkish first.

He wondered how his pilot was doing. The kid seemed to know his stuff with the F-111. As far as the kid or any of the young Turks knew, this was a training mission. The story of his life, he thought, was to know more— perhaps too much—than the world around him. Sometimes it gave him an edge, but more often, it spelled deep shit. This mission had that kind of smell. Still, he had to earn his gambling money somewhere. It was better than an office job.

Seven forty-five. Less than six hours until takeoff. Not enough time to go drinking and sober up. He'd already eaten. His sweet young thing was forty miles away. He took another swig of gin. Might as well go find the kid, throw dice or something. They'd better get Lady Luck on their side for the night. He finished off the gin and tossed the bottle toward the wastebasket. Two points, he thought as it landed dead center.

RUSSIA

Seven kilometers west of Yerevan

February 18

8:46 p.m.

They'd made progress slowly on the rough mountain roads. It was a solitary journey for the limousine. They'd passed no other vehicles. Peter explained that the route was used primarily in summer for obvious reasons. It was dangerous driving in winter months. Peter pulled toward the woodsy side of the road. He needed to rest. He got the extra blankets from the trunk. Despite the heater, it was cold in the car. The temperature had fallen quickly as they climbed higher in the mountains. The women brought out bread, cheese, smoked meat, and bottled water. Everyone was hungry. "We won't park long," promised Peter. "It is so cold I fear the engine or radiator might freeze." He'd been driving in circles, lights on dim. When they found the tracks in the morning, as he knew they would, it would slow their pursuit. But by then, it would be all over one way or the other. It was getting too cold. He resumed the journey.

Peter hadn't said exactly where they were heading, but Tasha knew they were extremely close to the Turkish border. The reality that they were leaving Russia became stronger for her, and she became frightened.

"Sergei, I mean Peter," she stammered, "how are we getting across the border? There are blockades, dogs, and guards on all the border roads."

"Yes," he agreed. "Especially now with the alert out for us. It would take a company of tanks to get through."

Frustrated, she shook her head. "Sergei Peter! Stop playing games and tell me how you plan to get us out of here!"

190

Peter replied, "You're certain you want to come with us?" His eyes remained on the road. "I can still give you the limousine at the last minute and you can go back."

Tasha was silent. Everyone else, filled with cheese and bread, was asleep. "Well?" he asked.

"I don't want out," she stated with quiet conviction. "Where you go, I shall go. Your home shall be mine, wherever."

"That has a familiar ring, love," Peter said softly. "From the Bible. The Book of Ruth. I remember my mother, my real mother, reading that to us."

"I don't know the Bible. We didn't study it in school." "I didn't study it at Harvard either."

"What's Harvard?"

"A school in Cambridge, Massachusetts, New England, USA." "A state school?"

"Not quite," chuckled Peter. "Peter?" she asked tentatively. "Yes?" he replied, eyes on the road.

"I thought I knew Sergei, my warm, loving Russian military man. Then I saw Colonel Padov, cold and frightening. And now there is another person, the Peter who is two people at the same time, with a past I know nothing about, from another country. I feel as though I'm suddenly standing on

the outside."

"Still coming with me?"

"If you help me come inside."

His hand reached for her inner thigh. "Anytime."

She playfully rubbed his knee. "You're a dirty-minded old man!"

"Right on all counts." He grinned, keeping his eyes on the road as he reached out his right arm and pulled her closer.

Little Vladimir moaned in his sleep. "Hush, everything's fine," comforted Nadia.

I hope she's right, thought Peter, slowing the car to a crawl. "We have over five hours," he told Tasha. "Try to rest. You can put your head in my lap and try to sleep."

Almost shyly, she put her head in his lap and closed her eyes. The suggestion was out of character for Sergei. As she drifted off, she thought she was going to like her new lover named Peter.

Peter considered turning around and heading back toward Yerevan, then doubling back toward Contact Point to waste more time driving. No, it would be better to move forward slowly. A turtle heading to meet the rabbit. He only hoped the rabbit had its hops straight. No, the Rabbit is Peter, he thought suddenly. I'm getting it backward.

"**D**amn it, Karl! What are you planning? You can't cancel a meeting with the president like that without letting me know! I stood around with my finger in my ear for half an hour, like an idiot! Thanks a lot!"

"Calm down, Charles. Guess my secretary flubbed up. I told her to call you. Sorry, I was only thinking of you. With everything that's happening, I thought you had enough to do without adding a tiresome meeting. I told the president we'd let him know the moment the team had defected and were at Andrews. Charles, I did personally come over here to proffer

proper apologies."

Mattimore sat back in his chair and tapped impatiently on the arm. "If you'd given me advance warning of your arrival, I'd have had the press here to record another historic event."

"Don't be caustic, Charles."

"We're sitting in the middle of a pile of powder kegs all over the world. At this moment, all I can do is sit here, check progress, and cross my fingers that nothing explodes. Oh yes, I forgot to add. I have as a partner in this venture a mad German chock full of mystery games—and it's beginning to smell gamy when you're around."

"Charles, you should relax. You're on edge, overreacting. It's not healthy.

I'll wager you're not getting your proper rest!"

"Rest! Since you tossed this operation in my lap, sleep is an archaic concept!"

"We have five hours to determine if you and your men have been successful. Once it's over tonight, you can sleep for a week."

"Thanks."

"I know this has been a pressure project, but the important ones always are. It'll be worth it."

Mattimore pulled himself straight to confront Karl. "Will it? If my part all works, then what?"

"Then we hold the cards."

"Fine. And then what game is played?"

"Game? No games." Bollinger raised his hands, palms up, in innocence.

"Simple negotiations from a position of power."

"You're playing a game with me, or you'd tell me the terms." "My terms are simple. Eighteen hockey stars for—"

The intercom interrupted. Mattimore pushed the button. "I said hold all calls." He listened a moment. "If Bob says it's urgent, put him on."

Bollinger rose, aware he was leaving his statement unfinished.

Mattimore raised his hand. "No, don't go." He addressed the receiver, "I didn't mean you, Bob. Secretary Bollinger is in the office."
"I must leave." A smile played on Bollinger's lips. "I'll talk to you later." Mattimore sighed in frustration. The slimy German had eluded him again.
"OK, Bob. He's gone." Charles adjusted his glasses and listened impatiently.

"It's too bad if the press wants to interview the team after Watson's out. Make the directive clear. Wings's interviews only before the official speeches. Period. Keep to the posture that they have an early plane and cannot be bothered once the dinner is in session. The wrong reporter getting too close to even one player once the deed is done could destroy the whole operation. Make damned certain they get all the time they want with the players during the cocktail hour! Work it out!" he snapped.

His face softened as he listened to Bob's defensive response. "Sorry, Bob. We're all on edge. It's going to be tense for the next couple of hours. We've done everything we can. All we can do now is wait to hear from Turkey.

# TURKEY STATION RHO
## February 18
## 10:00 p.m.

"**H**elluva time to get ready for work," commented Jim as he handed Pat the cream and sugar.

"You're telling me."

Pat poured out half his coffee into an empty glass, added four sugars, and filled it with milk.

"You don't like coffee much, do you?"

"Coffee ice cream. That's how I like it. Weak coffee and strong liquor and women."

"Remind me to mark your thermos with a big tape X so I can avoid it in the dark."

"We'll have lights, won't we?"

"Only as we're about to land. No main interior lights. They've been removed in case we forget."

"Not the instrument panel," Pat panicked.

Jim choked on his coffee and sputtered, "They tried to special order one in Braille, but can't get it in time so we'll have panel lights."

"Very funny."

"Come on, sir. Don't pack in your sense of humor. We have miles to go before we sleep," Jim quoted.

"I didn't know you were a Robert Frost fan, Sarge," Pat said in surprise. "Is that who said that?"

"The same poem also had something about promises to keep. We learned it in junior high. That's all I remember." Pat finished his lukewarm coffee. "The guys would never believe we're sitting here having a literary conversation." Pat grinned. "To change the subject to a more frivolous matter, you did get specific directions to the party tonight, didn't you?"

"Don't be a wiseass, sir, or I'll direct us to Volgograd where we can have a real party. They are etched in my mind, backward and forward. I think I could get us there with my eyes closed."

"Do me a favor, Sarge. Don't test that theory."

"Oh, if you insist. An extra pair of eyes never hurt." Jim studied the film floating on his coffee. "Shit! I wish we could take off now. Not enough time for a nap, too critical a mission for a drink. All we can do is sit around and try not to think about it, which, of course, makes us think about it more."

"Only a couple of hours to go. Less than that, really." Pat pulled out a dog- eared deck of cards."

"I hate to tempt Lady Luck tonight."

Pat's Irish blue eyes twinkled. "Don't worry . . . one of us has to win. This way we're sure to have a winner along."

"That's a tough argument. You deal while I fill our pot with fresh coffee." "I'll stack the deck while you're gone."

"Try it and you'll learn how it feels to fly with a broken arm." Jim headed for the coffee urn as Pat shuffled the cards. Curious, he cut the deck. Two of clubs. Clubs meant changes. He wished the card had been a heart or diamond or that he hadn't checked. They were crossing the border at two. He hoped it didn't mean "changes at two."

Jim banged the coffee pot on the table, arousing Pat from his reveries. "Daydreaming again! Caught-ya!"

"I wanted you to know I wasn't stacking the deck, all on the up and up." He re-shuffled and dealt ten cards each. He turned up the first card. The Ace of Spades. He stared, frozen for a moment.

"You don't want that one?" asked Jim. "Neither do I." He picked up another card. Pat shook his head to clear it. Superstition was ridiculous.

# RUSSIA

## Contact Point

## February 19

## 12:30 a.m.

"Peter?" yawned Tasha. "Could you turn the heater on again? My toes are frozen."

"OK but open your window a crack. We don't want to die of carbon monoxide."

Vladimir, sound asleep, huddled between Nadia and Berthe, his mother giving him psychological comfort and Berthe's bulk, the physical warmth. Berthe snored. Nadia stared out the window, wondering what waited for them in the United States. Aunt Katya cuddled like an old bird under her blanket, murmured an occasional prayer.

Peter turned on the engine and put the heater on high. Warm air began to fill the limousine. "I wonder what the temperature is out there?" he asked half to himself.

Tasha stared toward the small plateau that created a natural landing field. "How did you ever find this place?"

"Driving to a vacation house near the Black Sea. I took this road by accident. It was a beautiful day without a tight schedule. We kept driving until we found this spot, which seemed perfect for a picnic. It occurred to me then that it made a natural air strip. I made a note and included it in one of the exit plans."

For a passing moment, the use of the *we* bothered Tasha. She often wished she could have been there for all those previous years. Oh well, she consoled herself, I was probably two years old at the time.

"Two and a half hours," mused Peter. "It could be worse. We could have had twelve hours sitting here, pinned down for a patrol to track us." Tasha shuddered and moved closer to him. By now, he thought, the dogs and patrols must be spread out, searching for them. He dismissed the fear as useless. "What," he laughed, "could entertain us for the next two hours?" He stroked her inner thigh suggestively.

"After all we've been through in the past two days, you're ready for all that at . . ." She bit her tongue.

"At my age?" he finished for her. "Let me dream, love."

"Better than that, I'll let you sleep. Put your head in my lap. I'll watch the time." She moved right, allowing Peter room to stretch across the seat, head in her lap.

"If I were the least bit less tired," he muttered as he burrowed into her lap, "you'd be in real trouble. Don't let me sleep past twelve thirty. I want to be wide awake by Contact time." In less than a minute, he was snoring. Amazing, thought Tasha, watching him. He can turn it all on and off so quickly. She looked out the window. Pitch black by the woods. A slight overcast was moving west across the sky. She could make out a pale smudge of a moon. She turned gently and glanced into the backseat. The dark shapes were still, broken only by an occasional snore from Berthe, a wheeze from Aunt Katya, and the sound of Vladimir sucking his thumb in his sleep. The car was getting too hot. She quietly pulled the heater's lever off and switched off the ignition. The motion didn't wake Peter. She realized as she gently laid her hand on his shoulder that she could drive away and head back to Moscow with all of them. They might not waken until it was too late. She felt alone and claustrophobic at the same time. The weight of Peter's head and shoulder on her legs was becoming oppressive. It was a perfect opportunity, depending how she looked at it.

# PHILADELPHIA
## Penn Center Inn "Henry's"
## February 18
## 6:00 p.m.

"Cocktails begin at six forty-five, speeches at seven thirty, and dinner at eight. You can tape the speeches, but the press tables are set up on the outer edges of the banquet room so you can easily get up to follow Vice President Watson as he leaves. He'll be giving one of his traveling interviews from the dining room to his limousine. Get your player interviews early, because it's lights out for them following dinner. They have to make an early flight." Sally paused for breath.

"Which flight?" asked a young reporter from the Bulletin, thinking a shot of the players waving good-bye from the plane would take a nice photo for the sports page.

"That's classified. There are a lot of crazy Americans around, even crazier than you guys, if that's possible. And some of them can shoot straighter!"

"Is there room for our TV cables in the entry way for the traveling interview?"

Although she wasn't certain, Sally nodded cheerfully. "WHCA has that all taken care of." She'd find J. L. and check.

"Hey," asked the first young reporter, "who's that heavy set guy in the wicker chair by the dining room entrance? He really gave me the once-over!"

"You're the reporter, ask him," retorted Sally. "I can't brief you on every person in this place." She didn't want to comment on the KGB sticking out like wounded bears. "You'll have forty-five minutes with the team all to yourselves. And it's OK to tape or film the vice president's speech—player reaction and all that."

J. L. observed her from nearby the kitchen entrance. She'd been a dedicated campaign worker in Chicago who'd brought in more money per pound under her purple pantsuit than anyone else in the country. She'd majored in journalism at some midwestern university and worked on a Kansas City paper's social column for a few years. She'd probably pee in her pants with excitement if she knew what was happening behind those kitchen walls. If all went well, she'd never know anything about it to put in her gossip cache. He decided to double-check the audio cables and mike set-ups. She'd probably forget to ask about it until the press was ready to "plug in." This operation was like hopscotch. Playing soundboard for Bob Moore. Checking out the VP's set-ups, transatlantic cables, and blackouts, State Department tie lines with White House links, everything scrambled, even the wireless communications among the small interagency army of agents. Milk and bread trucks in the alley! It was insane. The upcoming campaign trail would be mild in comparison. J. L. still questioned the covert nature of the plan. It didn't make sense. Defections were usually plastered across headlines within hours, but orders were orders.

It would all begin in less than an hour. He decided to stay put in the Com Center in the early stages and let the reports come in from below. He was tempted to watch the whole operation from the kitchen, but he'd have greater mobility and communications upstairs until the last half hour, and he could wait in peace for word from the deities in D.C.

# ISTANBUL WEST
## February 19
## 12:45 a.m.

Forty-five minutes 'til take-off, thought Charlie Vickers as he listened to the drone of Turkish as the Officer of the Day gave the pilots a final pep talk.

It seemed to Charlie that the translator had twenty Turkish words for each English one. Maybe that's why their discussions drag on forever. He tried smiling at his young pilot. No response. This was a serious crew. Occasionally, he'd catch a phrase. Would they all be as eager if they knew he was leading them all astray into the land of the Red Bear? Probably, if their commander approved the order. It was far better for them to remain innocent in case one of them was shot down and survived. Nasty thought.

He pulled out his pocketknife and began cleaning his thumbnail. He put the knife away and lit a cigarette. At this rate the briefing would last through take-off.

He mentally ran down his schedule. Thirty minutes to fly around the mideast before crossing the border at 0100 ZULU, 0200 their time. Not too tough. Twenty minutes to play around the Russian skies and make it out the same day. No use worrying over that until they got there. It wasn't a difficult navigational problem. He'd best forget the Russians weren't friendly until they made unfriendly noises. Then worrying wouldn't help; fast maneuvering might.

# RUSSIA

## Contact Point

## February 19

## 2:00 a.m.

Peter awoke with a start. He'd been dreaming they were moving. "Tasha!" He looked around the limousine. Everyone was sleeping. Tasha wasn't there. Adrenaline shot through his body, bringing him to a state of total alertness. Outside, the thick cloud cover had blown away, leaving wisps like fine gauze covering the moon. He focused on the dark outline of the forest. Where was she? He got out of the car.

It was freezing. As he walked behind the limousine, he saw her standing ten yards away, staring up into the sky. "Tasha," he called softly, moving to her side and grabbing her shoulders, "what are you doing out here?"

"We are waiting like stones . . . cold stones. What if nobody comes for us?

Can we return to Moscow and make excuses? We could say we were kidnapped by the driver and couldn't escape until you killed him."

"No, my cover has been blown in twenty directions. There is no way I can go back to Moscow alive. If they don't show, we'll start thinking about going over these mountains in the morning."

She pulled away from him, agitated. "I don't want to go, Sergei. I'm afraid. It's all too fast, like a nightmare. I want out of this!" She began to sob hysterically.

"Hey." He moved close to her again. "Don't." He didn't know whether to reason gently or slap her into a calm. "You want to go back? Then don't come along. When they arrive, take the limousine and go back."

"I don't want to leave you," she wailed. "I want us all to go home." She ran to the edge of the woods, breathing hard, trying to regain control. She felt the rough bark of a tree and rubbed her palm against it with brutal disregard of the pain. At least it was real, solid.

"Tasha." Peter had followed her. "Don't break now. We're so close." Her sobbing was subsiding. He put his arms around her from behind. "I need you with me. I love you."

It was the first time he'd articulated it. She barely noticed. She spoke, still facing the tree. "It's easier to be strong when we're moving and doing things. The waiting gives me too much time to think. I want to explode."

"So, you've exploded. And we only have a few minutes . . ."
Peter glanced at his watch. "Less than an hour before they arrive." "Exactly who is coming for us?" Tasha was curious. "How did you contact them?"

"It's too cold out here. Let's go back to the car." Until they were safely out of Russia, the less he told her the better. There was still the possibility she could change her mind at the last minute. Peter put his arm around her shoulders and gently led her back to the battered limousine.

He doesn't trust me, thought Tasha. He didn't trust anyone, not a single Russian he'd known and lived with for over thirty years. Except perhaps Mother Padov . . . Aunt Katya. A lifetime disguise; it was difficult for her to comprehend. She felt a flush of shame as she remembered being a breath away from driving them back toward Moscow while they all slept. Perhaps he was right not to trust her. A few minutes ago, she would have run away if there had been a place to go. He was a man of many layers, many lives in a way. All she could do was try with her whole heart to build new trust between them.

"We have a long day ahead of us, whatever happens," Peter said as he turned the car heater on again.

She tried to read his expression in the shadows of the car. Did he doubt that those coming for them would arrive? She shuddered in the dark uncertainties of the night and slipped her hand in his.

# TURKEY
## Station RHO February 19
## 1:40 a.m.

The man called Adams called good luck to the closing helicopter doors. He hadn't briefed Blaire and McLaughlin on the border alert. Orders were to proceed as scheduled. No sense in adding tension.

"Well, here goes something, I hope," Pat muttered as he began the ascent.

Within minutes, they were all above the base, heading northeast into darkness. Jim busily scrawled figures and checked them against the compass readings. "Move a half a degree east." He watched the dials as Pat maneuvered. "Perfect."

The cloud cover had blown west in the past few hours, obscuring the moon and stars, leaving them the void, broken only by the sound of their own rotors and voices.

The radio crackled as foreign voices came through. They were on "receive" only. "Turkish squadron on course," Jim stated, reassured. "We should hear their engines a few minutes before we hit the border."

"That's nice to know."

"Nice?!" Jim objected. "To know some crazy Turks are flying around nearby? I hope none of them decide to get cute and swoop down into our props as we cross the border!"

"F-111's don't fly this low."

"A crazy Turk might," countered Jim.

"That's what I love about flying with you, Sarge. You're so cheerful and optimistic."

"Hey! Watch what you're doing. You're half a degree off course. Ease her west. OK, hold it there and keep her steady."

"Sorry."

"I don't want to set her down in the Black Sea in the middle of the ice floes," Jim protested. He hadn't flown a night mission for a couple of years. He hated flying blind. Although he normally relied on instruments for his navigation, he always liked to reinforce what the instruments told him he should know by what he saw. They were flying through a haze in the night, rotors echoing against the hollow body of the Huey. Jim could sense Pat's tension.

"Go ahead and set us down on the ice," Pat rattled. "I like ice fishing. It's the only time I catch fish."

"Cut the chatter and ease up," coached Jim. "We've got to cross the border at exactly 0200. Take it nice and easy."

"Nice and easy!" Pat protested. "Here we are in the middle of nothing, and you tell me to ease up. For all I know, we could be heading for Jupiter."

Let him chatter, thought Jim. It releases some tension. As long as we stay on course. He kept his eye on the instruments. They were doing fine, as long as the compass remained true. He pulled a pocket compass from his pocket and double-checked. Then he triple checked his calculations.

Pat was going on about the temperature, the lack of moon, and anything he could think of to break the silence. Jim ignored him and kept checking the instruments, occasionally telling Pat to alter speed or direction slightly. It was going to be a long fifteen minutes.

# PHILADELPHIA
## The Penn Center Inn "Henry's"
## February 18
## 7:40 p.m.

"Cooperation between the athletes of the world is opening up communications in many arenas for our nations. This competition signifies a great good will between our peoples . . ." Horace Watson, relishing his moment in the sun, smiled his way through his speech.

Vladimir squirmed in his padded chair. "Ivan," he whispered, "when is anything going to happen?"

"Shh," Ivan frowned. "We'll be contacted."

The NBC camera caught the pair whispering as it scanned the crowd for reaction shots. Ivan noticed the camera pointed at them out of the corner of his eye. "Pay attention," he hissed at Vladimir.

Vladimir took a bite of his shrimp cocktail and tried to listen to Watson. Watson, with his rapid style of delivery, was difficult for the young Russian to understand. He noticed Ivan's finger tapping slowly and steadily on the table as though Ivan was marking time to a ballad only he could hear. He stopped as he noticed Vladimir was staring at his finger and dug into his salad, although he hated salads. A minute later, as he was checking around the room, he noticed J. L. enter from the bar area, cross to the far corner of the banquet room and turn into the partition screening the kitchen area. Ivan stared after him. He saw a waiter emerge with a steaming trayful of prime ribs. Perhaps he was wrong about the man being an agent. He probably worked for the hotel. Ivan suppressed the temptation to excuse himself and follow, pretending to go to the men's room. But this was no time for idle curiosity.

Beside the complex bank of phones inside the kitchen, J. L. personally made a last-minute check of all the lines, refusing to accept his men's word that everything was operational. Ultimately, the function of the communications was his responsibility. He had to be certain. If the operation blew on the Philadelphia end, Rubin would be sitting in Turkey with a handful of Russian relatives who would have no one to meet in the United States. J. L. suddenly realized that would create a messier situation than if the Russian operation screwed up and the team refused to defect. They had no room for error in Philadelphia.

J. L. double-checked his watch with the Signal Board in Washington. They were maintaining base time for all ends. Two minutes before eight. Twenty- two minutes before he could expect to hear from Charles, at the earliest. Acid churned in his stomach as he turned down a plate of roast beef. He wondered if the players were half as tense as he was. They had not been told what time to expect action. Not knowing probably made it worse.

Inside the dining room, a waiter was helping Vasili to his feet. Vasili's eyes were watering; his face was a deadly shade of white. A KGB guard hurried over to them, questioning. Vasili groaned that he had been poisoned. The guard had no respect for the young athlete who doubled as a KGB source inside the team. His response was dubious as he assured Vasili it was probably indigestion. "If it were poison," he told him unsympathetically, "you'd be dead."

Bob Moore looked past Watson and saw Vasili wobbling out. One down, he thought with satisfaction, returning his attention to Watson's flowery remarks.

The atmosphere in the banquet room was electrified. The players shifted in their seats, glancing at one another, eyes darting from Watson around the room, edgy. A Bulletin reporter muttered to a Daily News crony that Watson was doing his usual bad job of holding attention. Brian Earle moved his chair farther back in the shadows, waiting for an opportunity to talk to Ivan or Yori. He'd come in with the veteran sportswriter for the Inquirer whom he'd told he wanted a chance to say farewell to Ivan and Yori. The half-truth wasn't questioned. The other sportswriters vaguely recognized him but didn't question his presence when he'd said his casual hellos. He'd stressed to his friend that he wanted no publicity.

The KGB guards were positioned near the restaurant entrance with one stationed in the outer hotel lobby. They'd checked the entrance earlier, noting the restrooms and ignoring the phone complex. It resembled a normal intercom system for a major hotel.

Ivan fiddled with his knife as the vice president concluded his remarks. With precise, heavily accented English, the coach gave the formal thank-you. Everyone rose and applauded.

Vladimir leaned toward Ivan. "When?!" he demanded.

"Shh!" replied Ivan, clapping louder. He concentrated on Watson's presentation to the coach of a sterling replica of the Liberty Bell. Ivan glanced around at the reporters and camera. It seemed the perfect moment for announcing the defection. What was the State Department waiting for? Had something gone wrong with getting his mother and Nadia out of Russia? He tried not to conjecture.

Watson apologized for leaving early as he stepped down from the head table. Reporters and cameras gathered around him and his Secret Service escort like gnats on a summer night. He passed through the banquet room and bar on his way to his waiting limousine, pausing to answer questions on the sidewalk.

In the kitchen, eighteen special agents tried to avoid tripping over the equally special kitchen staff. In the alley, the milk and bread trucks waited silently, carrying their token loaves and cartons. Waiting nervously by the phones, J. L. watched for a light to flash.

At the head table deserted by Watson and his entourage, Bob Moore tried to remain calm. The banquet had lost much of its formality with Watson's early departure. A few reporters had remained, preferring the thick prime rib to Watson's vacuous remarks. Canned music filtered in, softening the sounds of rattling silver and plates. Bob munched on his shrimp cocktail and turned to the coach, admiring the Liberty Bell replica in Russian. It was the best he could do at the moment. It was seven fifty-eight.

# RUSSIAN-TURKISH BORDER
## February 19
## 0100 ZULU (2:00 a.m. Turkey, 3:00 a.m. Russia, 8:00 p.m. Philadelphia)

They'd crossed the border within seconds of the schedule. The squadron flew above the thinning cloud cover, jets shrieking through the star-ridden sky. It was a piece of cake, thought Charlie. They'd heard nothing from the Russian ground patrol. They could as easily be flying over the Pacific. Suddenly, he listened carefully, his highly trained ears picking up an alien sound. "Hear that?" he asked his young pilot.

"I hear only our engines," the young man replied, his eyes on the instruments.

A slight frown crossed Charlie's forehead as he concentrated. There was something other than the squadron's steady engine noise out there. Was it a Russian patrol plane? He turned up the volume on the radio. It should start jabbering any second. "Someone's out there," Charlie stated firmly. "I know it." As he leaned over to double-check that they were on the right frequency, a great explosion rent the plane. "I was right" was his dying thought.

# RUSSIA CONTACT POINT
## February 19
## 3:01 a.m.

Tasha was leaning against the front fender while Peter paced, eyes searching the dark, hazy sky when the explosion echoed in the night sky. Above and to their left, a flaming ball plummeted toward the mountains. Without the noise, it might have been a falling meteor.

"The helicopter?" asked Tasha fearfully. "Too high. It could have been an F-111." "What are they?"

"A diversionary squadron to confuse the radar as the helicopter crosses the border. At least it tells us the plan is in motion. Someone was in position."

"The plane was American?" "Iranian."

"How did they get involved?"

"I'll tell you later, if you come along."

She followed him back to the limousine to get warm.

Five minutes away in the night sky above the travelers, Pat McLaughlin and Jim Blaire felt and saw the explosion. "That was one of the planes, Sarge. I know it. Do you think they've spotted us?"

"As long as they keep after the planes, they aren't after us." Yet, he added silently. "Hold your course. We should be less than four minutes away." Jim's own heart was pounding. Nice and easy, he counseled himself.

They began their descent to Contact Point.

Peter, Tasha, Katya, Berthe, Nadia, and even little Vladimir held their breaths as the noise of the rotors grew louder. Peter raced out to the plateau and signaled with an intense penlight. The dark mechanical creature, alien to the forests, descended on target. The door opened a crack. Peter half expected Martians. The unilluminated landing had looked so ominous.

Inside, Jim took his flashlight and caught Peter's taut face. "Peter," he heard him say. Jim responded, "Eater." Peter took a step closer, hair blowing in the wind from the rotors. "Pumpkin," he countered. Jim slid back the door and called, "Shell." Peter finished with "Koral" and relief. Then he turned to the others. "Quickly!"

Tasha held back, watching as Jim helped the others into the Huey.

Peter checked that the limousine was close enough to the woods that it couldn't be seen by air and looked around for Tasha. She was walking toward him, the tears in her eyes glistening in the low light from the helicopter. He reached in his pocket for the limousine keys and held them out to her. "With me or without me?" he spoke softly.

She took the keys and held them loosely in her hand. They slipped like sand through her fingers and dropped on the frozen ground between them. Her attention was completely on Peter.

"Come with me."

"I am Russian," she choked. "We are Russian."

She shook her head and choked through her tears. "No, Sergei, Peter, or whoever you are. You are not. Not the way I am. I cannot stand in your way, but your way is out there—a thousand miles and more—with Americans . . ." She took a step toward him. "What can you know about Americans today? You have been gone for thirty years! Sergei, we can make up a story to explain all this. Let them go. Let them go without you."

"You would rather have my grave to sit by in Russia than share a new adventure with me in America?" He searched her eyes.

"You're so certain that's the only choice . . ." she whispered, "but there must . . ." She froze, silenced by the resolution she saw in his face.

"I will never choose death or imprisonment, not consciously. There's no other choice for me."

"Maybe later," she stalled. "Maybe I can come later. Or maybe we could meet in Yugoslavia or somewhere. I can't just . . . defect."

The word hung in the icy air, forcing their attendance to the sound of the Huey's propellers.

"There is no time for debate," Peter said as the truth of his words pierced his emotions. It would be safer to kill her if she would not come, but the snake was out of the grass already. Fattening Taikov's background files could do no more harm. And Tanya could remain an innocent alone.

"Colonel!" The pilot's voice was urgent.

"Sergei . . ." Tanya began, her focus blurred as she blinked back tears. But she saw her lover's eyes soften and then go blank as though a shutter had closed.

"Are you coming?" he asked softly.

She closed her eyes and shook her head. "I can't," she breathed toward the frozen ground.

"The keys are where you dropped them," he said calmly. He might have been talking about her purse as they left for a party.

"Sergei!"

He stopped at the edge of his turn. "Just like that?"

"It's your choice." He forced a detachment as she sobbed. "Think of me as the traitor if you stay. It will make it easier for you with Taikov." A smile traced his lips. "He has a soft spot for pretty women." If she made it up the interrogation ladder to Taikov. The thought sobered him. Was there a choice for her at this juncture? She knew so much. And there was no time to sort out and analyze all potential damage.

"Sergei. We'll hide if we must, change identities, but it will be better here with our own people." Her lashes were dark and matted by tears, her eyes large and pleading.

Peter fingered the clasp of his watch, equipped with a hidden pneumatic injector, deadly when activated and touched against the soft skin he often held so completely. Killing was an old skill, but could he kill this new love for the faded old ideals?

"Being with you, Sergei . . . is all I want. I want . . . but not to leave our coun—"

"Colonel! Please!" Blaire shouted across the night. Time was running out. Sergei reached out, palm open. "Tasha . . . come with me."

Choked by tears, she could only shake her head in a convulsive rejection.

Peter's arm fell flat against his side. He spun sharply and walked toward the dark Huey.

Tasha pressed flat palms against her cheeks, holding her face together. In a breath, the form of Peter Sergei melted into the dark shadow of the helicopter. Within seconds, she knew the machine would rise up and away from Russia, away from her.

Mindless of the temperature beneath the moonless haze, she started into the sound of the whirling blades. Her sobs broke open again as she fell to the cold ground as in mourning, fumbling for the keys. Icy cold, the keys felt small but solid, real in contrast to the pilgrimage to this nowhere. "Sergei . . . Sergei . . ."

"Here." His arms were around her, shielding her from the frozen wind. "And you are coming with me."

Her thoughts tumbled with unspoken objections as she felt herself being lifted and carried toward the helicopter. Her protests had no value for her if Sergei were gone. She had to go with him.

Somewhere in that thirty-foot dash across the frozen ground, she made peace with the summary decision. From childhood on, her wont was to agonize over choices, but once the gear was meshed, she only went forward. As Peter handed her up the steps, her clenched fist opened, and the keys dropped with a final clink on Russian soil.

At the controls, Jim Blaire muttered that it was a good thing they had the big Huey the way the passengers were multiplying. Then he concentrated on the ascent, ears peeled for alien engines, eyes searching the mountain roads for headlights. The downed F-111 still had him on edge.

Peter approached the pilot. "Are you patched in directly to Eagle Three?"

Blaire's eyes did not waver from the night sky. "We have radio blackout until we're cleared."

"This is top priority, Lieutenant."

Jim's trained ear defined a jet engine in the distance. He glanced at Pat, noting the jaw muscles clenching. "Right now, sir, I think getting back alive is our first priority."

"Engines." Peter spoke softly. "Moving in around eight o'clock." "Roger." Jim nodded. "Pat, let's give those radars some real static."

Pat broke time records in crawling to the supply hatch, pushing a button to release dozens of aluminum balloons.

"Prayer time," Jim said mostly to himself. "Five minutes and we're home free."

The chatter in the relative security of the helicopter stopped as all ears turned to the steady chop of rotors counterpointed by the distant roar of jet engines, approaching.

Jim grabbed the mike and glanced at Peter. "Almost there, sir."

Behind them, the jet roar was closing in. Suddenly, the sound veered left and away. "The F-111s" Peter softly defined the relief.

Jim pushed the mike button. "Pumpkin eater coming home. Repeat.

Coming home. Over."

The speaker crackled. "Congratulations. Cleared for landing."

Jim backhanded the sweat on his chin. "Guess that's it." He grinned as Peter reached for the mike. "It's all yours, sir."

Peter requested Eagle Three. Eagle Three was standing by. "Kopall White—code four. Do you read me?"

"Loud and clear. Kopall White—code four—confirmed." Eagle Three signed off and Peter handed the mike back to Blaire. Within minutes, the untraceable call to Andrei Belsky, simple tailor, would start the rumors that Sergei Padov was in Warsaw. The audio tape for staged telephone calls relayed to Belsky should do the job. Belsky was good. Peter smiled mentally, picturing the gnomelike man he had recruited for CkO in the early sixties.

CkO. Crytak opasnos, snake in the grass. Slowly and meticulously, Peter had selected and trained his elite corps of agents, agents answerable only to him. Despite his assurances to Taikov that no CkO agents would be planted inside the KGB or GPU, Peter had place his CkO agents within all levels of both to prevent CkO operations from interference or inadvertent exposure. The network would be safe, he thought. Only Taikov had the failsafe code for CkO contact to use in the event of Sergei's death. A legacy from the grandson of Tietro Padov, gatekeeper, a.k.a. Alexis Rimnikov. Peter had changed the failsafe code in the message to Belsky.

"Are we there yet? Is Daddy waiting for us?" The sleepy voice of Vladimir brought Peter back to the present.

"Almost," Peter smiled at the boy as the landing lights brightened their faces. "You've been a real trouper. Your poppa will be proud of you." Then Peter turned to and spoke in English. "I finally feel like we're heading home."

Jim glanced curiously at Peter. How could this Russian colonel think of the United States as "home"?

The speaker instructed them to sit tight for a moment for a transmission from the United States, explaining that Nadia would be able to speak to Vladimir via the radio momentarily. Peter waved Nadia forward to the radio set, explaining to her in Russian. She gasped in disbelief. It didn't seem possible.

# PHILADELPHIA
## PENN CENTER INN
### February 18
### 8:22 p.m.

J. L. had the receiver to his ear. It had been there for five minutes. At the first flash of the button, J. L. punched and heard Charles say "systems go." Charles said he'd stay on the line so J. L. could keep him posted. J. L. picked up the RHO lines, spoke briefly with Rubin and learned Nadia was standing by in the helicopter to talk with Vladimir. That line remained open as J. L. nodded at an agent on his right. Rubin heard the signal, "Dessert alert."

The agent turned, nodded to J. L., picked up a pot of coffee, and headed into the banquet room. He walked directly to Vladimir, leaned close beside him, and freshened his coffee, saying softly, "Excuse yourself and go to the bathroom through the kitchen entrance."

Vladimir froze, his glance striking Ivan. It was happening. "Move!" Ivan hissed.

Vladimir opened his mouth to reply. The waiter interrupted, coaching softly, "Say thank you if you understand."

"Thank you," echoed Vladimir as he excused himself and headed across the room, turning into the kitchen entrance. The KGB guard at the door glanced at him for a second, noting his exit, then continued his watch of the crowd.

The moment Vladimir entered the kitchen, J. L. held out the phone to him while another agent explained in Russian that Nadia was on the phone to confirm her arrival in Turkey. They could talk for two minutes only. They had to move swiftly.

As Vladimir spoke to Nadia, thousands of miles away, Yori entered the kitchen. Vladimir noticed him, smiled, and nodded. Swiftly an agent moved to Yori and said, "Follow me." He guided Yori toward the back exit.

"The guards will notice I'm gone," worried Yori, stopping midway.

"Don't worry, you're covered," chuckled a tall agent dressed in clothes the same style and color as Yori's. Vladimir's double was already heading back into the banquet room. Yori took in the other sixteen doubles and grinned as the ruse became evident.

"It won't work for long if the guards talk to them. They know us well."

"It doesn't have to work for long," the first agent assured him. "As long as we keep moving."

J. L. had to pull Vladimir away from the phone and hurry him out toward the bread truck.

The KGB guard noticed Vladimir and then Yori return to their seats in the banquet room. Vladimir turned and chatted casually with Ivan. In ones and twos, the Wings were spirited out of the banquet room and into the waiting trucks while their doubles munched on their chocolate mousses and chatted in Russian among themselves.

Ivan was the last to be tapped. The first truck, emblazoned with "Pepperidge Farms," was already on the expressway, heading for the airport.

As Ivan entered the kitchen, J. L. relayed "all clear" to Mattimore and picked up the transatlantic phone with the other hand. Now for the tough part, he thought. "Line to Moscow all clear?" he asked the operator. Then, "Yes, Mr. Secretary," he said as he recognized Bollinger's voice. "I can hear you. The patch is working fine."

Brian quietly watched the Russians excuse themselves and head for the partition shielding them from the kitchen. He accepted their departures as bathroom visits as they returned shortly. When Yori resumed his seat, Brian looked for an opportunity to move closer. He noticed an empty chair at an adjacent table. Casually, he moved to the empty seat. He nodded at the others at that table, guessing they were local VIPs. Brian noticed Ivan rising to head for the bathroom a moment before Yori glanced at Brian. Brian looked in Yori's eye for recognition. There was none. It hit him like a brick.

The man was not Yori!

With a fluid grace for one so large, Brian swiftly followed Ivan past the partition into the kitchen. Brian brushed past J. L. as he saw Ivan at the far end of the kitchen, moving toward the exit. He raced toward them. J. L. saw him, but thought he was an agent from the rear; his attention was on the phone. In five minutes, he had to notify the KGB that there was a call for them.

Brian burst out the door, stopping for a second to adjust to the darkness. Ivan had one foot raised, about to enter the truck. "Ivan!" Brian shouted after him.

Ivan turned, half recognizing the voice. It was too dark to see who it was, backlit in the kitchen door. The escort agent hurried Ivan into the truck and slid the door shut quickly. At the same moment, the agent stationed outside the kitchen exit slid behind Brian and karate-chopped his neck before he could run after the truck. Brian fell, hitting his head against the hard metal edge of the dumpster by the door. He collapsed among the potato peels and rotten tomatoes that had escaped the bin, blood pouring from the deep gash in his head, above the crack in his skull.

As the truck accelerated and sped around the corner toward Market Street, a second agent ran over to assist. "What's going on?"

"I don't know," the first agent was on his knees beside Brian trying to determine the damage. "This guy comes dashing out of the kitchen screaming for Ivan. Obviously, he was on to something. And he wasn't one of us. I gave him a quick chop to stop him, and he fell against the dumpster." The agent pushed the hair off his forehead, leaving a bloody track.

"Who is he?" worried the second agent. "A reporter?"

"I can't find a pulse," the first agent glanced up. "I'm afraid the question is who was he?"

"Shit!" exclaimed the second agent. "Check his pockets."

# WASHINGTON, D.C.
## Georgetown
## February 18
## 8:45 p.m.

Bollinger smiled into the telephone. "Translator ready? Fine. Do they have the secretary on the line?" He frowned. "Tell them to wake him up! Or get the premier!" He frowned. "Tell them to wake him immediately. We haven't got all night!" He drummed his stubby fingers on his desk.

A full five minutes elapsed before a sleepy first secretary was on the line.

His grogginess evaporated as Bollinger spoke.

"So, you see, Secretary Provkin, you must have the premier immediately direct the KGB to say and do nothing. Only with complete secrecy can we consider negotiating a trade. We shall discuss details, conditions, and terms tomorrow. Meanwhile, we shall hold this line open so the premier can issue directives to the KGB here in Philadelphia." Provkin was speechless. "The initial suggested terms will be sent by coded telex tomorrow. The key to the code will be hand-delivered to the premier from our embassy. I apologize for disturbing your sleep, but some things cannot wait until morning." Bollinger waited as the translator caught up. "Excuse me, he interrupted, but I must know immediately if you plan to proceed as I have outlined."

Provkin interrupted the translator mid-sentence and replied in faultless English, "I see no other choice for us tonight. Tomorrow things might be different."

"Good," Bollinger curtly dropped the phone in its cradle. The line would remain open to Philadelphia. "These Russians always try to get one up on us," he grumbled still smarting from the put-down in English, "but in English, Russian, or Swahili, we hold the trump."

"Jeanne!" he called, "get your coat! It's the Leon D'or for dinner! Time to celebrate round 1!"

# PHILADELPHIA
## Penn Center Inn—"Henry's"
## February 189:00 p.m.

The stocky KGB security guard growled into the phone, "Impossible. The players are inside having coffee." He listened reluctantly while the CIA translator explained the illusion. The head guard turned to his second in command. "Go see." He turned back to the translator. "We shall know soon enough," he glared.

Within less than a minute, the guard returned ashen faced. "They are all imposters, dressed like our players. They look much the same, but we have been tricked."

The head guard flushed angrily. "We protest! You cannot . . ."

An American agent interrupted him by handing him the phone. "Your premier wishes to speak to you."

The guard spoke into the phone, "Captain Sardov here." He listened stolidly for a full two minutes, interjecting "yes, sir's." He handed the phone to the American agent and spoke to the other KGB guards, "We are to return to our Washington embassy, with Vasili, at once."

Bob Moore stepped forward. "Transportation is waiting for you outside. If you wish to go upstairs and get your bags and meet us in front . . ."

Captain Sardov nodded shortly and stomped out of the kitchen, followed by his subordinates.

J. L. held out his hand to Bob. "You guys think of everything."

Bob wearily accepted the handshake. "Major, we try to keep our asses covered. You might as well have your men start breaking down the equipment. At least the transatlantic stuff. Then let's go have eighteen  drinks

—one for each Wings."

"I'll drink to that," J. L. yawned. "But first we must check with one of the CIA guys waiting for us in the alley. He says it's urgent."

# MOSCOW
# KGB HEADQUARTERS
# February 19
# 4:00 a.m.

"We're fools!" Taikov was burning mad. "Why didn't we call for the instant recall of the team the moment we discovered Natalovya and Breinkov planted in Syktyvkar under Vladistock and Malitinsky papers?"

"We thought he was using them as a cover, not that they were using him," Omnarsky tried to fit the pieces together. "If Popov had turned in his report earlier, we might have caught it earlier."

"And we knew. We knew before they even slipped through our fingers. It's obvious those F-111s were cover. I ordered the recall of the team at two a.m. There was trouble with the lines at the American hotel. That was no accident, Colonel."

"I don't see how they got out. We tripled the border patrols. There was a red alert. The Turkish planes that made the navigational error were victims. Even innocents couldn't get through."

"I told you that was no accident. I wager they got out by air somehow. We'll get to the bottom of it, if it's the last thing I do." The general's face was white with mental exertion and anger. "I trusted that traitor for twenty years. I can't forget that." The pencil he held in his hand snapped in half. "I keep hearing that prig Bollinger assure the premier that Colonel Padov and the family members are safely on the way to the United States."

"But Bollinger's willing to bargain."

"I can't believe Padov is a traitor," the general continued to storm. "The service he has given us for thirty years makes it incredible to believe. Perhaps he was drugged or forced or . . ." He searched for another explanation.

"That double-dealing Bollinger could have hatched up the whole thing."

Omnarsky listened to the ranting without expression. There was no question in his mind. "That would not explain his behavior with Popov or, as important, why his files were missing from the army archives."

"He could have been hypnotized, his mother's life threatened."

"Such threats could not turn a good KGB officer," Omnarsky flatly stated. "Padov is our mole."

"Then we must get him back. We must change every agent or file he has ever touched. Our highest securities are in jeopardy if that is true." He stared at Omnarsky. "As chairman of Control, he had access to . . . everything." He pulled on his heavy overcoat. "I must get over to the Kremlin. The premier is upset at the loss of his star hockey team. He fears the press reaction if the defection is announced. That is all meaningless compared to allowing Padov to get into their hands."

"Padov has been in their hands for decades," Omnarsky said. Taikov glared at him for a moment. Omnarsky saluted as Taikov hurried from the room.

He was back within moments. "I need copies of the reports. And I want you to stay on top of the analysis of the wreckage and the tracking parties. I want to know the how, the when, and the where!"

"Yes, sir." The horse is out of the stable, thought Omnarsky. It is the time to plot revenge, not waste time sifting through the straw in the stable. The general would be calmer by morning. He would be more open to suggestions then. Omnarsky saluted smartly as the general made his second exit.

# SKIES ABOVE EASTERN PENNSYLVANIA
## February 18
## 9:20 p.m.

Accompanied by three State Department agents who'd been onboard when they reached the plane, the excited Wings flew through clear skies toward Andrews Air Force Base outside Washington.

"Where do we go from here?" Ivan asked agent Elmer Tynsdale.

"You'll be taken to a safe house, as we call them, and wait for your mother's arrival." Elmer was agent-in-charge of their safety.

"And Nadia and little Vladimir?" asked Vladimir. "They'll arrive with her."

"Will we have to talk to the newspapers about why we are leaving Russia?" asked Ivan. "Will reporters be there when we land?"

"Not until we know everyone is safe. No reporters will be aware until we get the go-ahead."

"If everything is OK and our families are on the way, why is everything such a secret?" asked Vladimir.

Elmer had no good answer for that in his pocket. He wondered if he should hedge an answer about procedures. He stalled simply, "I don't know. You'll be briefed more fully in Virginia."

"Virginia?" Yori was puzzled. "I thought we were going to Washington."
"The safe houses are in McLean, Virginia, a suburb of Washington, fifteen miles out."

"Will we meet your president? Will he welcome us?" Vladimir asked. Elmer shrugged. In his blue turtleneck top with his seventy-four-inch,

well-muscled frame and excellent Moscow accent, Elmer Tynsdale, belying his name, could have passed as one of the Wings. Silently, he joined in their questions. Why keep the press away? It could be the news story of the year. He bit his lip. His assignment was to keep them happy and assure them that the State Department had everything under control.

"Shall we all be in the same place?" asked Ivan.

"No." Elmer smiled. That one was easy to answer. Facts. He opened his notebook. "Since you and Vladimir are expecting your families, we have placed you in the same house. Don't worry, it's large. The rest are divided among three other houses."

"Are they close together? Can we walk back and forth?"

"They're in the same general area, but for the time being, you all must stay on your own grounds until everything is arranged."

Ivan frowned, a shadow darkening his normally peaceful gaze. "What arrangements? Once our families are here, can't we step out in the open? Talk to the American hockey teams? We have a great deal to discuss with them."

"Be patient," counseled Elmer. "You've waited this long. I'm sure all your questions will be answered soon."

Yori leaned forward. "You didn't answer my first question. Will we see your president when we get there?"

"Not right away."

# TURKEY STATION RHO
## February 19
## 4:25 a.m.

Nadia led the way up the steps of the military transport. Peter followed, carrying a sleepy Vladimir. The others were already inside.

"You're certain you want to leave now, rather than get a good night's sleep here and leave in the morning?"

"I'm certain, Colonel." "Peter," he corrected.

"It is hard for me to call you that. But it is best we go. The others are already on the plane and little Vladimir will sleep."

A male voice inside the plane added, "It's better that you immediately continue your journey home."

Still holding Vladimir, Peter headed toward the speaker. He saw a middle- aged man in a well-tailored pinstripe suit, silver-rimmed glasses shielding dark eyes. He stepped closer, searching the face. Where had he seen that face before? KGB files? The man looked close to his own age.

"Peter Porter! I doubt if you'd remember me." The man smiled. "If I hadn't seen your recent photos, I might have had trouble myself." Except for the eyes, he thought. Despite the sleepless journey, Peter's eyes held the same dark blue clear gaze. He reached out his arms. "Let me help you with the boy." Together, they laid Vladimir across two seats. Nadia claimed one beside him.

Peter turned back to the man. "Who are you? I know I've known you. Your voice . . ." Rubin had a distinct resonance in his voice. "Germany? During the war?"

"Go further back than that, Peter. Try the Harvard debating team. Rubin Silverstein, your nameless Washington contact."

Peter laughed heartily. "Rubin! That was a hundred lives ago! And no wonder you run NSC's Soviet desk. Your Russian was as good as mine back then." Peter knew that much about his main man. "I had not connected the name!"

Tasha, a few rows from the front, tried to catch Peter's eye. She patted the seat beside her. Rubin noticed and spoke rapidly. "That's why I'm here, to brief you. The report of the Turkish infraction has hit the wires. The Russians have officially protested to the Turks. The Russians suspect but haven't confirmed the connection, but your cover is blown sky high. The KGB has arrest orders out for Sergei Padov.

A smile creased Peter's lean cheeks. "I wonder if they'll bargain for extradition, not knowing I'm an American citizen. Taikov must be apoplectic!"

Rubin didn't comment. Taikov could remain Peter's business, for the moment. He stretched out his hand. "Anyway, I'll fill you in when we're in the air. Meanwhile, welcome to the free world, as we like to call it."

Peter hesitated, "Do you have any knowledge of my family?"

Straight facts would be best, Rubin decided, evaluating the strong, serious version of his old friend. "Your father died of a coronary in 1963. Your mother is well and living in New York, quite elegantly, I should add. Nathalie is married to an oral surgeon in Rye. Three children, the oldest one's at Princeton." He grinned. "Some families have no loyalty!"

"They haven't been told anything," Peter said it as a statement.

"No," Rubin removed his glasses and wiped them with a handkerchief, covering his emotion. "We wanted to be certain you made it out first." How calm he appears, thought Rubin. Yet beneath that measured exterior, he sensed the underlying tensions. Rubin had a sudden urge to laugh and cry with him, to agree it had all been beautiful and terrible, to explain he had read the files. To go on a binge like they had done in the early 1940s. The exodus, with women and the boy, must have been rough. He replaced his glasses. He too was well-schooled in self-control. "How was the trip?"

"Less relaxing than my last Black Sea vacation. The scenery wasn't bad for February." He smiled. "Read all about it in the debriefing."

Still the professional. He had no illusions that coming home meant wining, dining, and celebrating.

Rubin nodded to acknowledge Tasha while he spoke to Peter. "Better go fasten your seat belt. It's a long flight."

"It'll be a piece of cake compared to the last few days. A piece of cake," Peter repeated, pleased with himself for remembering the slang.


"Hmmm, that took long enough," Tasha commented as Peter joined her. "An old college classmate happened to be passing by."

"Sure," quipped Tasha. "Happens all the time. Divine coincidence."

"Little is."

"My stopping by that 'fatal morning' was." "Perhaps it was destiny."

"Don't be trite, Sergei . . . Peter."

"When we get back to the U.S. of A., you'll be surprised how corny I can be. 'I'm as corny as Kansas in August,'" he sang, then laughed.

Tasha laughed uncertainly. "Is that funny?"

"No, in America people laugh and sometimes sing when it's time to cry.

It's easier that way."

"Are you laughing now because you'd like to cry?"

"I'm not sure what I meant by that." He covered her hand with his as the plane rolled down the runway for take-off. "But this I do mean. I love you. And no more tears." There was so much beautiful in American he could show her. Cities and wilderness. Skiing in Vermont. Sailing on the Sound. So much catching up to do with time . . . and freedom . . .

"Sergei?"

He was lost in his thoughts. "Peter!"

"Yes?"

"Shall I like your America?" She sounded like a little girl on a trip to visit relatives.

"I hope so. We'll find out. I can't be certain. It's been so long for me." "And we can't go back home if we don't like it!"

He paused a long time. "Perhaps you can." He knew the only way he could return was by way of a tribunal. "I think the first thing I'll do is buy a Siberian husky in gratitude that we're not all headed for Siberia.

He patted her hand. "What do you think?"

"I'd rather not think about Siberia." Andre was still there.

# WASHINGTON, D.C.
## State Department February 18
## 11:30 p.m.

"They're back in the air, heading home? OK, let me know if any of the players gets too edgy. Sounds fine." Mattimore hung up the phone. The pieces were moving into place neatly, efficiently directed by half-truth. He knew he couldn't relax until he had full details on Bollinger's offer to the Soviets. He walked into the hall for a countless cup of coffee. Pulling off the complicated defection felt like a hollow victory, delivering innocents into the hands of a madman. He looked at the six-hour-old brew. It looked strong enough to tap dance on. He couldn't help wondering what Bollinger was scheming. He'd listened to the conversations with the Russians. Bollinger had revealed nothing more than Charles already knew. He wanted to make a trade. The persistent ring of his private line jangled his consciousness. Walk into the hall and the phone will ring. A fact of life. He decided against more coffee and headed back to the phone. "Yes?"

"I was about to give up and try you at home where you should be," Bob commented from Philadelphia.

"I was in the hall admiring our vintage coffee."

"I won't keep you. Is the line secure?" Bob paused. "Our scramblers are off on this end."

"Reasonably."

"I'll have to take the chance. You have to know. Brian Earle was accidentally killed in the back alley."

"What?! Impossible!" Charles was genuinely shocked. "I had it checked early this evening. He was at home with his children."

"We're 99 percent certain. He'd signed in at the banquet with an Inquirer reporter, slipped by in the last-minute crunch. Evidently, he caught on to the switch at the last minute and chased after Ivan into the alley. The agent gave him a chop to stop him. The order was that the escape had to be completely secure. The alley had been cordoned off." Bob paused, searching for words. "If it's any consolation, it wasn't the agent's blow that killed him. His skull was fractured on the dumpster beside the kitchen door when he fell."

"It's no consolation, Bob. It's all the same when a man's dead. Especially a good, loyal man who cared." He stopped. The platitudes ringing hollow to his own ears. "Have the police keep it under wraps until tomorrow. I'll have to talk with James and Earle's wife personally." He paused, thinking.

"Anything else, sir?"

"Yes. Have the boys make it look like a mugging in the alley. And on second thought, don't contact the police at all. Let them find the body on their own with no identification. It should take them until morning to identify it."

"Yes, sir." Bob's blood ran cold at the idea of leaving Brian's body in the alley, vulnerable to the rats he'd seen scurrying behind the dumpster.

"You'll be back in the morning?"

"On the seven-a.m. plane, but I'm not guaranteeing our condition. Rhodes and I have an appointment with our local bartender. I can't remember ever needing a drink more." Bob sighed.

"All right, I understand, but be sure the Earle matter is taken care of before you leave and take your beeper in case, I need you."

"All right, sir. We'll stay reachable, regardless of our condition." Bob suddenly felt totally drained. His shoulders ached. He waited for Mattimore to respond. Finally, to break the silence, he asked, "Are the Russians, OK?"

"Right on schedule so far." "Do we announce yet?" "No."

"Oh." Mattimore's short reply was answer in itself. Bollinger was in charge of the next phase, whatever it was.

"Commend everyone on doing a great job, especially the doubles. There was no trouble . . . other than Earle?" Mattimore forced himself to mention the name.

"By the time the KGB got even close to one of them, Moscow was on the line. We had the front bar cleared and gathered them for a last team picture while the 'waiters' cleared the crowd. They're all in the proper hotel rooms, maintaining the roles until they board the special charter to 'return to Moscow' tomorrow. They should be back at Langley by eleven," Bob summarized.

Mattimore almost chuckled. "Right under their noses like planned with only one casualty." The thought of the specific casualty quickly sobered him.

"Boss," Bob said, "I may be overstepping bounds, but would you get the hell out of there and go home for a change? You can't even get a decent cup of coffee in that place!"

"Good idea, but I'll be on call."

"So, what else is new? I'll see you in the morning."

# ANDOVER, MASSACHUSETTS
## February 19
## 1:00 a.m.

Mattie tossed restlessly, alone in the king-sized bed. The illuminated digital clock was a glaring reminder of the hour. Brian has a game tomorrow afternoon, she thought. He wouldn't stay out this late. She had listened to the eleven o'clock news. There was a clip on the banquet with the vice president making inane remarks, but nothing about a defection. She didn't see Brian in the crowd.

It was more than his absence that kept her awake. She was accustomed to his being gone on road trips. She was tempted to call Rob, late as it was. He could check with his friends at the State Department. She brushed the thought away. Brian had specifically instructed her not to tell Rob anything about his trip.

She grabbed a large pillow, trying to find a comfortable position. Finally, she got up and went to the medicine cabinet to get a sleeping pill. The only time she normally took them was the night before her period came when she turned into an insomniac. She took two for good measure and grabbed Sports Illustrated from Brian's dresser. The combination should put her to sleep quickly.

The colonel, small and trim in his Turkish uniform, extended his hand as Faeuil Al Rabu entered his office. "I am sorry," Colonel Mawal spoke, "Your Mr. Vickers was a valuable man. It is a great loss for both of us."

"If the Russians discover he was piloting the plane, it could be an embarrassment as well as a loss. Charlie was more than a mercenary. He was a former CIA operative. He was retired when his name appeared on a list published in a Parisian newspaper. But of course, he retained a certain contact."

"Through you." Mawal nodded sagely.

"It's rumored. Does your report indicate how badly the plane was hit?"
"The pilots and crew of the other planes stated the lead plane went down

completely in flames and crashed in the mountains. I doubt if anything survived to be recognized."

"That is good."

"To maintain the story you had given us, I have prepared an official protest for the Russian ambassador for their border patrol's failing to make radio contact and the proper inquiries. We are holding to the story of navigational error."

"Thank you, Colonel Mawal. Let us hope it works."

Faeuil bowed slightly and laid an unmarked white envelope on the colonel's desk. "Out of gratitude," he said without looking back at the envelope. Mawal knew the amount would be larger than usual. He smiled. "It is a pleasure to help the free nations. After all, we too are moving toward democracy."

# ANDOVER, MASSACHUSETTS
## February 19
## 6:00 a.m.

The cold winter morning light inched across the pillow. Mattie murmured in her sleep and tossed an arm out to find Brian. She sat up quickly, remembering as she looked at the shadow bars etched across Brian's empty pillow by the light filtering through the slatted shutters. She hadn't heard from him. She yawned as she slipped on a robe and grabbed her hairbrush for her hundred-stroke morning ritual. She wished he'd call. "Twenty-two, twenty-three, twenty-four." He was booked on the 7:00 a.m. plane. Maybe she could catch him at the hotel. She remembered he couldn't get a reservation at the Penn Center Inn where the players usually stayed. What hotel had he said? The Sheraton. She got the number from Philadelphia information and dialed quickly. The operator rang the room. He hadn't checked out yet. No answer. Maybe he was checking out right then. If so, he'd be heading for the airport directly. She made a mental note to have him paged at Logan when the plane arrived. Where was he? She picked up the brush—"Forty-six, forty-seven, forty-eight"—as Cloie stumbled in, sleepy- eyed, hugging her overstuffed Boston Teddy-Bruin, as she called it.

"Is Daddy home yet?"

"No, sweetheart, it's much too early! You don't have to get up for another hour!"

"May I crawl in your bed for a while?"

"Sure," she tucked Cloie in. She looked lost in the huge bed. "It's a cold morning. Snuggle in." She sat on the edge of the bed, quietly counting and brushing as Cloie fell back asleep.

Ivan sat down at the kitchen table while the middle-aged lady named Yosie scrambled eggs to go with the hickory-smoked bacon already on the table. "Looks good," he said in English.

"Wait until you taste them," she replied in Russian. She piled a golden mound of eggs on a plate and handed them to Ivan. "There is plenty more for seconds or thirds. Help yourself to bacon and toast."

"You're Russian!" He grinned. "I can tell a real accent."

"I've been here since 1944, but my work keeps my Russian fresh." She didn't explain she'd worked as a linguist and agent as well as a cook for the past twenty years. She'd been told to be discreet. "Your friend isn't up yet?" she asked.

"I didn't check," Ivan answered. Vladimir entered the room. "Better hurry," said Ivan between bites. "I'm trying to eat all the food in town."

"You could probably do it. Maybe you should give up hockey and become a professional eater." Yosie placed a plate piled high with fluffy eggs in front of him. "Looks great, thanks!" He was in high spirits. "Ivan! Only a few more hours!"

"True. Soon we shall start talking to the American teams to see where we shall play."

"It's exciting!"

"That's an understatement!" He stopped, fork midway to his mouth. "I wonder how the trip out of Russia went. It could have been rough."

Vladimir stopped chewing. "You're right. I hope they're OK."

"Elmer assured us everything was fine, but I'll feel better when they're here. Think, we might have been on our way back to Russia today."

"Eggs taste better here!"

"Freedom tastes better anywhere." Ivan tapped his fork against the rim of his plate for emphasis. Yosie responded to his tap with a generous second helping of eggs.

A man carrying a rake appeared at the back door asking Yosie if she could spare some of her world-famous eggs.

Ivan started at the man in shabby blue jeans and frayed hat. He looked familiar. "Elmer!" He jumped to his feet. "What are you doing dressed like that?"

"I'm one of your gardeners, today. Have to keep this a safe house. Sit down and eat your breakfast." He joined them.

"Is the KGB tracking us down?"

"Nothing like that. It's standard procedure for safe houses to have tight security." He grinned at Yosie. "Now I have to get down to something really important—like bacon and eggs!"

It struck Ivan that they could be back in Russia, except for the luxurious house. Everyone, including Elmer, spoke fluent Russian. Friendly or not, they were guards. He shook off the thought as Elmer reassured them Nadia, little Vladimir, and Berthe would be there by early afternoon. "Go easy," he advised, "they'll be exhausted."

General Taikov listened intently as Colonel Omnarsky gave his report. The KGB limousine had been recovered near the Turkish border. There was evidence of a helicopter landing nearby. It verified the U.S. based agent's information that Padov was out of the country with the Vladistocks, Berthe Malitinsky, his mother, and mistress. Taikov was beginning to accept the probability that Padov was the mole. They had to get him back quickly.

Taikov's mind drifted for a moment until he heard "American shoe found in the wreckage."

"What wreckage?"

"The Turkish F-111. An American shoe was found."

"The Americans sell many supplies to Turkey, but it is suspect."

"I believe the Turkish border violation was timed to cover Padov's exit. The reports show a smaller lower blip on the radar screen that wasn't checked at the time because of the pursuit of the F-111s. The squadron and the small blip, probably a helicopter, entered within seconds of each other."

"Clever," commented Taikov, "but I told you so last night."

Taikov's aide hurried into the room. "You're wanted at the Kremlin immediately, sir. They said a telex is coming through."

The general rose. "Perhaps we shall get a chance to see what Bollinger wants for the return of our team—and our turncoat."

Omnarsky joked, "Perhaps we should offer them Poland."

"This is no time for jests," snapped the general. He felt a sharp pain in his left shoulder and reached for a nitroglycerin pellet. It was a lot for his old heart to process.

WASHINGTON, D.C.

The White House

February 19

9:30 a.m.

J. L. passed through the corridor leading to the Oval Office. He noticed Mattimore and Bollinger deep in conversation outside. The door opened and they disappeared inside. J. L. wondered when they were going to announce the defection. Would the president call a special media conference? That could turn his day into total chaos again. He yawned. Morning had arrived too early following a late night with Rhodes celebrating their success and drowning their sorrow over the Brian Earle mishap. The VP was planning a series of minor whistle stops, ostensibly attending regional fundraisers for the GOP. In reality, some early campaigning. For J. L., it meant a lot of organizing.

He wondered if all the super security and disguises in Philadelphia was put in gear to save the announcement for Dodge. Politics. He sneezed as he hurried down the hall. He'd probably be the first to know. They'd need his mikes.

Rubin helped Aunt Katya into the backseat beside Tasha. "Climb in front," he told Peter as he entered the driver's side. "We're not using limousines—too conspicuous. We're all under wraps for a while."

"Where are the others going?" asked Tasha. She'd miss Nadia.

"To other safe houses as we call them. Their families are waiting for them."

"I won't mind being under wraps with Tasha for a while." Peter relaxed. "You'll have your own special wraps, my friend. Your house is lovely, with cook and houseboy. Lots of very secure gardeners. We'd like you to go into debriefing sessions immediately. I'd guess you're a lodestone of information about now."

"Bits and pieces, Rubin, but lots of them. But I don't know if I can still talk with a straight tongue. I've been a victim of my own double think for a lifetime."

"You'd better learn to talk straight," Tasha spoke from the backseat. "His heart has always been straight," Katya quietly defended him.

Events were still moving too fast for Tasha. The nightmare crawl of the limousine, the dash from the helicopter to the long plane ride and into this car heading God-knew-where to a place where Peter would be debriefed. She tried

245

to clear her mind.

Peter half turned and glanced in the back. "You ladies doing all right?"

"Fine," answered Tasha as unsought tears streamed down her cheeks.

Wordlessly, Aunt Katya handed her a handkerchief miraculously kept clean through the long journey. Tasha attempted a thank-you through her tears. Peter, his attention focused on Rubin, didn't notice.

"Now where do you go?" Peter asked.

"Downtown to my office. It's time to call the press and arrange the announcement."

"Not for me, thanks," Peter said with a shake of his head.

"No, not for you. For the team. You're not home free yet. You know as well as I do, if not better, that your old organization would like to find you before you can 'share' too much with us."

"It never ends, does it?" "Not yet. Maybe soon."

"I remember an old saying in this country that the only thing that is certain is death and taxes." He paused. "In Russia, we don't have taxes."

Rubin didn't smile.

In the long silence, Peter turned to smile at Tasha and found the tears. He reached back to give her hand a comforting squeeze. "We'll all be fine, my darling. You'll see."

"Peter." Rubin's voice was soft, but intent. "I don't think I'd talk about CkO . . . not just yet." Rubin took his eyes off the George Washington Parkway long enough to check Peter's reaction.

"You're the rabbi." Peter gave him a searching look. "Is it like that?" "Let's just say . . . a toe at a time . . . to test the water."

"For temperature or purity?"

"Maybe to find out if anything is fishy. Especially at State . . . with Herr Karl around, anything is possible."

J. L. exchanged the tiny wire disc lodged in the receiver of the presidential phone. The device was smaller than a dime. He slipped the used disc into his pocket, aware it had documented the meeting between Mattimore, Bollinger, and President Dodge. The disc burned in his pocket as he hurried next door to the Old Executive Office Building. By the time he reached his office, his curiosity was in high gear. Securing the door, J. L. pulled out his playback unit and earphones and settled down to eavesdrop on the high-level meeting.

Outside his half-opened window, he could hear the music of the Marine Marching Band playing for some ceremony on the White House lawn. "America the Beautiful," heard only by his left ear as he slipped the playback earpiece in his right, served as background music for the meeting. The irony was not lost on him as he listened to Bollinger's declamations. The man should have been a Nazi. It was outrageous to send the Wings back like bad merchandise in return for 7,500 Russian Jews and some American spies. He shut off the machine for a moment, gathering his thoughts. He felt like inviting Bollinger into a back alley for a Prince George's County discussion, fist to fist. His stomach growled.

J. L. made an exclamation point in the log and pushed the Play button back on. He heard Shields join the meeting and the discussion turn to the Earle incident. Shields, Mattimore, and Bollinger argued about whose agency should visit Mattie Earle with the official version of Earle's death. The ugly truth emerged in their discussions. Accustomed as J. L. was to political maneuverings, he blanched at the discussion of "reparations." Shields wanted the price high enough to insure silence. The CIA didn't need another angry citizen's crusade.

Bollinger chastised Mattimore for not having tighter security on Earle. "If your agents had screened the flight logs, they'd have stopped him at the airport."

"He booked under an assumed name," Mattimore quietly replied.

"It was foolish to take the word of his wife and base the report he was in the Boston area on that. Your carelessness cost him his life, Charles."

There was a long, twenty-second pause, broken only by a cough.

"So," Bollinger finally continued, "if Bob's agents had handled Earle earlier, I doubt if the problem would have arisen in Philadelphia. As it turned out, your agent did the correct thing. Had Earle gotten out of Philadelphia certain the team had defected, the whole operation would be in jeopardy. The incident is regrettable, but your agent is to be commended."

Shields raised a question, "How much does Earle's wife know? You said Whitehall and Carson were impressed with the confidentiality of the operation, but it would help to know if Earle would have discussed it with her."

Bollinger's voice jumped in, "We must assume she knew as much as he did up until the point of the switch. Our story must be developed accordingly. I'll work out the details with you, Bob, after this meeting and one of your agents can handle it personally."

"I would like to be able to express the sympathy of—" Mattimore began. Bollinger barked at him, "You'll stay out of it."

"Carson is my contact," protested Mattimore. "I'm the one he'll call!"

"You'll be briefed on the story Bob and I work out. Don't answer his calls until you have it," snapped Bollinger.

J. L. remembered Rubin was still on the way back from Turkey. If he'd been at the meeting, he would not have allowed it. J. L. wondered at the lack of participation by the president in this conversation. He reached in his breast pocket for a Rolaid before placing the incendiary disc in the NSA security packet, adding a small red dot indicating immediate attention.

# ANDOVER, MASSACHUSETTS
## February 19
## 2:00 p.m.

Mattie was getting frantic. There'd been no response to her page at Logan. Eastern airlines refused to confirm whether or not Brian had been on the flight. It was against their policy, which was for the privacy of their passengers. At ten, she'd called Rob whose initial reaction was anger at Brian for breaking his word. When he'd calmed down, he promised to call the State Department immediately. She called Cecily and cancelled their outlet shopping trip for the afternoon without explaining. Cecily recognized she was upset and offered to come over. Mattie declined the offer and promised to call her later. She called Rob again at eleven thirty. He told her to try to relax.

Their State Department contact was in a meeting, unreachable until early afternoon. He'd call her the second he heard anything. She knew something terrible had happened to Brian. He was the most reliable person she'd ever known. Not once, in a dozen years of marriage, had he not called at the promised time. The most he'd ever been late was two hours when the team bus had broken down outside of Milwaukee years ago.

At one, hearing nothing from Rob, she called the Philadelphia Police Department and asked to report a missing person. She explained the situation to the sergeant in charge. When he realized Brian had been missing less than twenty-four hours, he tried to reassure her. "Did Brian have friends in Philadelphia?"

She'd heard him talk about some reporters he liked in Philadelphia, but she couldn't remember names. The sergeant took detailed information on Brian and promised to call her if anything turned up.

She felt frustrated and scared. As she went to get a sheet of paper to list the Philadelphia hospitals, the phone rang. It was Sam, the Bruins' trainer, asking why Brian was late for practice. Sam was one of her favorites. As she started to tell him she didn't know, she broke into tears. Sam gently pulled the story out between sobs. She left out the defection part. Sam had a friend in the Fliers front office. He'd ask him to help by calling the hospitals. It'd be easier to do down there. Mattie felt relief, realizing Sam didn't think she was being hysterical or overreacting. But Sam knew Brian's reliability as well as she.

The children would be home from school by three thirty. She had to be under control before then. The phone rang again.

"Mrs. Earle, this is Bob Shields, director of the CIA." They'd decided to handle it from the top.

"Yes," she gasped. "Is it about Brian?"

"One of my agents will be there shortly to fill you in completely. I prefer not to discuss the details on the phone. I only wanted to personally express my sorrow and that of the president for what has happened."

"Then Brian is . . ." She couldn't say the word.

"Your husband is dead," Shields confirmed, wishing there were another way to break it to her, but he'd decided a phone call, followed by a special agent was better than the cold arrival of an unexpected agent. It would give her time to digest it a piece at a time. "I'm truly sorry," he added.

The doorbell chimed. "The doorbell," she mumbled into the phone.

The timing was perfect, Shields noted as he told her, "That should be our agent. His name is Tom Henry. I'll hold while you answer the door to make sure."

"Tom Henry," she echoed in a hollow voice as the doorbell chimed again, but she didn't move. She was in shock.

"Please answer the door, Mrs. Earle. I'll hold," Shields's firm voice directed her. Numbly, she placed the phone on the table and deliberately walked to the entrance and answered the door. She stared wordlessly at the tall, boyish-looking agent on her doorstep.

"Mrs. Earle?" he asked, looking as though he could have been little B's Cub Scout leader.

She felt the muscles in her face attempt to smile politely.

"Mrs. Earle?" he repeated. She nodded slightly and took a step back, trying to focus on him and remember who the man from the CIA had said.

"My name is Tom Henry," the young man said, wondering if Shields hadn't gotten through on the phone.

"Yes," she said softly. That was the name. "The man said you'd be here." She started slightly, remembering. "He's still waiting on the phone. Come in."

She turned and hurried back to the phone were Bob Shields was waiting. "If there is anything I can do to help, please feel free to call me personally. You have my deepest sympathy," he said. The word sympathy triggered hot tears. She fought them back as she wordlessly handed the phone to Tom. Tom spoke briefly with Shields, promising to report back in an hour, his eyes full of concern as he watched Mattie's agony.

"Would you like a drink?" he asked her. "Show me the bar," he gently requested. Getting her to perform a routine task might help her regain control.

She stopped at the bar and stared at the liquor. "Brian likes Scotch when he isn't in training," she said flatly, then corrected herself, "Brian liked Scotch." She broke down at the change in tense. Brian was gone. Tom quickly moved to her and held her, letting her sob freely.

She felt his young, muscular body. Like Brian's but different, she heard herself thinking. She broke away from him, slightly embarrassed as she thought about the children. What if they walked in and found her in the arms of a stranger? She blew her nose and wiped her eyes as Tom mixed her a gin and tonic and made a light scotch and water for himself.

They sat down in the living room, which suddenly seemed oversized and lonely to Mattie. Now she wanted details. What had happened in Philadelphia? Tom related the prepared story. Brian had been killed outside the hotel by the KGB. In the back alley. He'd been asking for Ivan earlier and the KGB must have suspected Brian was an agent. Somehow, Brian had tried to meet Ivan in an alley and the KGB had stopped him. They didn't believe the KGB had intended to kill him, but when the guard struck him, Brian fell against a dumpster and fractured his skull. He died without regaining consciousness, Tom assured her.

Mattie's mind fought through the haze of her grief. "How do you know so many details? Did the KGB tell you what happened?"

"One of our agents saw the KGB slip in the back entrance leading from the alley. Suspecting something irregular, he checked the alley and found Brian's body. He was dead. Our man went and questioned the KGB guard. The guard expressed his regrets for the incident, but insisted Brian had no clearance to contact the players. He wasn't on the approved State Department lists." Shields had decided the story had to include some guilt on Brian's part to minimize the outrage.

Mattie's lips tightened as the statement had the intended effect. Brian had been wrong not to tell Rob or anyone he was going. If he had told them, they might have been able to talk him out of it and he'd still be alive. But he had been so wrapped up in the Wings's defection plans, she thought. "What about the Wings?" she asked Tom. "Have they defected?" Nothing had been on the Boston late news the night before.

Tom explained that the Wings were returning to Moscow. It had been impossible to meet their conditions. Tom had not been told the truth at Bollinger's insistence. The secretary of state was totally confident his trade was assured and he insisted that Mattie be told they were gone to prevent her seeking out Ivan and raising embarrassing questions.

"Then Brian's death was meaningless," she spoke sadly.

"He was a good American. He took risks because he believed in our system and wanted the Russian players to share it," the young agent spoke with conviction. "That has meaning. His death was unfortunate, but it doesn't erase his loyalty and character."

"It was foolish for him to go there, but he felt he had to," Mattie spoke quietly, almost to herself. Then she realized she didn't know where Brian's body was. "Where is he . . . where is the body now?"

"In the Philadelphia morgue. The official story has to be that Brian was mugged in an alley, a simple robbery unrelated to the Russians. We have to avoid turning it into an international incident," Tom explained the CIA rationale.

Mattie's Irish temper flared. "You left his body in an alley for the police to find! Just left it! Without a priest or anything?!"

"There was no other way. For U.S. intelligence to have brought the body in would have raised suspicions. It wasn't there long, thanks to an anonymous phone call from a 'concerned citizen' who noticed a body in the alley." Tom reemphasized, "There really wasn't any other way to handle it."

"I need another drink," Mattie said darkly. "There had to have been a better way to do it."

"The agents were acting under pressure," Tom rationalized as he mixed another drink.

It hit Mattie that the Philadelphia police had no record of Brian's being there. She related her earlier conversation with the sergeant to Tom

"They hadn't identified him yet," Tom carefully explained. "His wallet had been removed to make it look like a robbery. He is listed as a John Doe."

Brian lying nameless in a city morgue. The thought turned Mattie cold. "We can't just leave him there like that!" she protested. We have to do something."

Tom assured her he'd make a follow-up call as a family friend and insist they check more carefully. He was surprised they hadn't made the connection from her earlier phone call; Brian was easy to describe since he was an athlete. Tom already had reservations for Mattie and himself for Philadelphia and arrangements were being made discreetly for flying the body back to Massachusetts. He told Mattie the Agency had arranged for a mature female agent, a "nice, middle-aged woman who loves children" to stay with little B and Cloie.

"No, I want my own mother." Mattie sounded like a child. Her mother was in Chicago.

Tom promised the Agency would arrange her mother's flight. Mattie's mother promised to take the next plane to Boston. She called her friend Cecily and asked her to stay with the children until her mother arrived. She told Cecily she didn't want to tell the children Brian was dead until she had seen Brian's body; she had to be absolutely certain there was no mistake. Cecily was to tell the children Mattie had gone to meet Brian in Philadelphia. It wasn't unusual for her to make last-minute decisions to join Brian on the road. They wouldn't be upset.

Rob called as they were waiting for Cecily. Charles had briefed him minutes before. He offered to bring Nancy and meet Mattie in Philadelphia. Mattie declined the offer. She preferred having a stranger help her through. It would be more difficult to maintain her composure with Rob and Nancy who had known and loved Brian too. Tom would add a composing detachment. She asked Rob to bring Nancy to Andover tomorrow and help with the children and arrangements. She realized by the next day when the shock wore off, she would need all the psychological reinforcement she could find.

On the way to the airport, she began to break down again. Tom kept talking to distract her. "I want you to know the U.S. government is not going to forget Brian . . . and you. In addition to the insurance the team carries on Brian, you'll own your home free and clear with taxes taken care of as long as you wish to remain there. Trust funds will be established for your children's education, and you'll receive $2,500 a month in consulting fees, with yearly cost of living increases until you reach retirement age."

She'd never thought about finances. Brian had handled them. But tuning in to details distracted her from her grief. "But why would they give me that?"

"Director Shields is according to Brian the same benefits given the family of one of our own field operatives. He believes it is the least we can do under the circumstances." The irony of Shields's statement was lost on both Tom and Mattie. It smacked of a "Bollinger-ism."

Tom continued, "Your area of consulting will be worked out at your leisure. We thought you might enjoy working with some of our American Indian programs. Nothing too time consuming unless you want it." Her file indicated she'd been active in championing the American Indians during the years Brian played with Minnesota.

"I can't deal with that now," she protested. "Not yet."

Tom assured her there was no hurry. He simply wanted her to know her future was of concern to Washington.

When they reached the airport, she called Cecily. The children had returned from school and were fine. There had been a call from a Sergeant Marino in Philadelphia. She gave Mattie the number and wished her love and luck.

Tom placed the return call to Sergeant Marino. The sergeant said that an unidentified body matched Mattie's description of Brian and the clothing labels were from Boston stores. The sergeant was surprised when Tom told him they'd be in Philadelphia before five. Tom asked him to make no statements to the press or announce Brian's identity until they arrived, explaining that Brian was a well-known athlete. Sergeant Marino made a mental note to stop home for a fresh uniform for the press interviews.

# WASHINGTON, D.C.
## State Department February 19
## 3:00 p.m.

Bollinger's bulk made Mattimore's office seem overcrowded as he joined Charles and Rubin. "Shields reports the Earle situation is under control," he grunted. "She's accepted the story."

Why wouldn't she? thought Rubin. The general public still believe the heads of their government wouldn't lie to them.

Bollinger pulled up the only upholstered chair and plunked down, stating, "So that's taken care of. She'll remain under surveillance twenty-four hours a day until our operation is successfully completed." He gave Charles a significant look as he added, "We don't want any more unfortunate accidents occurring from that direction, do we?"

Charles was too weary to take offense.

"With that out of our hair," Bollinger continued, "we must direct our attention to the critical matters of the day." He paused dramatically. The effect was lost as Rubin looked away to light a cigarette while Charles poured coffee for the three of them.

Bollinger leaned back in his padded chair and pressed his thumbs together. "It's unfortunate, but the Soviets want Padov and his women returned immediately. They'll dicker later on the Wings."

"No!" fumed Rubin, lighting another cigarette. "Do you know what they'd do to him?"

Bollinger stared unblinkingly at the Oliphant sketch behind Mattimore's desk while Mattimore quietly responded, "I have a general idea and it isn't pretty. Debriefing isn't the word for it."

Bollinger perked up at the word. "That reminds me. How is Padov's debriefing going? He must be a walking encyclopedia of KGB information. The Russians want him back first, as a sign of good faith." He smiled sardonically.

"Debriefings are to begin tomorrow."

"No, immediately. I'll stall the Soviets as long as I can by offering them the old woman and the girl first, then Padov."

"The name isn't Padov, Karl. It's Peter Porter, U.S. citizen. Your game is sick. These are people, not pawns for your political ploys. I only pulled Porter in because we'd gotten reports the search was on for a plant inside the KGB. He's worth more than three hockey teams."

"Interesting, interesting, but we must weigh all sides of the situation. What will benefit our president—and the nation—the most? And think of the 7,500 Russian Jews we'll free."

"In an election year," came from Mattimore's corner. He reached for a mint to counter the bad taste in his mouth. "Who knows? Perhaps the Russians will laugh at your terms, and everyone can stay."

Bollinger shot a frozen glance at Charles. "We'll come to terms unless you manage to foul things up."

"This is your operation now," snapped Charles. "I got the players over, with help from Rubin and the CIA. They're all together and accounted for. My efforts succeeded for your fraudulent defection. This next step is all yours."

Bollinger rose haughtily. He paused at the door. "Rubin, I want a progress report on the Padov debriefing first thing tomorrow."

Rubin flared, "I won't let you send Peter back for this hare-brained trade, Karl. Don't you realize what he's worth to us for future operations, all human and constitutional rights aside, Karl? It would be a stupid bargain."

Karl gave Rubin an icy stare. "First thing tomorrow." He didn't like being told his plans were stupid. The colonel would be sent back.

Rubin and Charles silently stared after him. Charles felt drained; Rubin, cheated. Bollinger reappeared briefly. "Almost forgot to tell you. I want written reports." The ponderous apparition disappeared as quickly as it had appeared.

"Now I can change my schedule for him again," noted Charles with disgust. "I'll have to stay late and dictate the report."

Rubin rose. "I'd better get moving." He had a lot of thinking to do. He leaned over to pick up his briefcase, turned to Charles, and asked, "Charles? Ever wonder why you didn't become a CPA?"

"Never." Charles's mouth turned up. "I was considering becoming an honest plumber."

"Ha." Rubin was gone.

Charles stared at the file on top of his desk. Peter Porter, alias Sergei Padov, about to be sold down the river when he didn't even know he was on the block. Charles took a sip of coffee, trying to stay alert. How did it all come to this? He'd spent years establishing himself with the State Department, moving from a bright young aide to deputy and then undersecretary. What had he become? Charles Mattimore, a man who could be counted on to put the Department first. The thought disgusted him. If he managed to last this crisis out and stay with State, he'd never have any self-respect. But if he violated direct orders from Bollinger, he'd be violating everything he believed was right for the organization. Damned either way.

The phone rang. It was Bollinger asking if Rubin was still there. When Charles reported he'd left five minutes before, Bollinger told him to be in the Oval Office at four thirty. He could forget the five o'clock meeting. Charles asked if Rubin should be there. Bollinger grunted that perhaps he should be, but it was too late to reach him. He expressed regrets that he hadn't known about it earlier. Charles had the distinct feeling that Bollinger was deliberately maneuvering so that Rubin would not be at the meeting. Charles left a message with Rubin's secretary on the slim hope that he might get it in time. But with or without Rubin, Charles decided, he wasn't going to sit silently by as Bollinger's yes man this time. No. He could be stronger than that.

# MacLean, VIRGINIA Safe House No.
# 1 February 19
# 3:38 p.m.

The debriefings were to begin sooner than Peter had anticipated. For all practical purposes, he had just walked in the door. He sighed wearily and turned to Tasha. "It's probably better to get it over with as fast as possible. It could take months."

"What are you talking about?" She dimpled. "Getting settled and outfitted?" She pulled out the front of the dress that had been waiting for her, showing the extra inches. "It had better come soon. If this is American fashion, let's go home to Moscow."

"Give us a chance. There was hardly a good opportunity to wire ahead with your sizes," he smiled at her. "You're like the woman who went on vacation and asked to go home before her bags were unpacked."

"She was lucky," Tasha retorted. "She had bags." She spread her arms wide. "But she didn't have you."

Peter quickly reached the waiting hug as the doorbell rang. "Damn. They wasted no time getting here."

"Who?"

"I have to go to a debriefing session. They want to be filled in on the last thirty years or so."

"Hmm. What time will you be home?" She used the word with pleasure. "I don't know. I'll call."

"Let me know if you want dinner. Maybe the cook will let me help."

For a moment, it all sounded cozy and suburban to Peter. Off to work, darling, with a promise to call about dinner. The doorbell rang again. He gave her a hard, fast kiss. "I love you."

"I love you," she echoed.

"I prayed that you would come with me the whole way south from Moscow." He was out the door before she could reply.

Tasha watched the dark car pull away, looking out the hall window. Then she turned and walked into the kitchen to ask the cook for a snack. If she kept eating the way she had done since they arrived in Turkey, she would soon fit the oversized dress.

Aunt Katya was sitting with the cook, having tea. "Hello, dear. Would you like some tea?"

"Would you read my tea leaves?" Tasha asked cheerfully. "You promised to do it months ago."

Katya gave her hand a motherly pat as she sat down with them. "Not today. We have tempted luck enough this week."

Tasha nodded.

Nadia, feeling revitalized by a bath and shampoo, hugged the senior Vladimir. "Is this where we shall live?"

"No," he grunted. "This is temporary until we talk to the team owners and know where I'll be playing."

"It's a charming house." She smiled, backing away to look around. She was too tired to ask important questions.

"There is a cook too!" announced Vladimir with pride. "Would you like a snack?"

"Not now." She walked over to the large picture window, facing the woods. "We're really in the woods." She wrapped her arms around her shoulders, feeling a sudden chill. "I had enough woods driving out of Russia."

"Tell me about your trip."

"There is too much to tell in a minute. Now, I'd like to see the kitchen and think of happy things. Maybe the cook would let me bake something."

Nadia often unwound from a long day at the hospital by baking. Beating the batter seemed to ease tension and the smell of baking cookies and cakes always put her in a good frame of mind.

The front door burst open and little Vladimir ran in, followed by Elmer. The boy shrieked "he won't let me play!" as he hurled his arms around Nadia's legs. Vladimir frowned. "What is going on?"

"Sorry, but the boy can't leave the grounds alone. Orders."

"Poppa," little Vladimir took a step toward his father, "I want to play in the woods."

"I can take him in the woods," offered Elmer, "but he can't go alone."

Nadia and Vladimir shot worried looks at each other. What is it? Nadia asked herself. Are we protected or prisoners? It was getting like the ride south from Moscow. Absurd. They were in a beautiful house with the agents who were their friends.

"Little Vladimir," instructed Vladimir, Sr., "you can go into the woods with Elmer. It isn't safe alone."

"Why?" asked the child wide-eyed.

"Bears," laughed Elmer. "Big red bears. Let's go look for some!"

As the door closed on the brave duo, Nadia took Vladimir by the hand and led him toward the kitchen. She stopped suddenly, eyes twinkling. "How do you like my new dress?"

He focused on the print dress hanging loosely on her slender body. "Ha, what do they think Russian women are? Tanks?"

"Elmer has promised he will take me shopping with Tasha tomorrow." That sounded better than red bears in the woods.

# WASHINGTON, D.C.
## The White House February 19
## 6:00 p.m.

All that remained for J. L. to do was pick up another disc and take it over to NSA. Then the evening was his. If he moved swiftly, he'd be out within the hour.

He slipped into the Oval Office, removed the old disc, and replaced it with a blank. Then motivated by curiosity, J. L. headed into his office to check the recording of the four thirty meeting in the Oval Office.

He listened carefully. Good lord, he thought. Bollinger is selling out all of them. An image of the tall Russian colonel with the easygoing smile flashed on his mind's screen. Bollinger claimed he was doing nothing illegal. He'd checked it out thoroughly with the Justice Department. They had no legal responsibility to accept the defectors. The legality of returning the American double-agent who was a citizen wasn't discussed.

For the first time since he'd entered the army in 1954, J. L. felt confronted by something too ugly to face, political manipulation at its worst. At least the Watergate victims knew what game they were playing.

"Think, Mr. President," he listened to Bollinger's unctuous presentation. "Think what those 7,500 liberated Russian Jews will mean for the election. Our polls show your support among the Jewish community is insignificant. The strongest financial political structure in the country is ignoring you." J.

L. felt his stomach churn. There was a brief silence, broken by Mattimore's reedy voice. "Sir, I'm concerned about the hockey players and their families and our integrity in the eyes of the world . . . and in our own eyes."

Bollinger countered, "The world will know nothing except that we've arranged for the release of 7,500 poor victimized Jews. And if Rubin's right about this spy Padov, I might push them up to 15,000."

"Surely you don't believe none of this will surface to haunt us?" Mattimore's voice was incredulous.

"That's part of your job," retorted Bollinger. "To make certain it doesn't. Considering we've come this far with only one minor mishap and no leaks; it doesn't seem impossible."

J. L. could hear the disgust in Mattimore's voice, the suppressed rage at times, the steady assurance in Bollinger's, and the indecision in President Dodge's. He found himself rooting strongly for Charles, hoping Dodge would reject Bollinger's scheme.

"Mr. Secretary," the president's voice interrupted the melee, "are you certain that bringing out 7,500 Jews will assure us the Jewish vote and financial support?"

"Mr. President," came Bollinger's smooth response, "I am certain of it. The releases will indicate you secretly and personally negotiated for their release—with my assistance. It could assure your reelection." Bollinger didn't have to mention that the incumbent Dodge was badly trailing in the polls; the president was well aware of it. "Unless you give me orders to the contrary," continued Bollinger, "I shall proceed as outlined, stalling the Russians as long as possible so the Padov briefings can continue as I negotiate the final details for the exchanges. And the public will never know of the exchange we made since the defection of the Wings will never hit the papers."

Mattimore continued to voice objections, Dodge questioning them, Bollinger holding firm for his plan. Finally, Dodge concluded the discussion, "I'm late for another meeting. If you think you can pull it off, Karl, go ahead." Sounds of chairs scraping.

The elation was audible in Bollinger's voice as he said, "Very good, Mr.

President."

J. L. noted Mattimore's reply came from a distance. He must have stopped by the door. "Mr. President," the voice sounded thin. "I want to go on record as believing this is dead wrong, immoral." He'd cleared his throat. "And illegal, in the case of Porter."

There was another silence, finally broken by Dodge. "We must do what we have to do," concluded the president grimly.

J. L. switched off the tape. He needed to get some fresh air. He felt an urge to burn the disc as though that could erase the meeting from ever having happened. Mattimore had said it. Bollinger's scheme was dead wrong. Why hadn't Rubin been at the meeting? Bollinger had muttered something about Rubin not being able to attend. Rubin wouldn't sit by like Mattimore and let it happen. Bollinger must be trying to maneuver behind Rubin's back.

J. L. reached for the phone to put in a Code 1 message for Rubin then stopped himself. He decided to mark the security packet "Code 1 Priority" and let Rubin hear it for himself. In his gut, J. L. knew Rubin would be outraged. But it could be hours before he'd listen to the tape. Something had to be done quickly; the less discussion the better. Rule 1 in the Intelligence world. And without putting it into words, J. L. realized that a deeper belief, the belief that there comes a time when a self-respecting man must act on what he considers right, also had to be followed.

Without hesitation, he dialed the number of a friend from his George Washington University days. As he placed the receiver to his ear, he realized he was still wearing the playback earpiece. It reminded him that he'd better place the call from outside.

# ANDREWS AIR FORCE BASE
## CIA "Secure" Debriefing Room
## February 19
## 10:30 p.m.

Peter closed his eyes as exhaustion flooded him. "I've about had it, friends," he said quietly.

Adams handed him a fresh pack of cigarettes. "I know you're tired, sir, but we have orders to continue until midnight, even later if you can take it."

Adams shut off the tape. He wasn't known for his compassion, but as Peter told his story, Adams's respect developed. He wished he could keep the tape off for the night and take Peter to a local bar for a couple of drinks. "Would you like some fresh coffee?"

"Please, and add a couple of memory pills!"

The telephone rang. "Yes?" Adams answered. "Yes, sir," he stated formally, "we are continuing until midnight."

"What time is it?" yawned Peter. "After ten. Not much longer."

Peter stretched. "Might as well get back to work. Incidentally, Fedora was KGB from day 1. Started with his seventh-grade history teacher."

Adams switched on the tape. "Would you like to repeat that for history?" Peter asked out of the blue, "I wonder how the Wings are doing?"

Nadia sat on the blue velvet couch, feet curled under her, hand resting on Vladimir's shoulder. The portrait of domesticity. Berthe Malitinsky looked at magazine ads while Ivan slowly read the Post.

"Ivan," Berthe asked in Russian, "when do we begin our English classes?

It is not enough for me to look at the pictures."

"I'll ask them tomorrow, Mother. I could use some more lessons myself.

The newspaper is difficult for me."

"Impossible for me," laughed Nadia. "Even Russian newspapers. I never know what to believe."

"Our story isn't in the papers yet?" Vladimir peered over Ivan's shoulder."
"No, I don't see it."

"What is all this waiting about?" stormed Vladimir. "When do we meet the head of their hockey league?"

"Let's not worry about that tonight. We are all together and safe in America. It is the first step."

"We've come many steps already," Nadia added.

Ivan continued, "I know the trip wasn't easy for you. But tonight, we are in a beautiful house with plenty of food, a cook, soft beds, friends."

"And guards outside," interrupted Vladimir. "Friends who are protecting us," corrected Ivan.

Berthe put aside the magazine. "None of you has ever been in a real prison.

You have no idea what it's like."

"We spent those two terrible nights in cells on the way out," Nadia reminded her.

"They were palace rooms compared with the prisons I've known! You have no idea of the filth and endless waiting. Vladimir, you are so angry and impatient. We've barely been here a day. We are being treated well."

"Mother is right," nodded Ivan. "They call this a safe house because they are protecting us."

Vladimir stared out at the dark, formless woods surrounding them. "It is late," he said to Nadia. "Let us go to bed." His disquiet had not been erased, only appeased for the night. It was difficult for him to feel free when he felt they were being kept in the dark.

## Safe House No. 1 Same time

Aunt Katya looked at Tasha, half-asleep on the couch. "I would like to call my sister in New York. Why do they keep telling me to wait? I don't understand. We are here safely. It is so many years since we were together. I don't know how many years we have left."

"Don't talk that way, Mother Padov—I mean, Aunt Katya. You'll live to be two hundred!"

Katya picked up her knitting. "It is only that I have waited so long I am tired of waiting."

"Me too." Tasha smiled. "I wonder how soon Peter will be back. Forgive me, I'm not making light of what you're saying. I know hours don't equal years. But if we must wait, this is a lovely place to do it."

"Yes, it is a peaceful place, but isolated. I would feel better if I could call Sophie."

Tasha's discomfiture had faded in the comfortable surroundings. For the moment, she luxuriated in a sense of safety. Katya, in a reverse of positions, had lost the security of understanding that had fortified her on the trek south.

Katya put aside her knitting. "It is late for me. I must put my old bones to bed." She walked over and patted Tasha's cheek. "Don't mind my worries. I am an old lady. Don't wait up too long."

"I won't," yawned Tasha. "Sleep well." She tucked a throw pillow under her head and promptly fell asleep until Peter returned and roused her well past midnight.

# WASHINGTON, D. C.
## The Class Reunion Bar
## February 20
## 12:30 a.m.

Alan Biddle blew the foam on top of his mug. "Do you have copies of the tapes?"

"You've got to be shitting me! They are single copies, eyes only. But I listened to them myself, and so help me God, that's what Bollinger plans to do. As far as the public is concerned, President Dodge and Bollinger will have negotiated for the release of 7,500 Russian Jews. The story of the Wings will be burned, forgotten, and perhaps buried."

"We can't print undocumented rumors."

"This is not a rumor, Alan! How about a what-ever-happened-to-the-Russian-hockey-team story in which you cite information from a reliable source. Ask State for comment. That might blow something open."

"Maybe, but it would be ten times stronger if I could interview one of the players. Get a photo or two." The shock of blond hair that was his trademark fell across his forehead. His hazel eyes darkened as he considered the problem of tracking down one of the defectors and getting close enough for an interview.

"They're all split up among safe houses in McLean. I don't know who's where." J. L. reached for another handful of dry, roasted peanuts.

"Do you know where the safe houses are?"

"I know where a couple are, but I don't know if they're using them for this operation." He rubbed his cheek as he yawned. "I'm getting too old for these twenty-hour days."

"Try drawing me a map, buddy. It's worth it for me to check them out and see if I can find myself a real live Russian hockey star. I'm on your team on this one, J. L. I believe you. I think the big boys should all be put in the penalty box!"

"Alan, you can't go up to those houses and knock on the door, saying, 'Hi there, I'm from the Post and I know this is a safe house. Just thought you might have a few Wings hanging around waiting to defect.'"

"I'm not that naive!" protested Alan.

"They've gone to ground with them. And the players themselves don't know they're being sold out."

"Maybe they should."

"Sure," muttered J. L., "and they'd start life here with a rotten taste in their mouths, like the one I have. I think if it hits the papers that they're going to defect, even Bollinger wouldn't have the balls to follow through with the double-cross."

"You're playing God a little," argued Alan.

"Not God. I'm pissed off with what the devils are plotting. I'm only trying to stay on the side of the angels."

"For openers, let's hope the angels stay with us long enough for me to swing an interview. Just keep me posted, so to speak, on the big boys' reactions." Alan pushed a notepad and fine line magic marker in front of J. L. and continued, "OK, tour director, give me a few celebrity homes to visit. I may have to dig up my pruning shears before this caper is over, so draw fast, but make it accurate."

J. L. slowly began drawing lines, searching his memory for street names. "You'll have to take your choice, fast or accurate."

"In that case, I'll have another brew. How about you?" "After I finish your map."

# GEORGETOWN
## Bollinger's Townhouse
## February 20
## 1:00 a.m.

When the agent-messenger rang the doorbell of the elegant townhouse, Bollinger answered in his monogrammed blue velvet dressing gown. "Thank you, my good man," he slammed the door in his face.

Bollinger poured himself four fingers of Courvoisier and settled down in his den. He skimmed the three pages of the decoded telex from the Russians. "Good, very good," he muttered. The first shipment would be made within six days provided the first of the defectors . . . They wanted Padov within seventy-two hours or no deal. His self-satisfaction faded. He didn't like to be pushed, even for 7,500 Jews. Why should he return their colonel before they made the first delivery?

He persisted in considering Peter the Russians' colonel.

Omnarsky crisply saluted. "Sir?"

"We have telexed our acceptance of terms to the Americans. I believe there is no doubt that we shall have Padov and the others back," Taikov reported.

Omnarsky's eyes gleamed. "Good."

"Interrogation shall begin immediately upon arrival. We don't know the extent of Padov's involvement. It may have been the girl."

"Impossible!" exploded Omnarsky. "It had to be him! What about the missing records? He was the only one in a position to arrange things."

"You would send him to Siberia before we examine the facts?" Taikov looked stern. "It is your job to compile records relating to Padov, his mother, and the girl. We seek facts, not scapegoats." Taikov believed Padov was the mole, but Omnarsky's vindictive eagerness revolted him.

"Yes, sir."

"Don't misinterpret. I will not go easy on him. Since he was a close associate, I am removing myself from direct involvement in the interrogations. You will also not be involved. You are too eager to convict him. It makes me wonder about your own possible involvement."

Omnarsky stiffened. Taikov shuffled through some papers on his desk. "You have a great deal to do. You are excused, Colonel."

The first two houses had revealed nothing. Alan checked J. L.'s map as he slowly drove around the block and parked. Removing hedge clippers from the backseat, he zipped his army green parka and headed for safe house no. 3.

The foliage was so thick he could glimpse only a distant windowpane. Quite an estate. The gate was locked, but he could see through the iron grillwork a large three-story colonial set well back with clusters of shrubs and trees closing in the lawns. He followed the hedge to the corner, searching for an opening. Around the corner, he spied a spot where the hedge thinned. A few decisive swings with his clippers, and he was inside the expansive yard. To his left was a clearing, broken by a stream edged with February ice.

"Hello," a heavily accented voice started him. He swung around face-to-face with Ivan Malitinsky, captain of the Wings. Alan recognized him from file photos. What a stroke of luck, he thought. Stay cool.

"Hello," Alan replied. "I'm one of the gardeners." "Like Elmer." Ivan smiled. "You have us surrounded."

"Indeed, we do. You're precious commodities." He reached for his inside pocket, casually scratching as he turned on the recorder. "What's your name? What position do you play?"

"Ivan Malitinsky. I'm the center." "And the star!"

"I'm OK," he acknowledged. "But it takes a team to do anything well, even defect."

"You've officially defected?"

"Do not joke. You know we are waiting for that."

Alan grinned ingenuously. "Sure, I just like to hear the word defection."

"I wish your people would get things settled so we can start living our new lives. It is time we begin talking to American team owners about playing. We will all get fat and lazy soon."

"What still must be settled?"

"Maybe you can tell me. I do not understand why we cannot talk to reporters to let the American people know we have chosen their freedoms."

Alan bit his lip. "That will come. Do you read the papers?"

"Your English newspapers are difficult for me. I'm thinking I should study English along with my mother and the others."

Alan wanted to ask more about the families. He had to be careful since Ivan obviously considered him an agent. "How are your mother and the others doing?"

"It was a rough trip for them. They are still tired. Mother is old and Vladimir's boy is only five. You haven't met them yet?"

Alan shook his head. "They flew directly from Russia?"

"They drove south from Moscow to the border . . ." Ivan stopped and looked at Alan curiously. "They don't tell you much."

"Elmer's told me nothing except to make sure everything around the property is clear," Alan remembered Ivan's reference to Elmer. "Are you getting restless here?"

"A little. It's not so bad. This is a nice house. Vladimir gets nervous and impatient, but he always does. You should have seen him before we left Philadelphia! I would be happy if we would start talking with the American hockey teams and not feel as though we are under guard all the time." He looked concerned. "I apologize. I do not mean to insult you. You are only doing your job."

"I understand." Alan smiled. He was rewarded by a smile in return.

Alan clicked his miniature camera, aimed up toward Ivan. He took three more in rapid succession for insurance. "I wasn't insulted. I understand—"

"Ivan!" A voice called from the house. "I think that is Elmer," Ivan said.

"Sure sounds like him," agreed Alan. "I'd better get back to work before he catches me off guard."

"I must go see what he wants. Good-bye." "I'll be here patrolling if anyone wants me."

"Ivan!" Elmer called again from the front porch. Ivan lengthened his strides and hurried through the trees. Alan snapped a series of photos of the grounds and house and high-tailed it through the hedge to his car.

"There you are," Elmer said with relief. "Everything OK?"

"Sure." Ivan grinned. "I was in the backyard talking to one of your agents."

"Oh, good." Elmer thought a moment. "In the backyard? Inside the hedge?"

Ivan nodded.

"What did he look like?"

"Tall with blond hair. Not fat. How do you say it. Little muscle. Skinny. I think that is the word."

Elmer frowned. "We don't have any blond agents assigned to this house. And our patrols are to stay outside the hedges. The cameras cover the grounds."

"He said if you needed him, he would be patrolling. It is a cold day to patrol."

Elmer had sent one of the patrol squads on an errand. He rubbed his hands together anxiously. "Let's go inside. I want to make a few calls and check this out. How long ago did he leave?"

"Just now, when you called. And he didn't say he was leaving, only getting back to his patrol job."

"Go on in. I'm going to check the backyard and be back shortly."

Charles coughed, a reflex brought on by his conversation with Bollinger. Karl didn't wait for him to finish the cough. "Answer me, Charles, how much longer is this going to take?"

"I don't know. Rubin's handling it. Peter's been privy to reams of highly classified KGB material for years. It could take months."

"I won't diffuse negotiations by waiting. We have seventy-two hours.

Period. Tell Rubin to run the debriefings twenty-four hours a day."

Bollinger was ignoring the fact he'd called for Charles's resignation because he still needed him. Charles considered telling Karl to stuff it, but he held his peace. Perhaps he could get President Dodge alone and make one last impassioned plea for reason. He sighed as Karl hung up on him.

Rubin finished reviewing the recording of the four thirty meeting in the Oval Office. Bollinger must be insane! He fully intended to trade them all back, he realized. Peter was on the top of the list. He couldn't protest directly to the president without revealing their surveillance system. He pondered on how to stop Bollinger. He'd begin by slowing down the debriefing. Maybe Dodge could be convinced to change his posture if there were more time to think about it. He picked up the phone and called Adams.

"Adams. Stop the debriefing and take Peter and the women out for a leisurely brunch. Go sightseeing. Pick up the debriefing around eleven tomorrow morning."

Rubin detected approval in Adams' voice. Good, he thought, Peter had Adams, the iceberg himself, on his side. Peter was remarkable. "And Adams, this is between you and me, period. The switchboard has instructions that no one, not even the president, can interrupt you without my authorization."

"Very good, sir. But sir," Adams added blithely, "don't call me. I'll call you."

Rubin smiled. Not enough people give Adams credit for his sense of humor.

He placed a call to Bollinger. He'd spend a few minutes assuring him that Peter was giving them a wealth of classified information. His mind was a KGB classified directory. There was truth in that. He wouldn't be lying to the crafty old bastard.

Yori restlessly tossed the playing cards on the table. He agreed with the others that the food was excellent and the house luxurious, but he was hungry for a taste of his new freedom. As far as he could determine, they hadn't officially defected. He'd expected some kind of ceremony or paper signing.

Normally, he was a patient man. Steady and methodical, even as a goalie.

Now he felt impatient, restrained in the plush setting. His teammates in the house were treating it like a vacation, enjoying the pool table in the paneled recreation room. They'd agreed training was off for the moment and toasted their agents with the free-flowing supply of Russian vodka.

Yori wanted to be able to walk down the streets of Washington and Philadelphia or any city alone. He wanted someone to tell him that he wasn't going to be a hockey player anymore. His teammates weren't enough. He wanted to meet Americans, working and living on the outside. He wanted to visit schools and talk about teaching Russian. Things were too contained here. The guards around their house were friendly, but they still were guards. A velvet prison. Where were the reporters? The defection had to be news.

He sipped his coffee, strong the way he preferred, and walked to the window, looking out at the sprinkling of snow. Moscow probably had three feet. Pictures of Russian winters projected in his mind. The old pond outside the city where he'd learned to skate, never dreaming he'd grow up to become a star on ice. The girl he'd almost married. He'd been away too much. She couldn't wait. He remembered their last meeting. He'd taken her skating, of course. There had been snow, soft flakes that caught in her lashes and hung like lace stars. They melted with her tears as he tried to explain that skating and hockey were his life. Now he'd had enough of it. And Russia. But how could he learn about his new country he'd chosen, locked away from it? He heard his fellow players laughing in the kitchen while he was worrying himself into an ulcer. He tried to shake it off, heading for the kitchen for more coffee and moral support. The "plunge into freedom" was not as he'd expected.

WASHINGTON, D.C.

B ollinger sat back in the padded armchair. His gaze seemed to cut through Mattimore and pierce the wall behind him. "Tomorrow I shall have Moscow's final terms and arrangements. We may ship the whole group as far as Turkey and stagger the return to balance their shipments."

"Absurd! According to Rubin, we've barely gotten into the debriefings. We're looking at thirty years' worth of classified information. You'll have to stall."

Bollinger licked his lips. "Impossible. You have lived without this so-called valuable information. The country will survive without it. When the final arrangements are made, he'll be sent—whatever stage the debriefing."

"Maybe you won't finalize terms." Charles was numb. "We've reached an agreement."

"Sure," snapped Rubin, "you'd make any concession to get your 7,500 political pawns to play with."

"The president has agreed to the plan and the number is now 15,000," Bollinger icily countered. "Your colonel proved to be a valuable man."

"Who will tell the team . . . and Peter?" Rubin played along, seeking details.

"They'll be told nothing until take-off. No use upsetting them ahead of time." Bollinger smiled.

"What do we tell them?" Charles implicitly accepted the dirty work.

Bollinger slapped his hand on the dark conference table. "Simple. We were unable to arrange for the defection and they are being recalled."

"Do you think they'll accept that?" asked Charles.

"They'll have no choice since they are in our custody," Karl replied.

"Safe house arrest?" Rubin questioned aloud. Neither Charles or Karl smiled at his joke. Rubin continued seriously, "Surely, you can hold the Russians off for a few more days."

"Why? To give you two time to hatch a counterplan? When I tell you to have them ready for take-off, I want immediate action! If not, I'll report to the president that you are dragging your feet and interfering with his operation!"

Rubin glared while Charles just stared.

"You won't get away with this," Rubin threatened.

"It's already done." Bollinger pulled himself ponderously from his chair. "You were kiting around Turkey at the time. Too bad. I'll let you know when it's time to move but expect it within forty-eight hours."

Rubin and Charles shared their anguish in silence for a full minute after Bollinger left. Rubin heaved a sigh and rose first. Charles asked listlessly, "Where are you going?"

"Back out to McLean to take Peter and the women to dinner. Hardly a joyful assignment tonight."

"Isn't there anything we can do to stop him?"

"We've tried arguing, hesitating. None of it works on Karl. He's a bull.

Maybe we should try talking to Dodge without him."

"I don't know." Charles's mind felt muddy. It seemed months since he'd had a good night's sleep. "Is there a way we could blow it open from the Russian end? Don't we have agents in place who could leak it to the Russian press?"

"You're getting tired, Charles. Their papers are State controlled."

"There must be a way, Rubin." Even if they had to leak it to the American press. He opened his mouth to suggest it then clicked his teeth shut. If he went that route, it was better no one else know. Besides, Bollinger might have a tap on this room by now. "How does Bob Shields feel about this?"

"I don't know if he's aware of it. And for all I know, he's tight on Bollinger's

side. His agents handled the Earle thing rather brutally from what I could tell."
Rubin gathered his papers. He still had the ultimate recourse of sanctioning
Bollinger. Better not to mention that to Charles.

J. L. tuned in the all-news station, hoping to hear a report on the Wings. He wondered how Alan had fared in McLean. He didn't want to risk calling from the office. He reached in his shirt pocket for his Tums. The tension was getting to him. Shit, he thought, Alan won't be at the paper, and I don't have his home number. He decided to head for his local legion. It was better than heading home to work on his ulcer.

# WASHINGTON, D.C.
## Washington Post Newsroom February 20
## 6:30 p.m.

Alan Biddle reached for his overcoat. Out late, up early, does it every time, he thought. It had been a tough day. Talking his editor into running the Wings's story on page 1, photo and all. Not enough facts, his editor kept saying. No comments from State. State had been unreachable, he'd argued, fingers crossed. And there was the interview. Nobody could deny the Russian was Ivan Malitinsky. What about the source privy to conversations between President Dodge and Secretary of State Bollinger? Can't be quoted, said the editor. "All you can do is verify information from other sources." Alan already knew that. "We have more solid information than the early Watergate stories," protested Alan. The editor finally capitulated on the condition that Alan handles all protest calls from State and the White House. "Love to." Alan had grinned. "I've been trying to get a statement from them anyway."

The old editor's blue eyes twinkled; he had reached out his large blue-veined hand and patted Alan's shoulder. "Good work, son. We'll make a reporter out of you yet."

Alan felt a let-down as he signed out. Somehow after winning the battle of position, the rest seemed anticlimactic. Maybe he'd feel better when the reactions started coming in. He wished he'd arranged a meeting with J. L. He might have picked up some new leads for the story. He needed something new for the second day's report. If he could get more of a line on the American-turned-Russian mole, that would be a great angle. J. L. had mentioned that the guy brought some of the Wings's families out of Russia, but he hadn't mentioned his name. If he could get the mole's real name, he might be able to track him down through his American family.

Alan gave up waiting for the elevator, turned back down the corridor, hurrying into the newsroom. He jerked open his top desk drawer and threw papers and cards out until he found the right one. White House Communications' switchboard. Stupid number to have unlisted. He hurried out of his office to the nearest public telephone.

J. L. was 1,500 points away from a free game with one more ball to shoot when his beeper went off. "Rats," he muttered to his friend Mark. "Wonder what the old man wants now." He headed for the telephone to call the switchboard.

"Hey," called Mark. "Want me to shoot for you?"

"No way. If the game is blown, I want to do it myself!"

Mark grinned and went to the bar to buy them another beer. No sense wasting time. He bought five dollars' worth of Las Vegas tickets and slowly pulled back the tabs that revealed bars, bells, lemons, and cherries— unfortunately not three in a row on the first eight tickets. J. L. had returned, grinning over his shoulder. "You look cheerful," Mark observed. "The general must have been in a good mood."

"Wasn't the general. It was an old friend I have to meet in a few minutes." He took a deep drink from the fresh draft. "Thanks."

"She must be something special to make you that cheerful . . . blond or brunette?"

"I'm not talking. I'm shooting." He returned to the pinball machine and pulled back the shooter to send the fifth and final ball bouncing around the board, setting off flashing lights and bells.

"Look at that!" Mark watched the score mount, staring in fascination as J.

L. continued to send the silver ball bouncing from one special to another.

"Keep it up, you'll set a new record."

J. L. continued, half-hypnotized by the ball's ricochets. He glanced at the scoreboard as another thousand was added to his score and missed the silver ball as it disappeared into the side exit. He'd already won two free games. "Oh well." He grinned at Mark. "You can't win them all."

"That one you did. Your luck's hot tonight." He handed J. L. the last Las Vegas card. J. L. pulled back the tab and asked, "Bells good enough for you?"

"Don't kid around. Bells are worth $10." "How many did you buy?"

"A dollar's worth."

Handing back the small card, J. L. said, "Not a bad return. And be my guest, play out the free games on the machine. I gotta go."

"Thanks, old man. For that, I hope you score yourself tonight." Mark winked suggestively.

"I intend to," J. L. took the last swig of his beer and headed out the door to meet his blond . . . named Alan.

"Thank you, Rubin." Aunt Katya smiled. "It was a lovely dinner. I forgot how nice restaurants can be. I'm afraid I ate too much."

"We all did." Peter patted his lean stomach. "Now we should go digest it in our sleep."

"Thank you for joining us, Aunt Katya." Rubin rose and held out his hand to help her up. "I may call you that, I hope."

"I'd be delighted." She took his hand in both of hers. Her hands felt dry and fragile, like old parchment. "Thank you, son."

"It's been years since anyone's called me son. You make me feel like a schoolboy!"

"Is that bad?"

"It's a compliment at this point!" He laughed.

She started to withdraw her hands then paused, looking into his eyes seriously. "Rubin, when may I call my sister and arrange to meet her?"

"Aunt Katya," interjected Peter, "Rubin told us at dinner we must wait until the State Department has everything arranged. He'll give us the go- ahead as soon as he can."

Rubin felt guilt as his half-truths overwhelmed him. Perhaps the only way out of this was to go after Bollinger . . . covertly. "Yes," he muttered. "As soon as I can." Rubin wondered what Karl's latest medical report showed. With luck, Karl had a history of high cholesterol and heart strain, enough to justify a terminal myocardial infarction.

The phone rang. Peter reached it first. "Yes?" He listened then held the receiver toward Rubin. "For you."

"I'll say good night again," said Aunt Katya. "Sleep well," said Rubin on his way to the phone.

"I hope so," she said as she headed toward the stairs.

Adams was on the other end of the phone. "Sorry to disturb you, sir, but there have been three inquiries from the secretary of state's aide about the debriefing. They refuse to accept the communications blackout. They demand an immediate report."

How dare Bollinger check up on his operation? Rubin raged to himself. Then he realized the cunning secretary of state had read him accurately and, from his perspective, was justified in his checks. "Call them back and inform them you're proceeding on schedule. It is dragging because of the complexity of the information. We are on the verge of critical information. Got that?"

"Yes. Will do, sir."

"Peter will be there about ten thirty a.m. I'll join you around noon. I have to go to the office first."

Peter was curious as Rubin finished the conversation, adding that the information was too highly classified for most NSA clericals to transcribe.

"What was that about?"

"Our secretary of state gets curious like a cat. He wanted a report on the debriefing, behind my back. Nothing to worry about." He tagged, "Not that part of it, anyway." He sat wearily.

"What do we worry about?" Peter caught his mood, realizing Rubin was holding back information.

Tasha glanced up from House Beautiful and asked, "Is there something we should worry about?"

"No, love," Peter shook his head. "Not for you."

Rubin spoke gravely to Peter, "I'd like to talk to you alone for a while."

Tasha was curled comfortably on the couch. She reluctantly agreed to head for bed. "Why can't I stay? I'm not tired. It seems I always am kept away from the interesting parts these days! You didn't send me away when I bashed the driver over the head!"

"I would have if I could have. This is classified, for old soldiers' ears only.

Right, Rubin?"
Rubin nodded solemnly, like an aging owl in his horned-rim glasses. "You're not a soldier anymore," she objected. "You're out of the KGB!" "As far as I know, I was never discharged from the U.S. Army," Peter countered.

"OK." She jumped to her feet. "I'll give you twenty minutes before I come back down and spy!" She turned to Rubin. "Thank you for the lovely dinner. I'm going upstairs to read about the Wings. There's a feature article about their success in the U.S. in Sports Illustrated!"

Rubin winced, then recovered with a smile. "It was a pleasure meeting you. Peter's a lucky man."

"Hmmm." She thought about his statement, her soft brown eyes steady on Peter's face. "In some ways, yes. In others, he has a tough time of it."

Both men watched Tasha gracefully turn the corner toward the stairs. "That's no weak-willed lady," commented Rubin.

"Hardly," acknowledged Peter.

"Sit down," said Rubin. "This might take a while."

For the next hour Rubin explained the situation, sparing Peter nothing. He tried to give him a full-dimensioned picture of President Dodge and Bollinger and the lines of power in the State Department, NSA, CIA, and the Executive Office. As Rubin faltered to a finish, Peter rubbed the deepening crease between his brows. "I can't quite digest all of this." He stretched his neck, chin reaching for the ceiling. "If I weren't right in the middle, I'd sit back and say 'Games within the games. Quelle fou!'" He paused, his mind searching for rational acceptance, a point of peace. He could find none. Rage engulfed him. "Jesus Christ!" He slammed his fist on the end table, violently shaking the brass lamp. "What kind of monsters are they? How much flesh do they want? Do you know how many deaths are on their heads already over this? I refuse to return and I won't sacrifice Aunt Katya or Tasha either. Do you know what they'd be put through when they got back?"

Rubin's lips turned into a fine line. He couldn't reply. The lump of national and personal guilt was too large for him to swallow.

"I think I'd shoot all of us before letting us go back." Peter raced on, "This is all supposed to happen day after tomorrow? Barely two days ago, we were heading south from Moscow, hoping against hope we would make it out of Russia. For what? To be sent back like common criminals by some power-hungry secretary of state. And for what? Some Russian Jews who may not even want to leave! Some mindless political campaign that may or may not be affected? It's insane! This double-dealing is what the Bolsheviks, the KGB, the Kremlin are supposed to do to each other. They're mild compared to you guys! This is supposed to be"—he slowed down to allow the sarcasm full reign—"the land of the brave and free . . . arms open wide for those wanting to breathe free. It was when I left it thirty years ago. I think they owe me for those thirty years." The scar on Peter's neck blazed red, but his blood had run dry. "I am still a citizen, Rubin."

"Katya and Tasha aren't."

"What are you saying? He'd send them back without me?"

"I don't know what he'd do. I put nothing past him. He'd find some slimy rule to allow extradition. So far all of this has been covert. The team thinks their defection is being accepted. We're under orders to say nothing until everyone is on the plane, heading east." Rubin was pale with his own anger. "If Bollinger were indicative of our entire government, I'd say fly the hell out of here fast." He paused, an idea forming in his mind. What if the return plane was diverted?

Peter walked to the window, gazed into the darkness, and banged his closed fist against the woodwork. "I could strangle him myself . . . personally."

"Or impersonally," added Rubin quietly. "Rubin, it can't end like this."

"There's one obvious thing to do, but I guess I'm looking for routes that preserve my position. But if he goes through with this, I won't have much fun looking at myself in the mirror."

"What are you talking about?"

"I can call a press conference, giving the story of your thirty years under cover. You'd have to be there, affirming your citizenship and happiness at being back in the U.S." He analyzed it briefly. "It might work. We could get some players there and Mattimore might cooperate."

"And it would cost both of you your jobs, right?"

"It's probably an ego thing, Peter, but I believe U.S. security is more honest and effective with me running NSA's Soviet desk."

"There could be other ways." Peter thought of the CkO network, remembering that Rudolph Kapinsky, Pentagon agent, was a most inventive man.

"Yes, but coming up with the right one is my responsibility. I'm the one who pulled you out. Israeli intelligence made it sound as though they were closing in on you."

So. The Israelis have a source inside, the KGB Sergei side of Peter's mind objected. Missed that one. His smile was wry. "Yes . . . I had the alert on. You see, Rubin, I was in charge of the search for the plant . . . the mole."

"Shit."

"Sooner or later . . . perhaps after I had retired as head of the KGB . . . You did know I was Taikov's heir apparent?"

Rubin's jaw dropped.

"But I hardly bargained for a confined vacation in the United States, finished off by a full-fledged court martial at best in the USSR." He stopped to light a cigarette. "Perhaps the only difference between the U.S. and the USSR is two initials."

Rubin also reached for a cigarette. "I don't blame you for feeling bitter. I feel damn bitter myself right now. I'd debated discussing this with you at all, Peter." He crushed an empty pack of cigarettes in frustration. "So help me, Peter, I'm going to do everything in my power to stop that madman if I have to." Rubin paused, biting off the thought. "You will be sent back over my dead body."

"Let's hope it doesn't come to that or we're both doomed," retorted Peter, trying to lighten the conversation and give room for reason. "It's better you've warned me of Bollinger's intent so I can be prepared for all eventualities." He deliberately quieted his thoughts. There was a lot to assimilate. "God, those poor innocent Wings," he said aloud.

"If you want to skip the debriefing tomorrow," Rubin spoke from his own dark thoughts without hearing Peter's comment. "I'll cover."

"I'd as soon stay busy. I think best while I'm working. And passing information is one of my specialties." He grinned. "I haven't come this far with so much to turn around, tuck my tail between my legs and go home, to use the word loosely. Now that I'm here, I want to observe for myself what's happened to our good old America, despite the Bollingers. One way or the other, Rubin, with you or without you, I'm going to put up a fight."

Rubin rose and placed his hand on Peter's strong shoulder. He adjusted his glasses. "I'll call you first thing in the morning. Until then, if you need me, the switchboard will track me down as long as you identify yourself."

"Rubin." Peter's voice was like ice. "If you don't have the stomach for it or don't want to involve your agents, I'd be willing to sanction Bollinger . . . for all of us." He still had a few double agents planted in the United States he could use. Rubin stopped short, realizing he'd finally caught a glimpse of Colonel Sergei Padov, code name Koral.

"As a last resort," Rubin's voice trailed off. It would be better to keepPeter clear of it if it came to that point. He didn't want anyone else put in a sacrificial position. Rubin said his good night quickly as he headed for his office to check J. L.'s packet and talk to NSA's medical experts.

Welcome home, Peter thought as he climbed the heavily carpeted stairs to join Tasha. He considered sharing the new twist to their adventure, a perverse political twist threatening all of them. He wanted to purge his highly classified brain, but he realized that if he told her now and they were able to remain, through whatever desperate measures required, she would share the bitter memory of the intended sellout. It was no way to begin a newlife.

Tasha lay on her back, Sports Illustrated bannering "Wings Fly Across America" on her chest. He smiled as he gently removed it. He'd looked forward to making love earlier in the evening. Now he would let her sleep.

His plans changed as she opened her eyes and reached her arms toward him. "Hello. I've been waiting for you."

Peter lost himself in passion, forcing his turmoil into his subconscious. It took him a long time, but Tasha didn't rush him, only clung tightly to him as though she were afraid, he'd disappear. Finally, spent with the many passions of the day, he fell into deep sleep.

# MOSCOW CENSUS BUREAU
## February 21
## 9:00 a.m.

Chief clerk Govorsky double-checked his lists. Fifteen thousand Jews. Sixteen junior clerks had worked around the clock, listing them by ages, addresses, and occupations. They had carefully honed the lists for the oldest, youngest, and least talented. The "most expendable" was the directive with priority given to those closest to the port. The list was now complete. Remembering the horrors of World War II, the list seemed ominous to Govorsky, but he quietly followed orders. It would reach the premier within the hour. He thought no further as he rang for the messenger, sealed the list in a secure envelope, and returned to his routine duties.

# MOSCOW

## The Kremlin

## February 21

## 9:40 a.m.

Taikov addressed the premier. "The list of Jews is being processed. We have telexed the Americans that our part of the trade is in order."

"Is it clear that we must have Colonel Padov returned within twenty-two hours or the trade is off?"

"Yes. You can read the telex yourself. The first five hundred Jews will be ready for shipment tomorrow. It is an unusual trade. I would think they'd do better to keep the Wings."

The premier nodded. "I don't understand it myself, but Bollinger is a crafty man. Whatever his motives, you can be assured he'll exploit his side of the trade. I am satisfied. We will have the Wings back without negative public reaction. They can be quietly punished and steadily replaced. Our people need never know."

"What they don't know, they cannot print. The defection was affected in complete secrecy. It was evidently planned from the inception with the trade in mind. At this point, we can't be sure if they coerced them into defecting only to double-cross them or if the team members initiated the defection and Bollinger hatched his plan subsequently. We must know that in time to determine the severity of the reprisals."

"We must know everything about their operation, everything," Taikov emphasized, rubbing the side of his nose where a small boil was forming. Nearly seventy, he was feeling the strain of the past several days.

"That is your area," the premier noted. "But I agree we must learn everything that can help put a stop to these defections that give Western journalists such pleasure."

"And I must know how and why Padov turned traitor. Where it all began. It is vital to our security that we know when he began working against us."

"Agreed." The premier rose. Taikov sprang to his feet. "Thanks to Mr. Bollinger, we shall have an opportunity to explore these areas. There is nothing else for the moment?"

"I'm personally attending to the arrangements to have Padov met in Turkey and returned in the style he deserves. I want no margin for error, no chance for him to reach anyone. His personal network of agents runs deep." He did not tell the premier that he knew of Padov's personal network generally but had never insisted Padov list the agents in the official KGB files. He'd agreed that an "unofficial" network could work to their advantage on many projects. He had trusted Padov as a son. But the CkO "Failsafe" had failed, indicting Sergei. Hardened as he was by a lifetime of callous intelligence operations, it hurt him deeply. Peter would have been surprised. The general had shown little emotion toward him in the last twenty years. And Peter was his handpicked successor.

Bob Moore arrived early. He'd picked up an early edition of the morning Post on his way home the night before. He was still recovering from the headline "SOVIET WINGS SECRETLY DEFECT." There was a two-column photo of Ivan Malitinsky and another photo of the "safe house." Bob dropped his briefcase and reached for the intercom.

Mattimore answered the ring himself. "Yes?"

"Bob here. Thought you might be in, sir. You've seen it?" "I'm glad you're early. Better get in here."

Bob hurried into Mattimore's office and sat down, paper in hand. "What do you think?"

"I think there has been a great big leak." "Putting it mildly."

"What do you think himself is going to do?"

"Our German weasel? Hard to say. Apoplexy seems probable."

Bob nodded. "I can't say I'm upset over the results. I liked the players, and I didn't like the double-cross."

"And I didn't like sending back Peter Porter."

They looked at each other, wondering if the other had been involved.

"He will have to accept the defection now, won't he? Has he given the go- ahead for comment?"

"Not yet, Bob. I have a call in to him. Officially, it's still no comment from the State Department. But that article is loaded with facts. There has to be an inside informant! Anyone who has that much information could be in a position to keep probing and get the whole dirty story. Bollinger wouldn't relish seeing his duplicity in headlines."

Mattimore looked at the article. "Alan Biddle. Know him?" Bob shook his head. "No. I wonder who his source was."

Mattimore laced his fingers across his narrow chest and looked across the bottom edge of his glasses at Bob. "I don't know. Period."

"End of story," finished Bob as the intercom buzzed.

Charles listened for a moment, then replied, "Right. I'll be there." He reached for his briefcase. "Emergency meeting in the Oval Office. It'll be interesting to see how Bollinger tries to maneuver at this point."

"I'll light a candle for you, boss."

"Better not. You might burn the place down before you have your report finished."

"I'll cross my fingers."

"Your handwriting's bad enough without crossed fingers!" He knew he'd be under fire for the leak, but his heartfelt relief infused him with good humor.

"OK, I'll keep it simple," Bob said. "Good luck." He watched his dedicated superior hurry from the office. Bob hoped his lighthearted mood wouldn't be crushed in the Oval Office. If Bollinger ran true to form, he'd put Mattimore's head on the block for the leak. Bob picked up his copy of the Post and crossed his fingers.

# WASHINGTON, D.C. THE OVAL OFFICE
## February 21
## 9:32 a.m.

Press Secretary Dave Kulper read the results of the poll he'd requested two hours before. "Mr. President," he summarized, "the public is overwhelmingly in favor of the defection. They love it."

"Good," the president nodded.

"Mr. Secretary," Dave addressed Bollinger, "what do I say if asked about the delay in announcing the defection?" He added with native sarcasm. "Were we saving it for George Washington's birthday?"

Bollinger glared at Dave.

The president looked at Bollinger. "It appears we must officially accept the defection." He looked steadily at Bollinger until Bollinger returned the look and slowly nodded.

"If we must announce it," grunted Bollinger, "it should be done here at the White House by the president himself."

"Good idea, Karl." Dodge smiled slightly. "It can't hurt our campaign. It might be as good as fifteen thousand Russian Jews and certainly much cleaner."

Dave's foot tapped impatiently. "When do we do this?"

"Noon would be good," said Bollinger. "If the deed were to be done, best it be done quickly."

"Impossible," advised Rubin. "The team and their families need more time to get ready."

"If we call it for two o'clock, the TV people will still have plenty of time to make the evening newscasts," Dave noted. "And it gives us more time to write the releases. I still haven't been given a good answer for why there was the delay between their disappearance in Philadelphia and the announcement."

Dodge looked at Bollinger for assistance. Bollinger carefully studied the crease in his trousers. Dodge turned next to Rubin who shrugged. Finally, he addressed Charles, "What can we say, Charles?"

"We could say," Charles began. He wanted to say Dave should tell them Karl tried to double-cross the team and the press blew it wide open. That would blow Dave out of the office. He continued calmly, "We had to wait until the families were safely in the U.S. It was part of their conditions for defecting." The half-truth should hold.

Dodge turned to Dave. "Got that?"

"Yes, Mr. President. If you don't need me for anything else, I'd like to get busy on this. We're only four hours away." He started to leave, then added, "I'll have your calendar cleared from two until three and make sure your remarks are on the teleprompter."

"Thanks, Dave. You keep me straight around here, and with this crew," Dodge indicated Charles, Rubin, and Karl. "I need that help."

And then some, added Dave silently as he said, "I'll have your draft remarks in to you by noon, Mr. President." "Fine."

As soon as the door closed behind Dave, Bollinger exploded, "I want to know where the leak came from! Charles! What do you know about this?"

Charles's lips tightened as he shook his head firmly. "Not a thing. I have my men investigating."

Bollinger's head swiveled toward Rubin. "What about your men? And who's checking with the CIA? They were involved too!"

Dodge, still comfortable with the image of the president publicly welcoming the Wings to freedom, raised his hand in protest. "Come, Karl, you can look into that later. What's done is done. And we gain from the defection this way. This version is fine."

Karl pounded his strong, plump fist on the arm of his chair. "Fine! Our security system is falling apart around us. We have got to get to the bottom of this immediately before anyone can cover their tracks. Whoever leaked information to the press is dangerous! Who knows what other information is in danger?"

"Yes," blandly agreed Dodge, "you must investigate, but right now we must worry about getting the team together and looking good for the two o'clock media conference."

"What do I tell the premier?" grumbled Bollinger. Dodge looked at Mattimore. "Charles?"

"We tell him, 'No deal,' Mr. President, and hope the press doesn't get its hands on the deal that was in the works."

Bollinger hefted himself to his feet. "Are we finished with this meeting?" He turned dramatically to Charles. "I am deeply disappointed in your performance. I placed you in charge of security, a security that appears to be nonexistent. I expect your resignation within twenty-four hours."

The president frowned. "Ease up, Karl. Charles has performed remarkably. You have no justification for blaming him. The leak could have come from dozens of directions."

Although the president had sprung to his defense, Charles didn't feel vindicated. His conscience would have felt better if he had been responsible for the leak.

Karl glared at Dodge. "I believe, Mr. President, I still run the State Department, unless you'd like my resignation?"

Dodge winced. "Of course, Karl. I have full confidence in you." Dodge turned to Rubin. "What about Major Porter? He's the real hero in all this."

"True, Mr. President, but I'd wager the KGB has a substantial price on his head. It's better to keep him quiet for now. They don't give up KGB colonels lightly."

"He intrigues me. What's his full name?"

"Peter Sergei Alexis Porter, Mr. President. His story is remarkable." "I must meet him soon."

"We can arrange for a private session at your convenience. I know he would be honored."

"Check with my appointment secretary as you leave, Rubin, and arrange it for this week. Maybe he'd enjoy a quiet dinner with Mrs. Dodge and myself."

The intercom buzzed. "Yes?" Dodge watched his ill-matched threesome as he listened. "Hold on a moment." He lowered the receiver. "Thank you, gentlemen. I'll see you again at quarter 'til two."

Bollinger led the small parade out of the office. Rubin stopped to set up an appointment for Peter. He dialed his switchboard and paged Elmer on the wireless. They made the connection. "Elmer?"

"Here, sir. What's up?"

"Take the ladies shopping immediately again for something to wear for a two o'clock press conference—at the White House. Nadia and Berthe." He grinned into the phone. "By the way, I think I figured out who the extra gardener was. Between you and me and the hedge."

"I'll bite. Who was he?"

"He wasn't a gardener. He was a stringer." "For all those 'posts' in the garden, right?" "You saw the paper!"

"Sure did, sir."

"Get going and have fun. Buy them the best." Rubin whistled his way along the White House corridors. He wanted to tell Peter personally. He believed he would have put his position on the line if it had become necessary or even taken more radical steps to remove Bollinger, but now it was not necessary. Bollinger had been overtrumped by the mysterious gardener-reporter guided by someone with access to the most private of conversations. Bollinger could push an investigation all he wanted to within the State Department. NSA had better things to do with its resources.

Taikov hurried into the premier's chambers. The portly leader greeted him with a telex, held in trembling fingers. "Read this! From Bollinger. I was on my way to a Hungarian dinner and almost missed it." The message was brief.

THE UNITED STATES OF AMERICA IS ACCEPTING THE DEFECTION OF THE WINGS OF THE SOVIET HOCKEY TEAM. NEGOTIATIONS HEREWITH CANCELLED.

"What kind of trick is this?" asked Taikov.

"No trick, it seems. It has been confirmed on diplomatic levels. Our Washington office is preparing a detailed report."

"I wonder," mused Taikov, "if Bollinger would negotiate separately for Padov and the women. The telex mentions only the team."

"We could demand it!"

Taikov coughed. The recent strain showed in the dark circles rimming his eyes and his gray complexion. He looked more like a hoary old bird than ever. "We can still find no satisfactory explanation of Padov's subversive involvement. We thought his girlfriend might be a Western agent, but her records check out clean. She had security clearance for her translating, also. With Padov's military records missing, we can't discount the possibility of a switch, that he was a long-term plant." "How critical is his return?"

"He had access to everything classified. If he is cooperating, already they could have detailed information on our international operations, names and stations of agents, codes. Already, we have recalled people and changed codes. But more important than that, I must know how our system failed— how and why he did whatever he did!"

The premier's eyes narrowed. "Our system did not fail. His did. Somewhere he became weak and corrupted." He slapped the desk with the telex. "Can't you immediately issue orders for his liquidation there, before they can drain all the information from him?"

"He is in a safe house, under tight security, we believe. We don't have an exact location yet."

"I shall bargain with Bollinger, but I also want the order out for his immediate liquidation—search, find, and destroy. We must make an example for others with the audacity to succumb to Western corruption."

"Yes, sir." Taikov hovered at the door, waiting to be dismissed. The premier shuffled through the papers on his desk. "Taikov!" without looking up.

"Yes, sir?"

"Wait before giving the order for extermination. I too am intrigued with what made this highly decorated hero of the State turn traitor. The answers to our questions could be exterminated along with him. We need him alive, long enough to question."

"We are investigating every small detail of his past. The missing files indicate he possibly was a plant, but we need to know when, if not how, he was placed. We need him."

"Then we must reopen negotiations with Bollinger, immediately."

# WASHINGTON, D.C. THE WHITE HOUSE
## February 21
## 12:45 p.m.

Bollinger read the decoded telex carefully. They wanted to reopen negotiations for Colonel Padov. Tempting. He could ask for the American spies and several thousand Jews, enough for a splash in the press at the right time. Padov was a heavyweight, he smiled to himself. Rubin was keeping him under wraps for security. Perhaps the game was not yet lost. Mattimore no longer was a problem. Silverstein would put up a fight side by side with Padov.

If only Dodge weren't aware of the man. He'd asked to meet him. Rubin had emphasized that the man was an American citizen with constitutional rights who could not, even if he wished, return to Russia. He searched the convoluted corners of his mind for another angle. Everything was too close to being brought out in the open. The leak had proven that someone had access to the most highly classified information. If that someone hadn't approved of dealing for the team's return, they might be equally unhappy with a Padov trade deal. Both Mattimore and Silverstein seemed too unconcerned about the leak. It wouldn't surprise him if they were behind it. He chewed on his fleshy underlip then scrawled his reply. "Working on plan to negotiate for Padov. Terms to follow." He coded it himself and hand carried it into the transmission room. No point in risking a leak at that end. He decided to do his thinking about terms over a large lunch before the press conference.

Little B raced into the living room and announced, "Mommy! Ivan and Yori are on TV! They're defecting! Come watch!"

Mattie's head swung toward Tom. "But you said," she began.

He'd been briefed earlier by Shields. He was prepared. He waited until B had pulled his grandmother out of the living room. Rob, Ellen, and Mattie waited for Tom to speak. "Your husband died a hero's death, Mattie. I had to give it to you backward until the official announcement. He was killed stopping a KGB guard from interfering with the defection."

"Why couldn't you tell me that? What was wrong with the truth?"

"We were under orders to say nothing until they were safely united with their families," Tom explained.

"Orders," Rob spoke derisively, "that turn fact to fiction and fiction to fact on command?"

Mattie had grown to trust Tom in the past twenty-four hours. She had to believe him. "I understand," she spoke quietly.

Ellen rose. "Shall we watch the ceremony? I'd like to see it."

"You go ahead," Mattie told them all. "I don't think I could bear to watch the . . . all that happiness today."

"Brian helped make it possible," Ellen spoke gently. "You don't even want to watch for posterity?"

"It's too personal. Posterity should be impersonal."

Ellen hesitated, not certain how to respond. Rob took her arm and directed her toward the TV room. "We'll give you a report later—if you want."

Mattie sat motionless. She was glad Brian's death was more than a meaningless gesture, but it really didn't matter that much. Either way, he was dead.

Tom left her to her silence. He picked up a copy of Children's Digest and skimmed it.

Mattie glanced up at him, gratefully. She was glad he was there. His presence was comforting, protective. Her vision of the CIA and Shields himself was colored by her positive picture of Tom. He had been selected carefully for the assignment for those very reasons.

She was feeling restless. "Tom?" He looked up from the magazine. "Would you drive me over to the church?"

"Sure."

"I want to go over the arrangements with the priest one last time. You called the papers and asked them to request donations to the children's hospitals rather than flowers, didn't you?"

"I made the call from Philadelphia last night." Bob Shields had told Tom there would be a wreath of white roses from the president. He hoped she'd be pleased.

McLean, Virginia

Safe House No. 1

February 21

2:20 p.m.

Peter, Tasha, Rubin, and Aunt Katya wordlessly watched the press conference. It was a first. The first time a major defection had occurred on national TV. The president himself was accepting the plea for asylum and welcoming the Wings. "In the spirit of our forefathers Abraham Lincoln and George Washington, you have chosen an appropriate month to accept the call to freedom." Dave Kulper had thoroughly briefed the president on the team. Dodge cited individual members' accomplishments, even mentioning the final score for the Wings-Capitals game. Few noticed, as Dodge shook each one's hand and mentioned them by name, that the players stood in careful order corresponding to the file cards on the podium. Nadia Vladistock and little Vladimir looked well dressed and rosy cheeked. Berthe Malitinsky was the image of the proud mother, dumpy enough to warm the hearts of aging overweight viewers.

As the Purina cat chow commercial replaced the presidential ceremonies, Tasha asked Rubin, "Why wasn't Peter there?"

Peter answered quickly. "First, I didn't defect. I'm already an American citizen. You and Aunt Katya have defected and there'll be some proceeding soon. Right?" He looked at Rubin.

"But we'll make it simple. I'll personally bring you forms and see to the processing." Rubin regretted telling Peter about Bollinger's plans. It put a cynical light on his return "home," but there had been no way to foresee this twist in events. Peter seemed calm, pleased with the events. "I probably shouldn't let the cat out of the bag, but I can't resist . . ." Rubin paused for effect.

"What does that mean?" asked Tasha. "'Cat out of the bag?'"

Rubin chuckled as the drama disappeared in the need for explanation. "It's an American expression that means revealing a secret. You are going to be invited to privately meet the president later this week so he can personally thank you."

A lot must have happened since Rubin warned me about Bollinger's counterplot, thought Peter, certain Rubin would fill him in later. He sighed softly. We begin our American life with a skeleton in the closet. "That will be an honor," he said.

In Russian, Katya asked for a translation, as they spoke too quickly for her. As Peter explained, she said seriously, "I am not so concerned, my Peter, with meeting your president as I am with meeting my sister—your mother— soon."

Peter took her hand, "We shall talk to her soon, but I think it's important that someone prepare her." Peter looked at Rubin. "Now that our cats are jumping out of bags, can you arrange to have someone personally talk with my mother, gently tell her we are alive?"

Rubin, switching into Russian for Katya's benefit, said, "I know just the person. I have business in New York, and although I was scheduled to go tomorrow, there are planes out all afternoon. I'll tell her myself, tonight." Peter smiled. "In fact, Peter, I'll call you from her apartment and put her on the phone. If you and she decided it's best, I'll even bring her back to Washington. How's that for service?"

"The best so far." Peter grinned.

Rubin checked his watch and quickly rose. "OK, I'm off to catch the next plane. I should be at your mother's by nine tonight. Expect a call no later than eleven. If I'm later than that, I'll call anyway."

"Thanks, Rubin." Peter walked him to the door. "You're going above and beyond—"

"Don't above and beyond me," interrupted Rubin. "You've been doing that for years." He hurried out the door. For the first time in years, he felt a sudden urge to cry. This strong, forgiving man was the one Bollinger wanted to send back to Russia like fodder. He stopped for a moment, letting the brisk February air clear his mind. He'd have to call his office first, get Mrs.

Porter's address and number, and let them know where he was heading. It should be an interesting evening, thanks to an interesting leak that had saved Karl's life. He'd called off Karl's early morning medical "checkout."

Inside the house, Aunt Katya spoke, "It is hard for me to understand English when it is spoken so quickly. I catch a few words and phrases, but no more. You and Tasha must speak to me in English, but slowly. Perhaps it will come back."

"I'll help," promised Tasha. "If you teach me to make your wonderful walnut cake!"

Peter laughed. "Less than a week in the United States and you're turning domestic. Last week you were claiming you could get a job anywhere!"

Tasha became serious. "Peter, what will we do for work here? Will Rubin find jobs for us?"

"I think I'm still in the U.S. Army. They probably owe me a pile of back benefits." He grinned. "Talk about double-dipping!"

"Peter!" interrupted Katya. "You know you have all the money you could ever need. "If your father didn't keep your trust funds for you, we still have our accounts in Switzerland. I have the numbers for mine and Sergei's as well as for Uncle Alexis's. Even without those, we have the jewels."

Peter gave Katya a big hug. "Mother," he began. "Aunt," she corrected.

"Mother-aunt, you are not to worry about any of this now. And you"—he turned to Tasha—"are to put job-hunting out of your head and concentrate on cake-baking."

Tasha was shocked. "Are you very rich?" "Very, very," Katya nodded.

"Then why . . ." began Tasha, but she couldn't put her thoughts into sufficient order to ask the questions. Her Party upbringing hadn't included dealing with being "very, very rich" in or out of Russia. "Are we going to stay in this house a long time? Will this be our home?"

"No, these are temporary quarters. But I believe we'll be here a while. The debriefing could take months. Filling them in on thirty years when I only have my old brain to help will take time." Names, faces, specialties flashed through his mind. He knew he was clear on current operatives in the United States; he'd made a point of staying current on those. Other places, other people would take more concentration. But they were not all clear. He knew the KGB too well to think they would write him off easily. They would sooner kill him than . . ."

"Peter?" Tasha broke into his reverie. "Yes? Sorry, my mind had wandered."

"Can we go out to an American restaurant tonight? I want to wear one of my new dresses."

"You're becoming Americanized quickly," Peter said. "But not tonight. We must wait for Rubin and my mother to call." They couldn't spend their lives holed up, afraid, but he knew they couldn't live in the open, using real names. If they did, he'd need heavy protection. Plastic surgery? New identities? Could they find a way to call off the inevitable KGB search? It hit him that he may have had greater freedom as the counterfeit Sergei Padov, recognized and accepted in Soviet society. For a moment, despite the luxury surrounding them, despite the prospect of seeing his family, despite the knowledge he was free from the cruel tasks of the KGB, he felt a strong sense of loss realizing his thirty years of undercover work for the United States had to be rewarded with restricted freedom. Perhaps it was knowing that even in the United States there had to be the Bollingers. If he had known thirty years ago what he knew now, would he have. . . ?

Tasha broke his thoughts with a hug as she asked, "Shall we have a good life in America, Peter?"

The phone rang, postponing an answer. "Hello," Peter answered. He listened, his forehead wrinkling with concern. "Right now?" He paused. "I'll be ready."

"Who was that?" Tasha asked. "Bad news?"

"I don't know. Bollinger wants a personal meeting with me this moment. I can't check it with Rubin. He's on his way to New York."

"What does that have to do with anything?"

"Rubin didn't mention any meeting with Bollinger." "May I come along and meet this pig Bollinger?"

"No." In some ways she was a child-woman, treating a meeting with Bollinger like late-night entertainment. "You are to remain here and learn to bake!"

She wrinkled her nose. "If I do, you will only get fat and round, like a capitalistic pig!"

Peter answered with a fast thwack on her rear. "To the kitchen. I must attend to matters of state."

B ollinger popped a cherry drop in his mouth and savored the burst of flavor. The terms: seven thousand Russian Jews ready to be shipped in twenty-four hours. That would still be good press. BOLLINGER  NEGOTIATES RECORD  RELEASE  OF SOVIET JEWS. Yes.

He would wait and send the telex as soon as that Padov fellow was half-way to Turkey. He felt his saliva thicken with the sweet cherry syrup. It would be magnificent.

# ANDREWS AIR FORCE BASE
## February 21
## 3:45 p.m.

The unmarked Mercury squealed to a halt beside the airfield. Peter leaned forward and tapped the driver's right shoulder. "Is Bollinger here?"

"I don't know, sir. My orders are to bring you to Captain Reynolds."

How these state department types like to play CIA games, thought Peter.

Secret meetings with Bollinger on a plane—his thoughts froze. Why the airfield? His defection . . . he slipped . . . his return had not been announced. The KGB must want him back. If Bollinger had been willing to sell out an entire hockey team, he'd be capable of side bets. Good poker. Cover yourself. Lose one, win another. His jaw tightened as a young captain approached. Peter glared at him.

"Colonel Padov, follow me."

Colonel Padov? Peter's mind raced. Here he was called Captain Porter. "Where is Mr. Bollinger?" he demanded.

The young captain tried to quickly size up the man half-shadowed in the car. Attractive middle-aged man. Looks straight. Good air of authority. Their spies were improving. "You are to follow me."

"Follow you where? I was told I was meeting with Secretary Bollinger. I demand to know what is going on."

As Peter's temper flared, the captain eyed him warily. Strong character. He might try something. Good English. He sounded American. He waved his hand and four MPs quickly stepped in position beside him. His orders were to take the man, by force if necessary. "You are to come with me."

"And I repeat, I demand to see Bollinger." He turned to the driver. "Take me back to McLean immediately."

The driver stared straight ahead, focusing on the airport lights. "My orders were to deliver you to Captain Reynolds. This is Captain Reynolds."

"I insist you contact Rubin Silverstein at once." Reynolds looked blank. "Who is he?"

"The director of the NSA!"

"Oh yes." The name had sounded vaguely familiar. "I am acting directly under the order of the secretary of state and the president. You are to contact no one."

There was no way Rubin could be aware of this latest switch. He was on his way to New York if he wasn't there already. Peter focused on the irony of Rubin visiting his mother to tell her he was alive and well and in the United States. How would it end?

J. L. couldn't stop grinning. He's been in charge of communications for the press conference. The press didn't know, he thought, just how much he'd been in charge. He slipped the wire disc into the NSA security pouch, not bothering to listen, called for a secure messenger, then headed for the elevators. Time to get wrecked. He'd told Alan to meet him at Jenkins Hill.

Alan, waiting at the bar, raised his arms in victory as J. L. entered. It struck

J. L. that Alan's byline was all over the stories. "Alan, pay the check and let's get out of here." A Capitol Hill press hang-out was no place for a covert source to celebrate with a reporter.

B ob Moore stuck his head into Mattimore's office, "Boss? You still here?"
"Come on in, Bob." Charles put down a file and gave Bob his undivided
attention. "You saw the press conference?" "Impressive."

Mattimore removed his glasses. "Politicians can change courses so blithely." He pictured Bollinger's smiles and congratulations. Dodge's perfect poise.
As though neither one would have considered a double-cross. "It's been a long,
long week. For the record, Bob, I have to ask you a question."

"Yes?"

"Have you made any progress tracking down the leak?"

Bob looked guilty. He'd been so gratified by the results of the leak, he'd
forgotten that directive. "I'm sorry, sir, I haven't done anything on it."

Charles looked fondly at his assistant. "Well, be sure you get around to
it"—he raised his eyebrows—"one of these years."

Bob got the message. "Yes, sir."

Mattimore began packing his briefcase to go home. "In a way it would
be nice to know . . ."

Bob waited for him to finish the thought.

"Know who had the guts to do what we all would have liked to do." He

319

snapped the catch on his briefcase. "Have a good night. Take your wife out, go dancing. And don't come in until noon tomorrow. That's an order!"

"Isn't there any freedom around here?"

Charles grinned. "Depends upon how you view things."

Bob looked at him, fascinated. He'd never seen Mattimore grin.

"And Bob, when you wander in around noon, be prepared for a long lunch.

"We have a lot to talk about." The grin had disappeared. "Serious?"

"I've been Bollingered—and I don't want it to happen to you in my wake. We need some honest men in this town." Without giving Bob time to reply, he called "see you tomorrow" as he briskly walked out the door.

# MID-ATLANTIC
## Inside a Boeing 707
## February 21
## 7:00 p.m.

"I am not at liberty to discuss either your destination or the purpose of the trip." Reynolds had been briefed that Sergei Padov was a KGB spy being sent back to the Russians for trying to bribe military officials.

"But I'm an American, as much a citizen as you are. You have no right to transport me anywhere without my permission." I'm still military, he thought, who knows where my rights lie? It was still worth a try.

Having been warned that Padov would try to concoct misleading stories, Reynolds turned a deaf ear. He'd been selected for this mission because of his unquestioning loyalty. He was more than intelligence; he was commando trained. Trusted no one. He prided himself on his gut reactions. He'd sworn over many a Thai brew that he could smell a traitor from a hundred yards. Padov didn't smell like one, but neither had that soft, fragrant Vietnamese whore. And he had slit her throat on orders one summer afternoon right after making the most fantastic love he'd ever known. He didn't feel normal guilt. He had memories—smooth golden honey skin dripping with fresh blood. Her face peaceful, a look of surprise frozen by death. She'd given him asylum among the black marketers and political whores of the steaming city, saving him more than once from enraged Vietcong who would as soon kill an American as a mosquito. The suggestion that he should feel guilt would have made him laugh. It had been an order. Someone knew something about her he didn't; she was a risk, and the order was executed on schedule.

# Code Coral

Peter sat back and enjoyed his last Winston 100. He'd been back long enough to prefer American cigarettes. It didn't take long. This Reynolds was real military. The MP cadre had joined them for the flight. Even if he could overpower Reynolds, it wouldn't do any good. Besides, his hand-to-hand combat training was rusty; Reynolds looked taut and trained. And not a cyanide capsule in sight. His last-minute call to Kapinsky to set up a Bollinger sanction was a flail against fate, a plan as lame as Rudolph's left leg. Peter was in no position to give the final command as planned. He sighed audibly.

"Do you want a drink?" Reynolds leaned toward him. "Shall I ring the stewardess?"

"Is she attractive?"

"She looked pretty good."

"Then get her and leave me alone for a while."

"Impossible. Where you go, I go until we reach our destination."

"Maybe a stiff drink will help." Peter watched Reynolds ring for the stewardess. "What is our destination?"

Can't hurt to tell him at this point, decided Reynolds. He's not going anywhere else. "Turkey. That's where I leave you and come back home."

Turkey, mused Peter. Sold out like a holiday turkey. Maybe there's an escape hatch before I get sent to the oven. There may be time. At least we're not heading directly to Moscow. There were two CkO Agents near Station Rho. If he could contact one of . . .

The stewardess, approaching with a rolling tray, interrupted his thoughts. "What would you like?"

"A double scotch, on the rocks."

The plane lurched in an air current. The smile remained fixed on the redhead's freckled face. "Coming up."

The metal desk lamp gleamed in the incandescent light. The premier's small round eyes bulged as his blood pressure rose. He crumpled the report in his little fist and banged it on the desk. "Rape! International rape, Taikov!"

"Let me see, sir." Taikov waited for the premier to recover himself and hand over the report. Taikov smoothed out the papers and skimmed, reading highlights aloud, "Charles Vickers . . . CIA . . . three fingerprints intact . . . Turkish ownership of F-111 confirmed . . ." His jaws muscles twitched as he read. "I knew it wasn't a navigational error, no green pilot's accident! Vickers was one of their best. We've followed his career for years." Taikov's explosion matched the premier's. "This whole thing was CIA instigated from the beginning!"

The premier enjoyed watching his icy cool KGB chief explode. He nodded, fanning the flame. "The U.S. thinks they can stomp over us like foolish beetles, playing games. Making terms, rescinding them. This puzzle begins to fit together making the picture of a cesspool. Bollinger must pay for his arrogance!"

"What about the Turkish traitors?"

"They're in their own hot water," the premier stated. "And they shall continue to pay for playing the puppets of the Americans, you can be certain." The wrinkled pouches above and below the premier's eyes moved closer together, his eyes becoming glimmers behind the slits. "We shall retaliate. Theirs was a navigational error." He spat the term.

"Ours shall be a terrible computer error. A technical accident. A nuclear missile accidentally released, aimed at their so-called secret Station Rho. An emergency message shall be dispatched immediately—through official diplomatic channels . . . due to trouble with our transatlantic lines. A bonus payback. It is unfortunate that diplomatic channels are so subject to delays. We ourselves shall dispatch a bomber squadron to attempt to intercept the missile, but alas, we cannot get air clearance to fly into Turkish air on such short notice. Our squadron, in obedience of international law, must turn back at the Turkish border. We would not want to make the mistake of being guilty of border violations. Mr. Vickers has taught us an important lesson in that regard." Angry sarcasm dripped from the premier's words. "It will be a most unfortunate incident. I shall personally cable my sincere regrets both to President Dodge and to Bollinger."

Taikov's rational nature gained the upperhand as he listened to the premier's scheme. "Those are extreme measures. They could backfire and set off a major holocaust."

"Our ambassador will be waiting at the White House door to assure Mr. Dodge and Mr. Bollinger that we consider the dreadful accident as evening the score. Any further action on the part of the U.S. will be considered hostile aggression and we shall respond accordingly."

"I have assurances that Bollinger will live up to his deal to trade back Padov for the Jews. It is reported that Padov is already headed for Turkey."

An evil smile creased the premier's lips. "Perhaps he shall land in time for our little surprise."

"He is scheduled to arrive tomorrow morning. One of our military planes is on orders to meet him at the Rho airfield. Shall I cancel the order?"

"No, we do nothing to arouse their suspicion. If everything can be arranged quickly enough, you may move up the accident accordingly."

"I would prefer to wait until we have Padov back in our hands in Moscow.

We still have many questions that are unresolved."

"And let Bollinger have his seven thousand Jews? Rot! May he rot! They have already milked Padov dry as a witch's teat. I don't want to give that low life another thing except something to think about next time he gets any clever ideas. I want that missile in the air before dawn! That's an order, General!"

The premier's mind was set. There was nothing to be gained by arguing, but Taikov could not let him unleash a nuclear warhead and trigger a holocaust. He began by reinforcing the premier's righteous anger and eased into the suggestion that the missile carry a nonnuclear conventional warhead. It would accomplish the object lesson without bringing adverse public reaction to potential nuclear fallout and avoid triggering an emotional and possibly devastating response.

The premier wasn't concerned with the mechanics, only his immediate result. "Put whatever kind of warhead on the thing you like, Taikov, as long as it blows that so-called secret base off the face of the globe!"

Taikov saluted and retreated.

Something was scratching in the attic. Leaves or rats or branches or ghosts. The windows rattled. The room was freezing. Tasha couldn't find an extra blanket. She pulled Peter's sweater on over her head. It was impossible to read or sleep. What was he doing? Where was he? Despite the luxury, the lonely bedroom was depressing. If he'd gone from the meeting with Bollinger to a debriefing session, he could have called, she thought irritably. She'd never liked Bollinger's looks from the photos in Pravda. She decided to go downstairs and make a cup of tea. Perhaps it would help.

No slippers. No lights. Guided by the smooth banister, she felt her way across the dark hall and down the stairs. She didn't reason out her stealthy descent. Somehow, she didn't want to disturb the empty rooms and halls.

The night light above the stove beaconed to her from the dark hallway. She scampered across the chilly hardwood toward the colder Spanish tiles in the kitchen and the teapot. As she neared her goal, the back door was flung open, and a bright light caught her in its beam.

"What?!" she started and froze, a fawn trapped by the hunter.

Elmer turned off his flashlight as he switched on the kitchen light. "What are you doing prowling around in the dark?" he asked angrily. "I could have shot you!"

"I came down for some tea!" Tasha replied equally angry. "You almost scared me to death!"

"If I hadn't looked in the back door, I'd never have seen you. You'd make a great cat burglar."

Tasha frowned. "What's a cat burglar? Someone who steals cats?"

Elmer guffawed, animating his face and creating elongated dimples creasing his cheeks. "No," he explained. "It's a burglar who moves like a cat, sneaking in and out of places."

"And scratches like a cat when challenged?" "Perhaps."

"Where is Peter?"

"Still with Bollinger as far as I know. It's a long session!" The phone rang. "Peter?" breathed Tasha.

"Want to get it?" The phone rang again.

"Yes, before it wakes Aunt Katya." She picked up the receiver, "Hello?" Disappointment filled her eyes. "Rubin. Yes. No, I was awake, waiting. Peter isn't back from his meeting."

From his suite in the Pierre, Rubin began filling her in on his attempts to reach Peter's mother. Her maid's English was terrible. Mrs. Porter was visiting friends in East Hampton. She hadn't left the number. The maid didn't know the names of the friends. She thought Mrs. Porter might be back tomorrow, but she wasn't certain. He'd already made a discreet call to the East Hampton chief of police but would wait until tomorrow before taking further action. Suddenly he stopped short. "Tasha, did you say Peter was at a meeting?"

"Yes, with Bollinger. He got a call hours ago and rushed off. Bollinger sent a car."

Rubin fought a red rage rising in him. Secret meeting with Karl! Why hadn't his men reported it? "Is Elmer there?"

"Right beside me. We were going to have tea." "Put him on!"

Elmer took the phone. "Yes, sir? Is there a problem?"
"Where's Peter?"

"At a meeting with Bollinger. He left before I came on duty. I assumed you knew."

"I wasn't informed. Somebody screwed up. Who was on before you?" "Fred Jameson."

"Don't let anyone else out of that house even if the president himself shows up in a limousine!" Rubin slammed down the phone. First Jameson. Then Bollinger. Something stanks.

# TURKEY
## Station RHO February 22
## 4:46 a.m.

Sergeant Jim Blaire wasn't dreaming of bombs flashing on Saipan mountains. He was sleeping like a long baby, mouth half open, pillow damp from his slight drool. Patrick McLaughlin tossed and turned, dreaming of Donna Anne Dougherty, his girl back home. The U.S. mail had delayed her latest letter.

They were innocents when the warheads hit, dead center.

Security systems went off worldwide. In Washington, alarms sounded at the Pentagon, triggered by signals from the NATO towers in Mons, Belgium. Within minutes, the secure phones beside the sleeping secretary of state and the president rang. Both were taken by surprise.

Tasha's knuckles whitened as she gripped her teacup and stared at Elmer. "I have a terrible premonition . . . something dreadful is happening."

"What do you mean?"

"I've gotten such feelings since childhood. They laughed at me in school. Old Russian superstition they would say. I was stupid. But whenever I get them, something terrible does happen."

"Such as?"

"Like when the Hungarians were all killed in the revolution, the uprising they called it. When my father died. Even when my supervisor had a stroke, which nearly killed him. I knew something was happening . . . it's a dark, hollow feeling in my stomach. I can't explain it. I only hope Peter is not . . ." Her voice trembled with sudden tears.

"You're upset because Peter isn't back. It can't be much longer. Rubin himself is tracking him down."

"But we haven't heard from Rubin."

"He'll call back," Elmer reassured her. Perhaps Tasha's premonition had merit. Rubin had sounded upset. "Why don't you go upstairs and try to get some rest. It's late. Peter can wake you himself when he gets in."

Tasha rubbed her neck. "I can't. I feel too helpless and afraid. I wish I knew what was going on . . . where he is!"

"OK, if you're not going to sleep, you might as well entertain me. Why don't I teach you to play some American cards?" He pulled a well-worn deck from his pocket, adorned with the presidential seal.

"I'm not in the mood to learn new American games. I'm afraid we're in the middle of one." She ran her fingers through her newly washed golden hair. She stared out the window. "It's so dark. I can't see a thing."

# GEORGETOWN
## February 22
## 11:00 p.m.

L ooking like a Prussian satyr, curly gray hair adorning his solid paunch, Bollinger growled into the phone, "You're certain it was a Russian missile?" The voice unscrambled electronically in Bollinger's ear.

"Yes, sir. They left so many clues. It's as though they wanted us to know." Bollinger grunted. "Like what?"

"First of all, the radar tracked one of the missiles from a launching site near Kirovavad. They know we monitor that one. We wiped it out midair, but the second one got through to Rho. Totalled. We have clean-up crews on the spot now. It's a mess. It appears there are no survivors."

Thinking half aloud, Bollinger muttered, "What can we tell the press?

What could have prompted it?" "What was that sir?"

"Any other clues?"

"After changing their codes for the past three days, they reverted back to the old codes, the ones we'd gotten keys for. They also broadcast the incident, calling it a misfire. According to our calculations, they aired the story three minutes before the missiles were fired. The broadcast was in all languages, obviously preplanned. The Turks are being besieged by the press. They've been in touch with us, asking how they should respond."

"Any mention of Rho?"

"No, the Russian broadcasts indicate the missile hit in a desolate mountain region. There was an official apology for border intrusion. The Turks want to know if they should confirm the story, avoiding the mention of Rho."

Bollinger's mind caught on his station chief's phrase, "apology for the border intrusion." They must have confirmed the U.S. intervention with the Turkish F-111 flights. "How" didn't matter anymore. The Soviets were ignoring the Red Phone alerts. Switchboards were stonewalls. Impersonal telexes sent in the clear stated that the premier and staff would not be available until the morning. There was no way of knowing if the shipment of Russian Jews was still on. Only he and a trusted few knew that Padov was . . . He had to move quickly.

The station chief was asking him what the Turks should tell the press. "Tell them to issue no comments other than that they recognize there has been an accident and an investigation has been called. The Russian ambassador has assured us we will receive a detailed technical report on the mishap. The premier is not answering phone calls. That's all I can tell you until tomorrow. Relay necessary information to the proper people!"

Jeanne, returning from the kitchen in Karl's favorite peignoir, went unnoticed. "Karl?" she hesitated as he slammed down the phone. "Is it serious?"

"I'm busy, can't you see? Go back to bed—in the spare bedroom" "Karl, I have security clearance, why must—"

"Leave me," he barked. He turned his hairy back and picked up the flashing phone. "Mr. President," he clipped into the direct line, "I'll call you back in five minutes. I must make a critical call." He turned to his frozen wife. "Move!"

"I forgot to tell you," she hesitated. "A Rubin Silver-something-or-other called and left a number. He sounded threatening. He said if you knew what was good for you, you'd call him back immediately. Is it important? The number's downstairs. Shall I get it?"

Karl hurled his Steuben crystal elephant against the wall beside her, missing her by inches. "Get out!" he screamed.

She left the room without another word as he grabbed the phone. "Get me General MacRimple!"

# Seven hundred Miles East of
# Tehran Boeing 707
# February 22
# 2:56 a.m.

The stewardess, trailed by an MP, approached Reynolds without a smile.

Reynolds looked up and raised his eyebrows. "Yes?" She leaned down and whispered in his ear. He rose and stepped back, giving the MP room to take his seat beside Peter. "I'll be back."

Now what? thought Peter as he watched Reynolds being swallowed by the silver curtains leading to the front cabin. Direct route to Moscow? No last chance in Turkey? If he could make it out of Rho, CkO Turkey might help. Becoming a renegade free agent would be preferable to returning to certain death in Moscow, but it would not be an easy choice.

He ignored the wooden-faced MP and stared out the window for nine eternal minutes. He traveled from childhood memories of playing ball in Central Park while his nursemaid cried dire warnings to Black Sea vacations to Tasha's arms and back before Reynolds returned, a hint of question in his cool gray eyes.

The MP rose, giving way to Reynolds who spoke as he sat down again next to Peter. "The State Department has ordered us back to Andrews. I also have a message for you from NSA Director Silverstein. I don't understand it at all. Perhaps it will mean something to you." Reynolds recited carefully, "Crimson outflanked the Bulldog in the last match."

Peter silently tried to decipher the message. Could crimson relate to his codename "Koral"? Was there a mistake in transmission? He let his mind go blank for a minute, letting his subconscious trigger his memory. It hit him. He chuckled aloud. Crimson was for Harvard! Bollinger had gone to Yale.

"You understand the message?"

"Indeed." Peter smiled. "What's today's date?" he asked Reynolds to change the subjectReynolds glanced at his watch. "Here, it's February 22. It's still the twenty-first in Washington."

"We'll be home by George Washington's birthday. Maybe I can find a cherry tree by the Potomac to chop down."

"What?" Reynolds gave him a puzzled look.

"To celebrate arriving home free. For the second time this week." "The second time?" Reynolds frowned.

"I cannot tell a lie. The second time. And, Captain, I also did not lie about being an American citizen. Whoever ordered this flight made a considerable mistake in judgment. I do not like mistakes in judgment." He knew too well who had issued the orders.

Something in Peter's tone sent a chill along Reynolds's spine. Reynolds looked away from Peter's dark eyes. He swallowed an urge to ask questions.

# BOLLINGER'S TOWNHOUSE GEORGETOWN, WASHINGTON, D.C.
## February 22
## 3:00 a.m.

The doorbell buzzed insistently. Karl turned restlessly in his sleep. Why didn't Jeanne rouse herself in the guest bedroom? Did she take sleeping pills again? Did he have to do everything himself?

His head felt swollen, and one last time, he swore off the extra good night brandies. Slowly he reached for his dressing gown and slippers to pad down the steps. The doorbell continued, unrelenting and yet strangely patient.

He stopped and peered through the small hole. The tall man was backlit by the streetlight, with an uncanny halo. "Who is it?" Bollinger rasped.

"Adams, NSC, CIA," replied the man who slipped his credentials through the mail slot. Bollinger turned on a light and carefully inspected the papers. "What do you want?"

"I have a message from Rubin Silverstein, crucial." "Why didn't Rubin call me himself?"

"He went to New York."

"Oh yes, that's right." Karl rubbed his sagging jowls. He turned off the burglar alarm and unlocked the door. Adams smiled, lifting one corner of his mouth slightly.

He moved toward Karl, stretching out his hand in greeting. "We haven't met, but I've heard so much about you, Mr. Secretary."

Karl reached groggily for the outstretched hand. Beneath Adams's strong grip he felt a nerve twitch with a sudden sharp itching at the base of one finger. Bollinger lifted his chins and shook his head to focus on Adams. The man was babbling.

"Mr. Secretary, I am to tell you the deal is off. Not even you can double-cross the Constitution. Porter will be staying here, where he belongs. Rubin wanted me to deliver this message. I think, if he hadn't been in New York tonight, he might have cancelled this meeting. But I thought it best that we keep our appointment."

Karl was puzzled and his face flushed with rage at this fool. "You—," he began, when his chest was squeezed in an iron clutch. His knees buckled, and he felt the floor come up and hit him against his face. His chest, his back were on fire. How could he, Karl Bollinger, mover of nations, be staring at this man's feet and his ugly brown Oxfords? He heard himself moan, and for the first time in his life, he felt embarrassed and suddenly afraid.

"Good-bye, Mr. Secretary," Adams said as he looked down at the classic case of cardiac arrest, stepped past Bollinger, reactivated the burglar alarm, and locked the door. On the street he glanced at his watch and felt again the weight of the school ring on his right hand, the class ring with the hidden Medici needle and the Latin inscription.

He stopped short, alert to a hidden presence. A short wiry man with a cane stepped from behind a large pot of impatiens beside a doorway and bowed politely. "My best to our colonel," he whispered before melting into the dark.

"So, we are to dine with the president of the United States?" Aunt Katya asked to be certain she had heard correctly. Tasha nodded. Rubin had called earlier to say Peter had stayed overnight in the debriefing center and would be back soon. Sophie had been located in South Hampton, and Rubin said she would be joining them at the White House later in the week. Katya's long night of fears had given way to a glowing morning.

Aunt Katya excused herself and went to her room, thinking it was like the old days, dining with the czar and czarina. Tasha was standing by the window, watching a cardinal perched on the lower branch of a blue spruce. She felt the older woman return and smiled. "It's a beautiful day."

"Turn around, child," said Katya. "I have a surprise for you."

As the old woman fastened the heavy necklace around her slender neck, Tasha gasped at the emeralds Prince Rudolph Padarovsky had given his young wife fifty-eight years before. "Oh," she said, "they are so beautiful."

"We must present ourselves as proper Russians before this president," Katya replied.

"Oh, Mother Padov." Tasha threw her arms around the fragile matriarch. "Thank you."

"Hello! I'm home," Peter called and stepped into the living room, followed by Rubin. Tasha, emeralds glittering, ran across the room into his arms. "Now I'm home," she whispered.

Peter kissed her. Out of one corner of his eye, he saw Rubin smile shyly. He must ask Rubin about the radio broadcast they'd heard in the car on

Bollinger's death. And thank him. Or Rudolph Kapinsky. It was good to have friends.

# WASHINGTON, D.C.
## Old Executive Office Building
## February 22
## 11:00 a.m.

J. L. didn't complain about his hangover as usual. Alan and he had made the rounds, blindly celebrating, without talking business. Dirty laundry like the Brian Earle accident wouldn't do anyone any good. The CIA's code of honor is a lot like the Mafia's, he thought. It was a dead issue.

Like Bollinger. A master stroke for a Machiavelli, he thought, to die at the "height of glory." J. L. winced as he contemplated the security and the communications, he would have to handle at the state funeral, premiers and princes paying tribute to a man who, even in death, was a hypocrite.

J. L. shuffled the papers in the "in" box. He had left the memo on Dodge's ski trip in March on top. Nothing like Colorado mountains. He would have to talk to General Bonekemper about getting assigned to that one. Beneath the itinerary, J. L. found the interagency memo Rubin had sent all intelligence personnel involved with the Philadelphia assignment. Rubin wanted information on any possible sources of the leak. J. L. recognized the request as pro forma.

He grinned, checked the "no" box, and scrawled at the bottom of the memo, below his initials, the newspaper symbol "-30-." Rubin would appreciate that, he thought.